FOOD AND FAMILIES IN THE MAKING

Food, Nutrition, and Culture

Published by Berghahn Books in Association with the Society for the Anthropology of Food and Nutrition (SAFN).

While eating is a biological necessity, the production, distribution, preparation, consumption, and disposal of food are all deeply culturally inscribed activities. Taking an anthropological perspective, this book series provides a forum for critically engaged, ethnographically grounded work on the cultural, social, political, economic, and ecological aspects of human nutrition and food habits. The monographs and edited collections in this series present timely, food-related scholarship intended for researchers, academics, students, and those involved in food policy, businesses, and activism. Covering a wide range of topics, geographic regions and mobilities across regions, the series decenters dominant, often western-centered approaches and assumptions in food studies.

Volume 8
FOOD AND FAMILIES IN THE MAKING
Knowledge Reproduction and Political Economy of Cooking in Morocco
Katharina Graf

Volume 7
NOURISHING LIFE
Foodways and Humanity in an African Town
Arianna Huhn

Volume 6
THE DANCE OF NURTURE
Negotiating Infant Feeding
Penny Van Esterik and Richard A. O'Connor

Volume 5
THE HERITAGE ARENA
Reinventing Cheese in the Italian Alps
Cristina Grasseni

Volume 4
FROM VIRTUE TO VICE
Negotiating Anorexia
Richard A. O'Connor and Penny Van Esterik

Volume 3
RE-ORIENTING CUISINE
East Asian Foodways in the Twenty-First Century
Edited by Kwang Ok Kim

Volume 2
RECONSTRUCTING OBESITY
The Meaning of Measures and the Measure of Meanings
Edited by Megan McCullough and Jessica Hardin

Volume 1
GREEK WHISKY
The Localization of a Global Commodity
Tryfon Bampilis

Food and Families in the Making

Knowledge Reproduction and Political Economy of Cooking in Morocco

Katharina Graf

berghahn
NEW YORK · OXFORD
www.berghahnbooks.com

First published in 2024 by
Berghahn Books
www.berghahnbooks.com

© 2024 Katharina Graf

All rights reserved. Except for the quotation of short passages for the purposes of criticism and review, no part of this book may be reproduced in any form or by any means, electronic or mechanical, including photocopying, recording, or any information storage and retrieval system now known or to be invented, without written permission of the publisher.

Library of Congress Cataloging-in-Publication Data

Names: Graf, Katharina, author.
Title: Food and families in the making : knowledge reproduction and political economy of cooking in Morocco / Katharina Graf.
Other titles: Food, nutrition, and culture ; 8.
Description: New York : Berghahn Books, 2024. | Series: Food, nutrition, and culture; 8 | Includes bibliographical references and index.
Identifiers: LCCN 2023051022 (print) | LCCN 2023051023 (ebook) | ISBN 9781805394679 (hardback) | ISBN 9781805394686 (epub) | ISBN 9781805394693 (pdf)
Subjects: LCSH: Cooking--Social aspects--Morocco. | Cooking--Political aspects--Morocco. | Cooking--Economic aspects--Morocco. | Women--Morocco--Social conditions. | Families--Morocco. | Cooking--Morocco. | Morocco--Social life and customs.
Classification: LCC GT2860 .G63 2024 (print) | LCC GT2860 (ebook) | DDC 392.3/70964--dc23
LC record available at https://lccn.loc.gov/2023051022
LC ebook record available at https://lccn.loc.gov/2023051023

British Library Cataloguing in Publication Data
A catalogue record for this book is available from the British Library

ISBN 978-1-80539-467-9 hardback
ISBN 978-1-80539-468-6 epub
ISBN 978-1-80539-469-3 web pdf

https://doi.org/10.3167/9781805394679

To my mother, and all mothers who cook, or do not

Contents

List of Figures	viii
Preface	x
Acknowledgements	xiii
Notes on Transliteration	xv
Introduction. Food and Families in the Making	1
Interlude 1. Kneading	27
Chapter 1. Taste Knowledge: Cooking with Six Senses	29
Interlude 2. Cooking	51
Chapter 2. Participant Perception: Learning to Cook	53
Interlude 3. Brewing	75
Chapter 3. Culinary Connectivity: Negotiating Womanhood and Family Meals	77
Interlude 4. Provisioning	101
Chapter 4. *Beldi* Foodways: Situating Food Quality	104
Interlude 5. Tasting	129
Chapter 5. Cereal Citizens: 'Bread Does Not Come from a Store'	131
Conclusion. Moroccans in the Making	155
Glossary	163
References	166
Index	179

Figures

0.1.	Food on sale in a medina street, Marrakech, 2013	xi
1.1.	Massaging couscous in a wooden *gsa'a*, Marrakech, 2012	33
1.2.	Couscous served with *lben*, Marrakech, 2012	35
1.3.	Combining with flour, yeast and water, Marrakech, 2012	41
1.4.	Electric blender, named after the brand Moulinex, Marrakech, 2012	44
2.1.	Child's hand asking for dough in a *qesriya*, Marrakech, 2013	55
2.2.	Mixing batter by hand, Marrakech, 2012	60
2.3.	Making pizza, Marrakech, 2013	67
3.1.	Placing meat in the *tanjiya*, a Marrakchi speciality prepared by men, Marrakech, 2013	81
3.2.	Grinding almonds and oil with the *raha* to make *amlou*, Marrakech, 2013	89
3.3.	Learning to mix ingredients for *sellou*, a Ramadan sweet, Marrakech, 2013	92
4.1.	Shop selling live *rumi* and *beldi* chicken, Marrakech, 2012	102
4.2.	Corner shop (*hanut*) selling daily needs items, Marrakech, 2013	106
4.3.	Spices and herbs on sale in the *suq* (market), Marrakech, 2012	109
4.4.	Earthenware *tajine*, which describes the cooking vessel and the dish, Marrakech, 2013	118
5.1.	Inspecting grains at a weekly grain market, Beni Mellal, 2018	134
5.2.	Small-scale *gemh* farming in the Haouz, near Marrakech, 2018	140

5.3. Baker wielding homemade bread loaves at a small *ferran* (public oven), Marrakech, 2013 — 142

5.4. Homemade bread ready to be picked up from the *ferran*, Marrakech, 2013 — 143

5.5. Socoma, one of many newly built neighbourhoods, Marrakech, 2012 — 146

Preface

I visited Morocco for the first time in March 2006, spending my days discovering the buzzing medina of Marrakech, the vast historic centre that was walled in nearly 1,000 years ago. Among large groups of international and national tourists, and an even bigger crowd of local shoppers, sellers and strollers, I meandered through the main thoroughfares and markets, sometimes getting lost as I followed the whiff of a scent or the fraction of a sound. I devoted these days as a solo traveller to absorbing the sounds, smells, sights, tastes and feelings of medina life: the regular calls to prayer and the lyrical market cries of hawkers advertising their food; the smells of noisy scooters and freshly baked bread mingling with that of slow-cooking *tajines*; the colourful stalls and shop fronts selling artfully arranged spices or fruits; the exhilarating taste of a date or of sweet mint tea; and the oily heat of roasted meat that burned my tongue as I sat down to eat in the sunset light on the medina's main square Jemaa el-fna.

At the end of each day, I was overwhelmed and exhausted, but every morning I dived anew into the ebb and flow of the medina's daily rhythms. In one way or another, food always seemed to be involved in these multisensory rhythms. Indeed, any visitor to the medina will note the constant presence of food, and not only in the medina; its ubiquity betrays its importance in everyday life across Marrakech (Figure 0.1). The way in which one perceives food in the streets and squares also betrays its multisensorial appeal for everybody – or should I say every body: one cannot help but notice the many activities around it and become part of this material and social rhythm. I joined this rhythm when I got lost one day in a small alley and knocked at a random door to ask for the way out. I met Aicha who worked there. When I returned in 2007 as a visiting student at Cadi Ayyad University and stayed with Aicha's employer, I also met her neighbours Fatimzahra and Hajja.

The more familiar I got with Marrakech, the more my sensory perception of food revealed something about the rhythms of everyday life in the city. The damp smell of peppery milk soup (*harira al-bieda*), sold at crossroads by ragged peddlers, marks the deceivingly calm beginning of the day after the first call to

Preface xi

Figure 0.1. Food on sale in a medina street, Marrakech, 2013. © Katharina Graf

prayer at dawn (*al-fajr*). The real buzz begins after sunrise, when honking scooters and donkey carts selling seasonal vegetables or fruits emerge from the alleys and the surrounding suburbs and villages, mingling with the smell of locally baked baguettes that are transported to the many corner shops in time for breakfast before school and work. Soon after, the deliveries of hundreds of litres of milk and yoghurt and of whole meat carcasses block the high streets just when the first shoppers bring homemade bread to the public oven on the way to the market. By the time tourists begin to explore the medina, most children are in school, most workers are at work and most cooks are preparing lunch; the city calms down while the aromas of lunch preparations penetrate the air.

As soon as the *muezzin* calls for midday prayer (*al-dhuhr*), shops and stalls close, but the buzz begins anew as schoolchildren and workers rush home for lunch, picking up their homemade bread from the public oven on their way. After lunch, the city calms down momentarily. By the time shops reopen and peddlers re-emerge, snack food stalls begin to make food for those on the move again or those expecting visitors around the afternoon prayer (*al-asr*). Until the prayer at sunset (*al-maghrib*), the entire city remains noisy, smelly and dense with shoppers searching for a cheap bargain, schoolchildren and workers returning home again, cooks processing food for dinner or the next day's lunch, and with those who can afford to sit down at one of the many open-air food stalls or cafés. Eventually, the city slowly quiets down after the last call for prayer at nightfall (*al-ishha*).

While I clearly already perceived the centrality of food in everyday Marrakchi life on my first walks through the medina, it took a few more visits and many months of living and working with three Marrakchi families between 2012 and 2013 to realize that domestic cooks, especially wives and mothers who often also had paid employment, were key contributors to these daily rhythms and to the reproduction of everyday life. Even though one cannot see the meals being prepared in the labyrinthine medina or in the many new, purpose-built neighbourhoods, one can still smell and often also hear them sizzle in *tajines* or whistle in pressure cookers.[1] The sounds and smells produced by domestic food practices contribute to the multisensory experience of Marrakech, while the meals prepared therein sustain life.

In sourcing raw ingredients and processing them by hand, in making their own flour and bread, and in serving a Moroccan meal rather than 'fast food', domestic cooks shape not only themselves but also the material and social infrastructure of Marrakech. When sitting down to eat with the hands from a shared platter, many of these daily activities were condensed into a shared multisensory feeling of food.[2] As the ethnographer that I was becoming by then, I tasted the work and the knowledge these women invested into what they deemed to be good food. And by joining my research participants when they sourced, processed, prepared and served food for their families and friends I, too, learned to cook the Moroccan way.

Notes

1. In more spacious middle- or upper-income neighbourhoods and homes, the presence of food's smells, sounds and sights is more limited (Newcomb 2009: 1).
2. Eating with the hands and a general multisensorial engagement with food is of course not limited to Marrakech or Morocco (e.g. Adapon 2008; Janeja 2010; Meneley 1983; Naguib 2015; Staples 2020). Indeed, Ray (2022) reminds us that hands are central in anthropological theories around cooking.

Acknowledgements

This book has been many years in the making, and it is impossible to thank everyone who contributed to it along the way. If anything, the following is an approximation. First and foremost, I must thank the protagonists of this book, Hajja, Rachida and Aicha and their daughters and families, for sharing their knowledge, their food and their everyday life with me. Without their hospitality and generosity, my fieldwork would never have been possible; working and living with them was an immensely enriching and memorable experience for life. I would like to extend my thanks to the many other families I have worked with over the years of fieldwork in Marrakech, Beni Mellal and elsewhere in Morocco. I am so grateful that they have welcomed me into their homes. To a large extent, this was also due to Monia Alazali's invaluable and tireless assistance during my fieldwork, whom I include in thanking. Furthermore, I would like to thank all the other people who participated in my research, ranging from family friends to extended family networks across Marrakech and Morocco. I also owe thanks to many interview partners as well as friends and colleagues in Marrakech, Beni Mellal and the rest of Morocco. Our conversations, debates and shared meals have contributed in many subtle ways to this book. Special thanks are due to Chloé Pellegrini and Philippe Chéoux for providing thoughtful comments and comfort particularly when fieldwork was difficult.

Putting in words my gratitude to my mentor Harry West is more difficult. His supervision took many forms: at times he was supportive and encouraging, whilst at other times he was critical and challenging. I don't know how, but he always knew when either was needed without ever imposing his experience and knowledge upon me. Speaking to Harry still inspires and comforts me. I am immensely grateful for his advice throughout my project and beyond and feel very fortunate to experience his unwavering support. At SOAS University of London, I would like to especially thank the members of the SOAS Food Studies Centre, many of whom have contributed with questions and their comparative perspectives to furthering my project. Special thanks are due to my peers Giulia Baldinelli, Kat Cagat, Jess Chu, Anna Cohen, Mukta Das, Camelia Dewan, Jamila Dorner, Petra

Matijevic, Hannah Roberson, Brandi Simpson-Miller, Chenjia Xu and many more fellow students at SOAS, particularly in the seminars under Trevor Marchand's and Kit Davis' invaluable guidance, all of whom have made this book project so enjoyable from the start. I am also grateful for Elizabeth Hull's mentorship during my postdoctoral research at SOAS, particularly for helping me to expand my understanding of cooking beyond the domestic realm. I would also like to thank Anna Colquhoun for enabling me to hone my Moroccan cooking skills in her London and Istrian kitchens, and for continuing our enriching comparative conversations. Last but not least, I would like to thank Zofia Boni, my closest companion since day one as a SOAS doctoral student, and Nafsika Papacharalampous, my partner in crime when it comes to finalizing a book manuscript.

I am also indebted to the Institute of Cultural Anthropology and European Ethnology at Goethe University Frankfurt, Germany, where I finally managed to finish the book and where many unexpected conversations contributed to doing so. I would also like to thank the many colleagues and friends who over the years have shaped my thinking and have contributed to this book in various ways and on various occasions, in particular Johannes Arens, Hande Birkalan-Gedik, Francesca Bray, Nora Faltmann, Laura McAdam-Otto, Anne Meneley, Anne Murcott, Nefissa Naguib, Yotam Ottolenghi, Heather Paxson, Johan Pottier, Krishnendu Ray, Claudia Roden, Ruba Salih, Sebastian Schellhaas, Peter Scholliers, James Staples, David Sutton, Gisela Welz, Richard Wilk and Sami Zubaida.

Many close friends have supported me throughout the project in one way or another. I would like to especially thank Lisann Heyse, Julia Pfitzner, Diana Quirmbach and Jana Witt. Of course, as in everything, my parents and my sisters have encouraged and supported me whenever needed. A big thank you to you and to my extended family in Germany, Italy and Slovakia. Properly thanking my biggest supporters, Andrej, Emil and Alba, is impossible, so let me just say thanks for cooking for me in the widest sense.

Conceptualizing, researching and writing this book would not have been possible without the financial support of the following funding bodies. The Foundation of German Business supported me within the Klaus Murmann Fellowship Programme for doctoral students. I was granted the RAI/Sutasoma 2016 Award by the Royal Anthropological Institute in recognition of the potentially outstanding merit of my doctoral project. I also received funding from SOAS in the form of a fieldwork award and childcare fund. My postdoctoral research on Moroccan bread and political stability was financed by the AXA Research Fund.

Finally, I would like to thank the whole team at Berghahn for their professional and kind support along the way. I would also like to thank Melissa L. Caldwell and Jakob A. Klein for being the most enthusiast and supportive series editors one could hope for.

Notes on Transliteration

It is notoriously difficult to provide consistent transliteration in a context of linguistic diversity such as Moroccan. Depending on the situation, Moroccans use Modern Standard Arabic, a regional dialect of Arabic, three Tamazight dialects as well as French, English and other languages in Latin script such as Spanish. Modern Standard Arabic, referred to as *fusha*, is mostly used in writing and was not commonly used by my research participants. For the spelling of words in *darija*, the Moroccan regional dialect of Arabic, I mostly follow the spelling conventions in Harrell (2004), unless a word or expression is more established in Latin script. I use French spelling conventions when it is the most established form, for instance, *couscous*, and English spelling conventions when words are less established, for instance, *suq*. Because it is more commonly used in English or French, I divert from Harrell (2004) by indicating the letter *ayn* with " ' " as in *'Id*; by indicating the letter *ghayn* with 'gh' as in *Maghrib* and by indicating the letter *jim* with 'j' as in *tajine*. Italics have been used for non-English words, except for place names, which have not been italicized. Translations into English or specifications have been provided in brackets following the italicized word. When in doubt about rendering a word, I have tried to use the form that is most recognizable to Moroccans. I hope for the reader's indulgence regarding any inconsistencies.

INTRODUCTION

Food and Families in the Making

This is a book about domestic food preparation. It asks how we know cooking. Yet, this seemingly simple question raises many more questions, such as who is cooking, where and for whom, or, indeed, why one should cook at all in view of continuous technological change and women's emancipation. In the low-income Marrakchi homes where the experiences recounted here took shape, women made tremendous efforts to prepare good food for their families and were proud of doing so, despite their limited temporal and financial resources. In the absence of savings in a bank account and of health insurance, coupled with a cultural emphasis on social connectivity via food, domestic cooking assured the reproduction of everyday family life in the context of widespread poverty and food insecurity. In exploring these questions and driven by the desire to understand why many low-income women continue to make so many meals from scratch even when they worked for a wage, this book turned out to be not only a foray into the making of food and of everyday family life but also a political economy of cooking that departs from previous studies of food and cooking and from ethnographies of everyday life in Morocco and the Middle East and North Africa in three different ways.

Domestic cooking is a bodily practice that is often difficult to verbalize and to describe. At the same time, it is mundane and familiar to many. As a result, cooking knowledge is often labelled as nonverbal or embodied knowledge. Yet, while there exist some studies of *what* cooks do or know, *how* they do or know still remains nebulous. Rather than describe what it is or is not and take for granted that readers understand what is meant by embodied knowledge, I first propose to consider the engagement of the cook with food as a form of multisensory knowledge that might not surprise those who have been to Marrakech, or to places with a similarly dynamic food culture, and who perceived food and everyday life through all their senses. In this context, understanding how a person learns and knows cooking requires immersing oneself with all senses in everyday life. Thus, based on my own experience of learning to cook, this book endeavours to understand and make accessible the bodily knowledge of the domestic cook and how it is reproduced in the context of material and social change. It does so through the thick description of my own engagement with food in the interludes and that of my research participants in the main chapters. Learning to cook and understanding it – method and theory – are thus one and the same. Ideally, in reading this book, my words will resonate with the experiences of everyone who cooks, yet struggles to express precisely what it is they know.

Although my focus is on everyday practices and bodily knowledge, this book does not stop there. Just like a bite of homemade flatbread can expose the whole cosmology of Moroccan foodways, this book also attends to the multiple nested layers and scalar relationships of people's interactions with the material substances of food. These interactions are manifested not only in idiosyncratic bodily experiences but also in family and social relations, in transactions in the streets, shops and markets of a rapidly urbanizing society, which are, in turn, situated in a much broader national and global context. In other words, the study of cooking knowledge connects and condenses the social, cultural, spiritual, ecological, economic and political dimensions of everyday life in a way that can be experienced phenomenologically. For instance, bodily practices of food preparation also always relate to changing norms and values about womanhood and family life, which depend on income, class and identity more broadly. In the monotheistic context of Muslim Morocco, food is also sacred and cooking establishes a connection to God, which more abstractly helps cooks to account for the unpredictability that is inherent in any activity. Equally, Marrakchi cooking practices shape and are shaped by the wider Moroccan food system, which in the context of a drought-prone climate is based on a historically grown 'participatory paternalism' (Holden 2009), whereby the state heeds the preferences and practices of the urban poor on the one hand, while, on the other hand, marginalizing them economically and politically. Through its engaged attention to the lived experience of a handful of low-income Marrakchi cooks – at the confluence of the materiality of food and the sociality of the family – this book contributes a political economy of cooking that considers women's food knowledge as not only *shaped by* but also *shaping* broader debates about health, poverty and political stability in Morocco and the region.

This approach is based on the more general theoretical argument that the ethnographic attention to bodily knowledge as multisensory resonance with one's material and social environment necessarily involves dissonance too, which leads me to the third major contribution. Although it champions women and the knowledge of the cook, this book is not simply a romantic depiction of everyday food and family life; domestic food work is hard work.[1] Rather, it argues that in the absence of reliable food standards and affordable health insurance, making good food, as my research participants strove to do, is the single strongest lever low-income women have to ensure the health and wellbeing of themselves and their families. In other words, if these women do not care, nobody does. In showcasing the mostly hidden but hard work that especially low-income women across the globe do in order to reproduce their families and everyday culture, this book seeks to give these people – and all women who cook – dignity for what they do and in which many take pride doing, not despite but *because of* material and social change.

Overall, the making of Moroccan foods and families teaches us something important, namely, that reproducing bodily knowledge and the family is worth it. This message is especially salient in the context of the so-called enlightened West, where bodily work especially in domestic contexts – and thus predominantly women's knowledge – has been systematically devalued for centuries (cf. Smith 2004; Spiekermann 2018), amounting to a double devaluation of what women continue to (know how to) do the world over: making good food and making the family. This double devaluation has never been more evident than now, in crisis. Writing this book in the middle of a global pandemic caused by COVID-19 – while also cooking for my own children more often than I am used to due to repeated nursery and school closures – revealed a common faultline that marks not only Moroccan but also my own society: willingly or not, women are called on to cook and care for their families, while governmental institutions fail us.

Three Marrakchi Families

During more than ten years of research, I have encountered and worked with many low-income families in both rural and urban Morocco. But the three families I have learned cooking with and from during my fieldwork between the summers of 2012 and 2013 are the protagonists of this book. At the time, they all lived in the medina, the historic centre of Marrakech. I revisited all three families repeatedly between 2016 and 2018, during my research project on bread in Marrakech and Beni Mellal, and remain in touch with them today. To gain a deeper insight into everyday food preparations and family life, I adopt Miller's portrait approach (2008, cited in Sutton 2014: 152), which contends that individual people can display a pattern in their approach to everyday life that is representative of the society in which they live. Each individual or family portrait synthesizes larger, recognizable themes that resonate with different aspects of daily life. In other words, I follow Geertz's motto that 'We hope to find in the little what eludes us in the large, to stumble upon general truths while sorting through special cases' (1971: 4).

I first lived and worked with the family of Fatimzahra between September and December 2012. I met her in 2007 when she was my neighbour and – thanks to having attended secondary school – taught me *darija* (Moroccan Arabic dialect) while I attended a French-taught course at the University of Marrakech.[2] When

I began fieldwork with them, Fatimzahra lived with her mother Hajja and her older brother Mohamed in the same old *riad* (a house with an open courtyard) in the south of the medina. Her younger brother Hassan had recently bought a small, newly built flat in Socoma, one of many purpose-built quarters on the city's periphery, where he spent most of his spare time. During the period of my fieldwork, Fatimzahra was in her mid-forties and unmarried. Hajja was in her late sixties and had been widowed for more than ten years. Fatimzahra's brothers, fifty-year-old Mohamed and thirty-five-year-old Hassan, were also unmarried. Although Fatimzahra earned some money mending clothes for neighbours or teaching *darija* to foreigners, the family relied on the income of Hassan from his low-paying but stable and respectable government job. Mohamed held only occasional and low-paid jobs, mainly to finance his fondness for alcohol. His alcohol addiction caused occasional domestic disturbances during my stay, such as loud nightly singing and arguments when Hajja tried to prevent him from doing so. To soothe these tensions, Hassan occasionally invited Fatimzahra, Hajja and myself to stay at his new apartment for a period of days or weeks, as was the case when I joined Fatimzahra and Hajja upon my arrival in Marrakech in early September 2012. Most of the time, however, I occupied my own room in their medina *riad* for which I contributed a monthly rent.

As the senior woman in the household, Hajja was the lead cook. She managed food supplies and provisioning, and planned and prepared lunch, the main meal of the day. Despite her illiteracy, she remembered hundreds of detailed recipes and food prices, and seamlessly switched between the three currencies still in use at the time.[3] Because of her rheumatic legs, Hajja did not usually go shopping herself, as lead cooks tend to do in urban Morocco. Instead, she discussed a shopping list with Fatimzahra, who went shopping nearly every day despite her own disability.[4] Fatimzahra was also in charge of breakfast, snack and dinner preparations as well as most other domestic chores. This task allocation changed when Hajja went on the *haj*, a month-long pilgrimage to Mecca – one of the five obligations or 'pillars' of Islam – and Fatimzahra replaced her in the role of lead cook throughout October 2012.[5] I advanced to the position of second cook and became much more involved in cooking and domestic work than I would have otherwise been in this constellation. Indeed, my extra pair of hands was needed when entire days were devoted to the preparation of food to celebrate Hajja's safe return with her extended family throughout November and December 2012.

Their family speaks to broader processes in Morocco in several ways. Fatimzahra's maternal family originated and was still based in Taroudant, in the Souss Valley south of Marrakech. Although the Souss and the surrounding Atlas Mountains are predominantly Amazigh (indigenous peoples) territory, Hajja's origin is urban and Arab just like her husband's.[6] The moving of Hajja to Marrakech as a bride in the early 1960s is exemplary of the first major wave of urbanization after independence from the French Protectorate in 1956.[7] Her children claimed *sharifi* descent through their father, materialized in the fading beauty of her family's old *riad* and manifest in a sense of social superiority.[8] Hajja sometimes reminisced of the past when she still cooked elaborate meals for her husband's many visitors. Since his death, the family struggled financially and lost much of their social status in the neighbourhood. Like many formerly noble Marrakchi families before them, they contributed to the medina's gentrification and Marrakech's urban sprawl when they eventually sold their family *riad* to a foreign neighbour and relocated to a much smaller but newly built flat in close proximity to Hassan and his own young family in 2016 (cf. Coslado, McGuinness and Miller 2013; Ernst 2013). Although they missed life in the medina, in the context of the COVID-19 pandemic, Fatimzahra and Hajja rejoiced in having moved out of their crumbling *riad* and the dense medina. Thanks to Hassan's government job, the family have weathered the pandemic and food price inflation thus far.

Between January and May 2013, I worked with Rachida. She had moved from the surrounding Haouz plains to Marrakech in the 1990s to marry Mohamed, a distant relative of her family. During the period of my fieldwork, they still lived in the same tiny house in Bab Ailen in the western medina. Rachida is Amazigh, whereas Mohamed is Arab. I met her at the beginning of my fieldwork through her work as a cleaner in the house of friends in the former colonial French neighbourhood Gueliz, derived from the French term *église* for church. At the time, Rachida was forty years old and had two daughters, twenty-year-old Zakia and fifteen-year-old Ibtissam. Mohamed was twenty years older than Rachida and had been unemployed for roughly fifteen years. Rachida was partially literate; she had also learned to speak French during her full-time work as a self-employed cleaner mostly in houses owned by European foreigners. As for many low-income rural migrants, her children's education had been a main reason for marrying into the city. Indeed, Zakia went to Marrakech's public university during my stay, while Ibtissam attended a nearby public high school. As is often the case in low-income households, Rachida was the sole income earner in her household. She earned less than the monthly national minimum wage of 2,500 Dh at the time.[9] Her only insurance was her extended family spread across Morocco.

Their busy routines outside of the home were one reason why I did not live with Rachida's family. Moreover, their house had only one bedroom and was very small overall. In order to work with them, I rented a small studio in Gueliz. However, as a consequence of not living with them, neither Rachida nor Zakia allowed me to participate properly in food preparation or contribute financially besides small gifts such as fruits. I was considered their guest throughout my fieldwork. I observed rather than joined Rachida's or Zakia's food preparation whenever they invited me and I shopped, ate and occasionally cleaned up with them. This happened once or twice on a weekly basis, typically during weekends when Rachida did not work or whenever Zakia had a day off from university. Although Rachida was the lead cook and managed all food work, Zakia often prepared lunch on the days when Rachida returned late from her wage work. Ibtissam regularly cleaned up and tidied the kitchen. Occasionally she also helped to process ingredients, mainly cutting and peeling vegetables, but she did not cook. Mohamed was sometimes asked to bring homemade bread to the public oven or to make last-minute purchases of milk or eggs at the local corner shop, but generally he did not help with the household chores. Meriem, a younger unmarried sister of Rachida, also temporarily lived with them and took over lunch preparations whenever she stayed there. I sometimes observed her cook. She had helped raise Zakia and Ibtissam years ago when Rachida took over the role of breadwinner after her husband became unemployed.

In the spring of 2013 Meriem suddenly fell ill and stayed with Rachida to go to a hospital for diagnostic tests. She died one month before my fieldwork ended of an undiagnosed illness, causing immense grief and sadness. In 2017, thanks also to Zakia's income from her new job as a teacher in a private primary school, Rachida finally managed to secure a government grant to rebuild the old adobe house in cement, gaining valuable space and a refurbished kitchen. It is thanks to Zakia's, and later also Ibtissam's, steady incomes that Rachida and her family weathered the uncertainty of the pandemic. In fact, compared to the time of my fieldwork with them and to the other two families at the time of writing, the family thrives and was able to afford the weddings of both Zakia and Ibtissam in 2021.

The third family I lived and worked with was that of thirty-year-old Aicha and her husband Hassan, ten years her senior, with their four- and one-year-old daughters Zahra and Rita. I met Aicha in 2007 in the *riad* I was staying at during my university studies, where she was working as a cleaner and where she also met her future husband. She migrated to Marrakech from the Tadla plains below the Middle Atlas Mountains at the age of seventeen to support her natal family financially, waitressing in restaurants and bars until she found the more socially acceptable work as a cleaner. Aicha also befriended Fatimzahra during my second stay in Marrakech in 2007. By September 2012, Aicha had married Hassan, had just given birth to their second daughter Rita and was about to move out of her mother-in-law's house with her small family. Aicha and Hassan are Imazighen (plural of Amazigh), yet they belong to two different dialect groups and thus spoke mostly *darija* with each other and with their daughters. While her husband worked in a nearby tourist boutique and earned their main income, Aicha's income paid for items such as fresh fruits, children's clothes or household appliances. Like Rachida, Aicha had no contract or social security, but she participated in a local women's saving group (*jama'a daret*). Aicha had not completed her primary school education because at the age of seven, when her father was incapacitated to work due to a work accident, she had to run the household while her mother started to work as a picker in the surrounding agricultural fields. After moving to Marrakech, Aicha learned to read and write in Arabic script at an evening school and learned to speak French at her workplace through interacting with foreign guests.

Although I had not intended it, Aicha invited me to live and work with her in her rented flat in the south of the medina when no other suitable family was willing to accommodate me in their household.[10] I lived with her family from June until late August 2013 and paid Aicha a monthly rent. During the first two months, we lived in their two-bedroom flat, but for the period of Ramadan, the month when Muslims fast during daylight hours, we moved to her employer's *riad*, who had gone on holiday. Because she worked afternoons only, Aicha had more time for daily food preparation than Rachida, and I had more occasions to join her. Even though Aicha's family was small at the time of my fieldwork and she was the only cook in her household, her extended family was a constant presence in her daily life. Aicha's parents – whom she still supported financially – and her two younger brothers visited regularly. Most memorable was their visit during that year's Ramadan, the first Aicha hosted, for it temporarily resembled multigenerational food preparation. Since both Aicha's mother and Halima, her twenty-year-old sister-in-law, only spoke *tamazight*, Aicha had to translate when I was present. After my fieldwork, Aicha and Hassan moved into a larger rented flat in the same neighbourhood and had three more children. Fully dependent on employment in tourism, both her and her husband's sources of income collapsed in the spring of 2020. As the quasi-family member that I had become over the years, I stepped in to partially compensate for their losses.

My own familial situation was also relevant during my fieldwork. Although I undertook my fieldwork alone, many of my research participants knew or got to know my visiting partner as well as my parents, my two sisters and various friends. Later on, I also brought my own children. This allowed them to conceptualize me as a social and cultural being, a hugely important dimension in relationship building in Morocco, as this book will illustrate. The different stages of my life – from being an unmarried woman to being a wife and mother – mattered on both practical and ideological levels. For instance, although my research participants acknowledged that I was 'like' married at the time of my fieldwork, my partner, with whom I shared a household back home, was not able to stay with me at any of the families. We travelled instead. When meeting with other men in the neighbourhood – whether for fieldwork or not – I risked losing not only my own reputation but also that of my host family, which was a regular source of tension.[11] At the same time, not yet having any children of my own, I was considered an inexperienced woman, even a girl (cf. Zvan Elliott 2015). This status facilitated my research in the intimate context of family life, where I was conceptualized as a learning daughter and sister, but it made movement outside of the immediate neighbourhood unpleasant. I was often verbally harassed by male strangers. To prevent this, Aicha sometimes sent her daughters with me on errands, substituting for the children I did not yet have.[12] The importance

Moroccans attach to children and their mark of mature womanhood became even more pronounced during my later fieldwork on bread. Being a mother gave me trustworthiness when interviewing numerous unknown women in their homes, places that are often guarded from foreigners. It also enabled me to speak to male millers and bakers as well as wheat traders and farmers without incurring a loss of anyone's reputation.

Although my portrayal is necessarily partial and remains temporally and spatially situated in the unique life trajectories of my research participants and their families, these three families represent an important subset of Moroccan society for two reasons. First, in relation to similarly sized cities, especially Rabat and Casablanca, the hubs of major government institutions and of industries and services respectively, Marrakech itself is special. A commercial hub on trade routes between western Africa, the Atlantic and the Mediterranean, the former royal city has a thousand-year-long history as a cosmopolitan marketplace. Because of its rich architectural heritage, its oasis-like urban ecology and climate, and its location below the High Atlas Mountains, the city has more recently developed into a national and international tourist hotspot and became a favoured residence of European and American expats (Ernst 2013).[13] The city's daily life and infrastructure reflect this. Low-income Marrakchis in the medina are routinely exposed to foreigners, often working in the related informal tourist economy. Compared to precolonial neighbourhoods elsewhere in Morocco, Marrakech's medina is well preserved and its tourist hotspots benefited from electricity and running water relatively early, following its declaration as a United Nations Educational, Scientific and Cultural Organization (UNESCO) cultural world heritage site in 1984 (Schmidt 2005). The downsides are, according to my research participants, higher rents, reduced amenities and reduced security in daily life in the main tourist thoroughfares. Those who do not earn in this sector, and who can afford to, move from the medina into the fast-growing urban peripheries, as Hajja and Fatimzahra eventually did.

Second, low-income Marrakchis differ from other urban or rural Moroccans described in the literature. For instance, contrary to the low-income Casaouis described by Strava (2021) and the middle-income Casaouis, Rbatis and Fassis described by Cohen (2004), Montgomery (2019) and Newcomb (2009, 2017) respectively, who are either long-term urban inhabitants or lived for more than one generation in the city, many of Marrakech's low- and middle-income families are more recent migrants, whose rural origins still shape their contemporary urban life. At the same time, by moving to the city, their material and social lives differ markedly from the lives and the relatives they have left behind (cf. Crawford 2008; Zvan Elliott 2015); between a material life marked by scarcity and by abundance for those who can afford it; between a generation of unschooled mothers born in the countryside and a generation of schooled daughters born in the city. Despite their actively maintained migrant origins, the three families were socially and economically embedded in their respective neighbourhoods. They earned their livelihoods largely in the informal economy and their children had access to public education, but hardly any other state services, reflecting the broader context of poverty and general uncertainty that mark their lives. Yet, none of the three families self-identified as poor or – for a lack of identification with their wage work – as working class, hence why I refrain from calling them either. For them, poverty is considered as more than just financial dearth: in the absence of social welfare institutions, really poor is someone who has no one to rely on if things go wrong.[14]

Like low-income Casaouis (Strava 2021) and Rbatis (Bogaert 2018), most Marrakchi inhabitants have neither benefited from the many urban redevelopment projects over the last decades nor from the International Monetary Fund (IMF)-induced economic liberalization since the 1980s.[15] Not surprisingly, Marrakchis fundamentally distrust governmental institutions and political actors (Citron 2004). More so than other Moroccan cities, which boast a small but important middle class and a largely functioning urban infrastructure, Marrakech is marked by a strong divide between its wealthy minority and its poor majority. This divide is perceptible across the city: oasis villas, ostentatious malls and luxurious cars coexist with slums, street markets and carts pulled by donkeys. These two worlds meet within the walls of the medina (see Preface). While perhaps contributing to its (inter)national charm and appeal of 'authenticity', Marrakech's political economy is determined by informality and a lack of urban policies around urban infrastructures ranging from markets and housing to industries (Citron 2004; Sebti et al. 2009). In everyday life this translates into poorly paid and insecure jobs in the informal (tourist) economy such as Rachida's, unaffordable medical treatment, causing Meriem's premature death, or inadequate housing for lower-income families and a push into the urban peripheries, as eventually happened to Fatimzahra's family. Needless to say, the financial situations of low-income Moroccans like them remain highly insecure, as the COVID-19 pandemic between 2020 and 2022 made eminently clear, when Marrakech's booming tourist economy collapsed and many Marrakchis like Aicha and her husband lost their incomes. The current global inflation of food prices further exacerbates this enduring sense of a state of crisis. And yet, the Moroccan monarchy remains a paradox paragon of political stability amid perpetual regional and global instability. Paying attention to the domestic work and life of low-income Marrakchi cooks and their families will provide an original and urgently needed understanding of why this may be so.

Material and Social Continuity and Change

Domestic cooking is not only central to the reproduction of family life, but also contributes to reproducing society and culture at large. This becomes evident when considering all networks, discourses and practices enabling contemporary provisioning, processing, preparing, serving, eating and disposing of food, which together constitute a domestic cook's knowledge. All are relevant to the making of a meal, as this book will illustrate. At the same time, what the preparation of food entails is radically changing the world over. My research participants are no exception. Thus, in order to understand contemporary food preparation and how it is continuous and changing at the same time, it is important to consider the past.

Of the three families, Hajja's and Fatimzahra's foodways can be described as more urban and thus royal, with more distinctly pan-Arab influences marked by saffron or sweet and savoury combinations (cf. Aylwin 1999; Rosenberger 1999). Not only is Hajja's hometown in the Souss Valley well known for its regional cuisine, it is also reputed to produce excellent cooks who in the past used to be employed as cooks in the royal kitchens (Hal 1996). This found expression in Hajja's access to and knowledgeable use of regional ingredients such as saffron or argan oil, the combination of sugar and meat in dishes such as *bastila* (almond and chicken pie) or prune and almond stew, and her command of complex recipes for *haluwat* (sweets, especially patisserie-style pastries) such as *shebbakiya* or *mhancha*.[16] The family's foodways changed after the death of Hajja's husband. Although Hajja owns fruit trees near her hometown and receives a share of the annual harvest through her maternal family, during the period of my fieldwork she could not afford to buy and prepare many of the speciality foods that she and her children grew up with. As a result, her daughter did not fully acquire a Soussi taste. Rather, Fatimzahra introduced new recipes from television shows, cookbooks and her neighbours and friends to complement her mother's Soussi cuisine.

Rachida's foodways can be described as more rural than those of Hajja and Fatimzahra. They were marked by a smaller repertoire of specialty ingredients due to her growing up in the Haouz plains surrounding Marrakech and her role as sole breadwinner with less time and money for cooking. Her Amazigh heritage and family connections influenced her wide-ranging use of cereals and herbs for cooking, such as barley or wild thyme, which she received from her natal family in the Haouz plains and the Ourika Valley close to Marrakech. At the same time, Rachida did not know how to prepare typical urban Moroccan dishes such as *bastila* or *shebbakiya*. Nevertheless, despite her full-time work as a cleaner, she spent much of her spare time processing and preparing food, including homemade bread. Not surprisingly, her daughters both hoped they would not have to cook as much when they would marry. Although Rachida insisted that they learn to prepare everything 'the way it should be', in exchange for help, Rachida's daughters employed their digital literacy to introduce new recipes such as homemade pizza or pound cakes.

Aicha's foodways were also marked by her rural Amazigh origins. However, since her husband was an Amazigh from the Souss with a distinct taste, as Hajja's case also shows, Aicha learned to incorporate his childhood tastes into her cooking, such as *amlou* (a spread containing almonds, argan oil and honey). Perhaps due to her relative youth and the fact that she had just established her own household when I began my fieldwork, Aicha reached out more actively to widen her cooking knowledge to include Soussi regional cuisine and royal urban dishes like *bastila* or the Marrakchi specialty *terda* (a lentil dish based on leftover bread). It was only when her first child was born, nearly ten years after she moved to Marrakech, that Aicha began to regularly prepare homemade foods again and was proud of doing so. She worked to have her own money for buying relatively valued and artisanal foods such as fruits or honey, so that her daughters would grow into healthy and clever women.

Although marked by different life trajectories, these families' daily food routines and diets also point to shared routines and patterns. Most daily meals were remarkably similar among my research participants. For most breakfasts, leftover flatbread from the day before was briefly warmed up in the pan, dipped into butter or olive oil and served with either tea or coffee. When no bread was left, fresh bread was usually bought and quickly spread with butter or cream cheese in a nearby *hanut* (corner shop), often on the way to school and/or work. Lunch was considered the main meal of the day, even if it was not always consumed every day, as was the case in Rachida's household up to three times a week depending on their busy schedules of work, school and university. Most days, my research participants prepared a *tajine* (stew) in the name-giving earthenware pan or in a pressure cooker to speed up cooking time, using seasonal vegetables and a little bit of meat 'for the taste', except on Fridays or Sundays, when couscous was prepared for lunch. *Tajine* was always accompanied by and eaten with bread, ideally homemade during the morning. Whenever available, a small salad, a self-squeezed juice or fresh fruit were served too.

In the afternoon, a shared snack (*kaskrut*, from the French term *casse-croûte*) was common in all three families consisting of heavily sugared tea or coffee as well as more bread or *msemen* (a layered pancake) with butter and honey or, increasingly, a pound cake or even pizza. If other commitments such as wage work prevented a lunch, this snack could be replaced by a more substantial meal based on *tajine*. Generally, *kaskrut* was a commensal moment that often involved visiting neighbours, friends or extended family members and reflects the strong cultural emphasis on hospitality common to Muslim societies. Dinners were considered the least important of daily meals and often consisted of leftovers from lunch, sometimes a quick pasta or rice dish and, more rarely still, convenience foods such as yoghurts or street food bought spontaneously. For all three families – as well as for all other low-income Moroccans I worked with – bread was the main staple of their everyday diet and was revered as such. At the same time, my research participants often blamed bread – along with sugar, another daily staple of the urban poor (Mintz 1986) – for the rising rates of noncommunicable diseases such as diabetes and heart diseases among urban Moroccans (cf. Food and Agriculture Organization et al. 2020; Mokhtar et al. 2001).

As in most low-income Marrakchi households where my research took me over the years, Hajja, Rachida and Aicha had had access to reliable electricity only for roughly one decade. Still, refrigerator-freezers and smaller electric household appliances such as handheld blenders were a common sight in 2012 and 2013. Although potable running water was also common by then, with one single tap in the kitchen and one in the bathroom, central heating systems and hot running water were largely absent across low-income medina homes. While Rachida and Aicha had recently bought semi-automatic washing machines and rejoiced at the reduced workload, dishwashers were not common (cf. Dike 2021). Bigger kitchens like Hajja's often contained a low plastic table with a few stools around it. Smaller ones often resembled fitted kitchens with a countertop, hanging cabinets and a 'modern', i.e. high table with a few chairs as in Aicha's home. For cooking, most households relied on subsidized liquid petroleum gas (LPG) sold in cylinders of two sizes.[17] The larger cylinders were used for a two- or four-stove combined hob and oven, while the smaller ones were used as a single, mobile LPG burner. Most cooks also owned a small adobe frame to grill over charcoal, mostly for special occasions such as Ramadan or 'Id al-kebir, the feast of the great sacrifice. With widespread 3G internet access, smartphones became common among younger Moroccans towards the end of my fieldwork. These often served as kitchen tools to communicate, entertain or research recipes online.

Material continuity and change is also manifest in the broader urban infrastructure. Although Marrakech boasts a number of smaller and larger supermarkets, traditional markets were very popular among low-income Marrakchis. These latter supplied all the daily, weekly and monthly necessities of food and drink, making food provisioning a local practice. Like all transport hubs and marketplaces, Marrakech also offered a vast range of affordable street foods, which provided occasional alternatives to homemade food for low-income families, albeit in the form of snacks rather than complete meals. Although a huge range of restaurants and cafés exist throughout the city, these were generally not frequented by my research participants, and certainly not by the women among them. Rather, most low-income cooks strove to bake their own bread and cook at least one meal every day, shaping the city's infrastructure in subtle ways. For instance, each neighbourhood boasts an electric mill and at least one public oven to grind wheat grains into flour and bake the characteristic large homemade bread loaves. Fresh food is sold at nearly every corner, meeting the general preference for raw, unprocessed ingredients. In addition, mobile peddlers travel through every little alley to sell seasonal foods such as fish or barbary figs door to door.

Social change is less obvious to the eye, but it can still be perceived in the city. For instance, school attendance is compulsory for all children until the age of thirteen and it was common for girls of low-income backgrounds to attend secondary school and increasingly also university. Since many low-income women work for a wage, women of all ages are present in the streets and markets at all times, which marks a decisive break with urban life in the past (Mernissi 1987). This is also due to structural adjustment programmes and agricultural reforms in the 1980s, pushing large numbers of impoverished rural Moroccans to try their luck in the cities. The prospect of an independent income lured predominantly younger generations (Crawford 2008), women were particularly attracted by education and the promises of a capitalist labour market in fast-growing cities such as Rabat, Casablanca and Marrakech (Kapchan 1996; Montgomery 2019; Sadiqi and Ennaji 2006). Women like Rachida and Aicha, and even Hajja one generation earlier, gained some freedom when they left behind their natal families – and the tight social control – yet without losing their rural kin and sense of identity, as was evident in the constant flow of regional knowledge, of foods and of people in and out of Marrakech (cf. Graf 2018).

Education in general and literacy in particular divide generations of women most notably.[18] Despite the Arabization programmes that have been running since Moroccan independence, everyday communication and literacy in Morocco is largely based on the oral Arabic dialect *darija* and the Latin script, which includes absorbed French terms dating from the Protectorate. Until today, French and the Latin script remain important tools in the professional and business world, and increasingly also English. At the same time, many rural migrants to Moroccan cities speak Tamazight as a first language, which only became an official national language in 2011.[19] They grew up speaking one of the three distinct Tamazight dialects depending on their regional origins, which bear no linguistic resemblance to *darija* or to *fusha*, the Modern Standard Arabic that many Moroccans still scarcely use in their daily lives (cf. Boutieri 2016; Sadiqi 2014). In an increasingly visually and digitally mediated world, generational differences in literacy acquire yet more nuanced meanings. What exactly being literate means in Morocco is thus highly varied and context-specific, as the protagonists of this book also demonstrate.

Furthermore, for poor, unmarried 'girls', it is nothing new to work for a wage both in rural and in urban Morocco (Cairoli 2011; Montgomery 2019; Zvan Elliott 2015).[20] However, in the last couple of decades it has become much more common for married urban women to also continue to work for a wage after marriage and childbirth (Conway-Long 2006; Kapchan 1996; Sadiqi and Ennaji 2006). These latter women, including those I conducted research with, work for financial reasons and not because they seek to realize a professional career or identify with their jobs like the 'global middle class' described by Cohen (2004). Rather, earning an income allows them to buy 'treats' such as fruits or clothes for their children, and, in the longer term, to establish their own conjugal household and manage all food work independent of their mothers-in-law, who have often exclusive control over younger women's domestic work and life. Although policy reforms since the early 2000s, like that of the family law (*mudawana*) advocating women's right to divorce among others, are fostering awareness and discussions about women's emancipation, they have not (yet) contributed to changing the everyday lives of young low-income women or unmarried 'girls' (Zvan Elliott 2015). Patriarchal values based on the dominance of men and seniors still rule, despite palpable social change in the city, and play an important role in contemporary domestic cooking.

Living and Thinking Domestic Cooking

The above descriptions point to the tremendous cultural importance of food work in everyday family life in Morocco. However, no food-centred monographs exist; even in the Middle East and North Africa, very few anthropologists have studied everyday domestic food practices.[21] Although food figures in some ethnographies of everyday life in Morocco, it is often studied rather casually and within different contexts. For example, in rural Morocco the familial production and processing of food are central to low-income families' economic livelihoods, especially in the absence of alternative incomes (Crawford 2008). By contrast, in middle- and upper-income families in urban Morocco, food preparation plays an increasingly minor role in everyday domestic work due to a professionalization of women, access to supermarkets and kitchen technologies or the ability to employ other women to do the work (Kapchan 1996; Montgomery 2019; Newcomb 2017). My ethnographic research with low-income Marrakchi families fills this gap by bringing together the study of food and of the family. It shows how and why cooking continues to be important.

To understand the reproduction of food and of the family in this context, I draw on anthropological food studies from across the world, an ever-growing research field since the 1990s (Mintz and du Bois 2002; Sutton 2010; Wilk 2006). Yet, even within anthropological food scholarship, ethnographic studies of cooking are relatively scarce and focus mostly on the United States, Europe or other highly industrialized countries like Israel. In various ways, these studies attempt to understand *what* cooking knowledge is, describing it as embodied and largely nonverbal. The knowledge to cook is either reported to be transmitted from older to younger women or men, or acquired from cookbooks and other written sources. However, these authors do not agree about the effects of material and social change on cooking knowledge and its reproduction. Some conclude that bodily practices are gradually being lost (Abarca 2006; Counihan 2004, 2009; Giard 1998; Gvion 2012) – and to some extent echo the public perception of cooking skills declining with the advent of affordable technology and the individualization of societies. Others focus on cooking practices and their reproduction as being in constant flux and reflective of changing technologies and societies (Adapon 2008; Short 2006; Sutton 2014; Trubek 2017).[22] I follow in the footsteps of the latter perspective, with emphasis on *how* cooking knowledge is constituted and reproduced in the context of change.

Studying domestic cooking knowledge lends itself to a phenomenological approach to sharing the lived experience of domestic cooks. As Ingold put it: 'We do not have to think the world in order to live in it, but we do have to live in the world in order to think it' (2011: 418). Although critiquing the emphasis on societal continuity rather than change, phenomenologically inspired anthropologists like him draw on Mauss' concept of techniques of the body as 'the ways in which from society to society men [*sic*] know how to use their bodies' (1973: 70), coupled with Bourdieu's (1977) analysis of how people learn and share a practical sense of the world. According to practice theory, routine practices such as the use of space or the daily preparation of food are internalized structures, a habitus, which disposes people to do something in a certain way without the need to reflect upon it. Since the late 1980s, anthropologists combined practice theory with Merleau-Ponty's (2001) phenomenology by focusing on embodiment and the subjective experience of the world as lived (Csordas 1994; Jackson 1996; Stoller 1997; Weiss 1996).

Ethnographies of craft learning prove particularly helpful, since they argue that understanding a nonverbal practice requires doing, and advocate for apprenticeship as an ethnographic method (e.g. Coy 1989; Grasseni 2008; Marchand 2009; Portisch 2010; Wacquant 2004). Not surprisingly, methodology is key to these ethnographies. The ethnographer joins in the transmission of craft skills and a broader conditioning of the artisan body through the 'integration of morals, muscles and mind' (Marchand 2009: 6). Wacquant describes such an approach as anthropology 'from the body' (2004: viii); a form of 'surrender' through immersing oneself in the practice that is being studied, what he calls 'observant participation' (2004: 4 fn. 3, 11 fn. 16). And so I surrendered to Moroccan cooking.

Yet, in doing so, I realized that learning to cook also differs from more formal or semi-formal craft apprenticeships. Learning to cook – as well as understanding learning – is often done without deliberation by the cook-to-be as it is in more formal apprenticeships such as carpet weaving (Portisch 2010), masonry (Marchand 2009) or boxing (Wacquant 2004). Equally, because it is such a mundane practice, embedded in everyday family life, learning to cook has no beginning or end point; it always takes place as we hear, smell, touch, taste and see food in the making around us, even in the womb. Thus, some form of learning takes place whether we seek it out or not.

My own experience is indicative of this. After fieldwork, when I began analysing my ethnographic materials, I was puzzled and seemingly unable to fully heed my learning body (see the interludes). It took a while before I understood that my methodological attention had been biased by vision and sight as my main perceptive tools. In fact, most ethnographic craft apprenticeships rely primarily on participant *observation*, in particular through focusing on imitation. Yet, my fieldnotes hardly contain any material based on direct observation and even less on imitation. It was only after fieldwork, when noticing this absence and grappling with whether I had learned to cook the Moroccan way at all, that I realized how the study of cooking engages all senses, often beyond what I could observe or verbalize in fieldnotes; my bodily experience had become ethnographic material.[23]

Participant Perception as Theory and Method

A collection of such different practices as provisioning, processing, preparing, serving, eating and disposing of food, domestic cooking involves a cook's multisensory, often synesthetic perception of the entire material and social environment that makes cooking possible (cf. Korsmeyer and Sutton 2011). In this context, where, when and how does the knowledge of the domestic cook and its apprenticeship begin, and does it ever end? To take seriously and account for this open-endedness and the sensory multiplicity of bodily experience and learning, I suggest speaking of 'participant perception', both of the research participant and of the ethnographer. Participant perception captures not only a way of learning to cook, as I describe throughout the main chapters; it also captures my own growing understanding of domestic cooking as I describe in the interludes and in Chapter 2. Participant perception provides the methodological and theoretical basis for my understanding of the reproduction of cooking knowledge.

By incorporating the ethnographer's multisensory experience during and after fieldwork, participant perception joins the methodological attention to practices with the theoretical attention to the senses.[24] In its successful attempt to end the 'hegemony of sight' (Howes 1991: 4) – which is deeply engrained in Western culture and in anthropological scholarship since Enlightenment (Stoller 1989) – the anthropology of the senses places all senses at the centre of bodily modes of knowing.[25] Stoller (1989: 7) was an early proponent of 'epistemological humility', teaching us that the ethnographer should not only observe, but also touch, taste, smell and hear along during fieldwork. Stoller (1997) describes the dialectic between the sensory and the analytical as a form of 'sensuous scholarship'. Yet, participant perception brings the understanding of the cook and the understanding of the ethnographer closer together, without at the same time equalling what are necessarily vastly different experiences. It recognizes much more forcefully that I – just like my research participants – can only know what is opened up to me by my experience, and that in learning to cook, I also understand cooking. As a result, participant perception manifests itself in many different ways during and after fieldwork.

In practice, the notion of participant perception means that the ethnographer's involvement extends far beyond direct observation and involves participation at various distances. Since many daily practices are gendered in Morocco, as a woman I spent much of my time with other women, participating in the domestic activities that women of various ages do, including but not limited to provisioning, processing, cooking, baking and eating food. While I often joined the engagement of a cook with her material and social environment, especially when shopping food or baking, depending on the tasks I took on in each family, I did not always share practices in a direct manner. Sometimes I was physically unable to join, especially when I went shopping while another member of the family processed ingredients for lunch. In other cases, I was tasked with processing herbs in the salon, while the lead cook was cooking in the kitchen. In such moments, although I was not observing the cook, I was still able to smell and listen to her activities or touch and taste the result of her work, enabling me to share some of her bodily engagement. Lastly, in handling and eating the meal around the communal plate, everyone was drawn back into the shared experience of food in the making. In short, participant perception involves joining in and co-producing a social multisensory routine that goes far beyond food preparation itself.[26] Taken together, these food practices produce a shared multisensory life that involves family members, friends and guests, cooks and noncooks alike.[27]

The spatial and temporal boundaries of my participant perception were equally fluid. Apart from 're-membering' (Connerton 1989: 72) or storing procedures and processes in my body through repeated practice, which I describe primarily in the interludes, I also kept a food diary and jotted down small notes, recipes or techniques in a small notebook throughout the day, followed by writing more detailed fieldnotes at the end of each day. As I joined in the many activities of daily life, I asked a wide range of questions and discussed topics as they arose and mattered to my research participants and their wider social network. These informal and often spontaneous conversations, carried out in *darija*, French or – more often – a mix of the two, were part and parcel of my participant perception. In fact, casual conversations proved to be the most meaningful way of interviewing especially older women due to a widespread suspicion towards formal information gathering and voice recording. With family members, friends or acquaintances who were less familiar with me and my research, already the presence of a pen and paper altered the flow of a conversation to the extent that I learned to remember entire conversations for later note taking.[28]

This verbalization and sharing of multisensory experiences complement my own bodily understanding of cooking and allow me to relate my participant perception to the lived experience of my research participants and to that of their friends and extended family in Marrakech and beyond. To further a more generalized understanding of food, I also interviewed, accompanied or sat with other experts such as ethnobotanists, chefs and shopkeepers, as well as various friends and acquaintances in Marrakech and beyond. Given that many of these encounters involved sharing food and a bodily engagement with a certain environment, I was able to expand my participant perception beyond the circle of the three families and their social networks. Even as I write these lines, I still remember the smell, sight, sound, taste or touch of many of these interviews or walk-alongs through the meals or the food environment that I shared with others. It is in this context of shared encounters that photographs, video and audio recordings can capture certain domestic gestures and procedures or urban rhythms and routines, and thus complement and enrich the analysis and representation of my research participants' and my own experiences.[29]

Participant perception also allows us to attune to nonhuman materialities and their relations with humans in an activity such as cooking. After all, food is organic and also transforms without human intervention, and so does the nonorganic environment, including such different elements as climate, temperature and kitchen appliances. The materiality of food and its inherent transformative capacities – what Sutton calls the 'mutinous unpredictability of matter' (2014: 125) – make it a collaborator in the production of a meal, just as the material environment such as tools, appliances and/or the specific space and microclimate of the kitchen facilitate and contribute to this production.[30] Multisensory immersion through participant perception helps us to understand the co-production between cook, food and the material environment as it unfolds in practice. It can manifest itself in cut fingers, sticky hands, stench and disgust as well as intense physical pleasure, which trigger different and unpredictable reactions and adjustments by the cook. My Marrakchi research participants conceptualized the co-production between a cook, food and the material environment, and the inherent unpredictability of every meal making through *baraka* (God's blessing); a meal that turned out well is considered to have *baraka*. Importantly, *baraka* refers not only to a spiritual force and human intention, as the literal translation suggests, but also relates everyday practices to socially negotiated values, which are embedded in various relations of power, as I will illustrate in Chapters 1 and 3.

It is evident by now that understanding food preparation through participant perception takes time, intimacy and patience. It is thus not surprising that in food studies – ethnographic or not – the main methodological approach to cooking has often been via verbal and visual methods such as interviews, surveys and observation rather than via apprenticeship-style and bodily experience, even though cooking knowledge is often described as a largely nonverbal, embodied form of knowledge. My own experience of learning to cook the Moroccan way without fully understanding that I did, which I relate in the interludes and in Chapter 2, makes a strong case for long-term participation in the everyday lives of cooks through deeply immersive perception. Participant perception emphasizes and, indeed, requires the building not only of relationships of trust but also of intimacy with one's research participants and the stuff they use and engage with and that matter to them (Miller 2010).

At the same time, participant perception does not stop at the level of domestic intimacy and everyday lived experience. Although cooking knowledge is anchored in the body of the cook, it is also intersubjective and embedded in family life within a given neighbourhood and urban market, which are, in turn, emplaced in the broader context of a globalized food system. Thus, I consider cooking knowledge as much more than embodied knowledge. It is also a spiritual, a cultural, an economic and a political way of knowing, and as such also involves dissonance and conflict, a dimension that is notoriously absent in phenomenological approaches to practice. Participant perception allows one to *feel* the political economy of life with a low income. Without access to cars and supermarkets, without paid help and convenience foods like many of their middle-class counterparts, the hard work of making food can be acutely felt. Carrying groceries in heavy plastic bags from the market while the sun is scorching and the fingers are being cut by the plastic, being assigned the tedious task of sorting and cleaning herbs or of peeling piles of vegetables every day until the fingers, hands, arms and eyes hurt, and being chastised for being too slow or too wasteful of precious ingredients made me and other novice cooks experience through all perceptual channels of the body the broader social, economic and political context of cooking.

Not only was my participant perception alongside other learning cooks an often painful reminder of the hierarchies of domestic labour requiring young and unexperienced women to submit to the power of older women, it was also a physical reminder of the economic vulnerability and political marginalization of low-income families in Morocco. Of course, relative to other novice cooks, as a relatively affluent foreigner interested in understanding – yet also able to distance myself from – the lives of less affluent and less privileged Moroccans, my position is vastly different. I address this by following Crawford's example to feel *with* and *for* others by bringing our 'fleshy selves' to the ethnographic encounter so as not to overlook the 'hard surfaces of life' (2009: 524, referencing Geertz). By bringing my fleshy self to the daily experience of urban life with a low income, I came to understand just how aware and critical my research participants were of the faultlines of the Moroccan food system and of the government at large. Indeed, as I will show in Chapters 4 and 5, many of their routine provisioning decisions and processing practices should be understood as political acts in response to a government that they hold partially accountable for their plight. As a result of this regular but largely hidden form of political economic participation, domestic cooks and their everyday food practices contribute to political stability in Morocco amidst global food prices hikes and regional upheaval.

Participant perception also has implications for thinking about and representing research. During my fieldwork, it was often impossible to extract myself from the immediate bodily and emotional experience of cooking within a given material and social environment; as my body ached at the end of the day, my mind struggled to express in fieldnotes what had happened. After fieldwork, back home, analysing this experience distances me from the lived experience of cooking in Marrakech. At the same time, it still reverberates in my body when thinking and writing about it; I continue to re-create sensory engagements and emotions old and new. Equally, by preparing Moroccan dishes for my own family and friends, I re-enact past experiences in the present. While my postfieldwork endeavour to analyse cooking requires me to step back from immediate experience in the field, participant perception cannot be removed from bodily experience; it becomes a part of the ethnographer just as I become a part of the ethnography.[31]

Finally, while the representation of domestic cooking in this book threatens to objectify not only my own subjective experience but also that of my research participants, through interweaving my experience of cooking in the interludes with that of my Marrakchi research participants in the main chapters, it also stands for and embraces what all ethnographies ultimately must be: a situated encounter between the anthropologist and her field, including not only other people's often incommensurable experiences but also the ethnographer's thoughts and feelings within a broader context of particular scents, sights, sounds and tastes enmeshed within a constant flow of events and emotions, producing necessarily 'partial connections' (Strathern 2004) and 'situated knowledges' (Haraway 1988). Participant perception is thus both theory and method; it is a way of learning and of understanding; and of making sense of it as we do.

Outline of the Book

Although cooking knowledge is anchored in the body of the cook, it is also intersubjective and embedded in family life within a given neighbourhood and city, which is, in turn, emplaced in Morocco and in the world. As I trace these layers in each chapter, from the body to the globe and back, I demonstrate how low-income Marrakchi cooks engage each layer in their daily food work and that each matters to understanding cooking. While I differentiate between these layers for the sake of representing them in writing, each chapter and interlude also emphasizes the many entanglements between individual and social human and nonhuman bodies, between the urban and the rural, between local and global processes, and between the material and the social. This becomes particularly evident in the making of homemade bread, the staple of the Moroccan diet and of food culture at large. Throughout the interludes and the chapters, different aspects of making bread are used to highlight these entanglements and how seemingly distanced layers are also always connected.

It is thus no accident that the first and the last interlude are about bread. Like all the following interludes, Interlude 1 on kneading describes one of the most routine practices of a low-income domestic cook in Morocco, albeit from my position as a female ethnographer and keen, if not always adept, learner. Interlude 5 points to the very material centrality of bread in preparing and eating a Moroccan meal; without bread, a *tajine* tastes nothing like *tajine*. Furthermore, although these and each intermittent interlude – on cooking couscous, brewing tea and provisioning food – hone in on my participant perception in the reproduction of cooking knowledge in Marrakech at a particular time and place, they also always relate to broader contexts and analytical questions. Thus, each interlude also anticipates the main analytical emphasis and theme of the following chapter. At the same time, the splitting of chapters is sometimes forced. In particular, Chapters 1 and 2 on cooking and on knowledge, and Chapters 3 and 4 on food work and on the family should be thought of as one respectively. Chapter 5 on homemade bread and cereal citizenship will bring all the layers together.

There seems to be no doubt that the knowledge of the cook is grounded in the body, but *how* the domestic cook knows is less clear. To explore the bodiliness of this practice, I propose to consider cooking knowledge as *taste knowledge* in Chapter 1. The notion of taste knowledge allows us to grasp how cooking knowledge is constituted in, through and beyond the sensing body of the cook. Importantly, rather than taste with her tongue, she tastes and knows food also with her fingers, her nose, her eyes and her ears, often jointly. Bodily perception through taste is rarely verbalized in Morocco, though often invoked when the cook vaguely explains she cooks 'according to taste'. At the same time, taste conjures social evaluation and serves as a moral compass in times of change. The expression 'as long as it takes' captures this social dimension and also points towards the temporality of cooking knowledge. A sense of temporality guides all cooking practices in the confluence of cook, food and environment, both as a cook's *sixth sense* or bodily perception, and as an *extrasensory* ability to understand the moral universe around food. In other words, cultural values of good and bad food are deeply implicated in the bodily experience of temporality in cooking. These values pertain to widely shared ideas of health and wellbeing, womanhood and family life, as well as spiritual and ethical behaviour towards God and other creatures.[32] In combination with *baraka*, the notion of taste knowledge highlights that there is much more to a cook's knowledge than the mere act of preparing food and that it requires hard work. As such, taste knowledge is not only marked by bodily resonance with the material environment; in the context of change and persisting socioeconomic uncertainty, it also involves a cook's negotiation of deeply held social values and thus necessarily includes conflict.

In Chapter 2 I then ask how taste knowledge is reproduced and apply the concept of participant perception as both a theory and a method of learning and understanding cooking knowledge. A cook's participant perception is composed of three distinct elements of learning, which taken together illustrate that knowledge is not simply transmitted from one generation of cooks to the next, but rather is regrown in each in a material and social taste environment dominated by older generations of domestic cooks. However, this chapter also shows how new technologies and media such as smartphones and social media initiate a reversal of the flow of knowledge from younger cooks to older ones, and thereby contribute to altering the reproduction of taste knowledge and, ultimately, the making of a cook too. At the same time, since participant perception understands learning from the particular vantage point of situated encounters between humans as well as between humans and nonhumans, how, when and what a cook learns is the result of manifold situated negotiations and defies any form of temporal, technological or cultural determinism. Taken together, the notion of taste knowledge coupled with attention to the multisensory dimensions of learning and understanding learning highlight how a cook's sense of taste is attuned to the unpredictable and constantly changing workings of her material and social environment, and, as such, constitutes a highly accurate and adaptive form of knowledge that is anything but fading with the advent of affordable electric and digital technology.

In Chapter 3 I move on to focus on social change in low-income Marrakech. Low-income women increasingly work for a wage in order to gain independence from patriarchal family relations. I analyse and make sense of women's emancipation and their continuous motivation to cook for the family through the notion of 'culinary connectivity'. This concept illustrates how Moroccans define themselves in relation to others and how mature womanhood is reached through making good food for the family. It allows me to explore the crucial role that food plays in making the low-income urban family. The preparation and consumption of family meals is central to creating, maintaining or challenging the material and symbolic bonds that hold families and friends together. Culinary connectivity thus emphasizes the knowledgeable practices of the cook in connecting the materiality and the sociality of food. Although gender plays an important role in the domestic division of labour, as I will show, culinary connectivity focuses attention on intergenerational gendered negotiations of what it means to be a woman and a family in low-income Morocco. In establishing the link between making food and making the family, culinary connectivity helps in understanding why domestic cooking remains an important cultural practice that is central to notions of womanhood and of the family in urban Morocco.

To widen our understanding of why these women still bother to cook for their families, in Chapter 4 I propose to attend to the whole range of networks, discourses and practices that matter to ensuring that food is not just any food, but *good* food. During my fieldwork over the years, my research participants often emphasized the quality of the food they bought, processed, prepared, served and ate. They used the vernacular pair of *beldi* and *rumi* to describe food quality. Depending on the context, *beldi* indexes regional or homemade food, whereas *rumi* indexes imported or industrial food. Yet, even though there is a widely shared idea of the 'Moroccan way of cooking' – even described as part of the 'Mediterranean diet' by UNESCO – 'beldi foodways' stand for a situated and bodily understanding of food quality that connects rural and urban Morocco.[33] By widening what defines Moroccan food practices through attention to more than just the domestic preparation and consumption of food, the notion of *beldi* foodways shifts attention towards the material and social network that makes the preparation of a good family meal possible. Tracing the connections and disconnections between *beldi* and *rumi* foods points to the broader political economy of domestic cooking, showing how low-income urban Moroccans engage with the entire food system and their government as they cook.

Indeed, food and those who provision, process, prepare and eat it every day play a central role in national stability in Morocco, as I will argue in Chapter 5. This chapter draws on my research on bread in Marrakech and Beni Mellal to bring together the bodily and cultural dimensions of food preparation with the broader ecological, economic and political aspects of daily sustenance. Through a historical approach to wheat production and distribution in Morocco, it first reveals the main coordinates of poverty and food insecurity in Morocco and situates mundane practices around homemade bread in the larger political economy of life. I argue that in provisioning domestically produced grains and processing them into wholemeal flour, low-income domestic cooks become 'cereal citizens'. In valuing homemade bread over store-bought alternatives and in carefully reproducing the knowledge it takes to make their own flour, recently urbanized Moroccans contribute to the social contract that has ensured the political legitimacy of the Moroccan monarchy for four centuries. I further describe how through baking and eating homemade bread, cereal citizens also shape and maintain the urban food infrastructure and, in doing so, ensure the health and wellbeing of themselves and their families. Overall, Chapter 5 suggests that phenomenological attention to low-income women's bodily knowledge helps us to understand the paradoxes of political stability within a national context of authoritarianism and a global context of ecological, economic and political crises.

Notes

1. Other ethnographies recounting how hard food work is include Bowen, Brenton and Elliott (2019); Carney (2015); Garth (2020); and Holtzman (2009). Overall, however, there is still not enough research, ethnographic or not, that showcases this aspect of everyday food work.

2. I also took a course on Modern Standard Arabic at SOAS prior to my main fieldwork and learned to converse independently in *darija* thanks to five months of paid weekly individual lessons in Marrakech in 2013.
3. During my fieldwork, three currencies circulated in traditional markets: the riyal was officially operative between 1882 and 1921, and continues to be used in Marrakech, mostly by shopkeepers with their older female clients. The franc was introduced during the French Protectorate (1912–56). Though officially in use between 1921 and 1960, during my fieldwork it was still used by all older urban shoppers, women and men alike. The dirham is the current official currency in Morocco and the only one in print. It was used by shopkeepers in interaction with children and high-income shoppers or foreigners. The women I worked with were fluent in all three currencies and easily switched between them, using whichever was more convenient (cf. Wagner 1993).
4. Fatimzahra is burdened with a physical disability she has had since birth. She suffers daily from pain, which affects but does not impair her body movements. In 2007 I accompanied her and paid for various medical check-ups to see whether her pains could be alleviated permanently; they could not. To some extent, after more than forty years of living with it, pain had become a normal part of her life and Fatimzahra had developed the 'expertise' to normalize her disability for others (Hartblay 2020).
5. My presence – coupled with the successful bid for a coveted plane ticket – was a main driver in Hajja's decision to undertake the journey. She would not have left her daughter without female support for such a long period of time. Hajja, which is not her given name, acquired this honourable new name upon her safe return to Morocco, like all returnees from the *haj*. Like everyone else, henceforth I only called her by this name.
6. Among the low-income Moroccans I met over the years, language and ethnicity were rarely a topic of conversation or contestation. Rather, regional origin served as a marker to identify with others. Still, it is important to note that Amazigh language and identity, including that of other ethnic minorities such as the Haratin (El Hamel 2013), have been systematically devalued in the past. Despite more recent political activism that led to recognizing *tamazight* (the generic name for all Amazigh dialects) as a national language in the early 2000s, this is still the case today (Silverstein and Crawford 2004).
7. A total of 29% of the Moroccan population lived in cities in 1960. In 2014 60% of the population was urbanized (Royaume du Maroc 2014). Gaul (2019) reminds us that rural-to-urban migration is not always direct; it often involves multiple stops and movements.
8. *Sharifi* designates descendance from the Prophet Mohamed and bestows a religiously endowed nobility. It is only passed on via the patrilineage. While it used to imply a certain economic and political power, today it tends to carry mostly symbolic weight.
9. This amount equals roughly €250 (€1 = 10 dirham).
10. My search criteria included at least two generations of low-income women and a small room for myself – an almost contradictory pair of conditions. Although several women I met had agreed to participate, their husbands objected to my stay in their homes.
11. Neighbourhoods are closely monitored spaces, as I learned on several occasions. Not only did both families I lived with register my presence with the local authorities, I was also warned by the local imam not to spend too much time with male shopkeepers of the neighbourhood as this could compromise everyone's reputation.
12. Despite women's widespread presence in urban Moroccan public space, many low-income women considered leaving the house as trespassing into male space and thus avoided going

out alone or lingering in streets or public squares (cf. Graouid 2004). Especially when unmarried and unaccompanied, both Moroccan and foreign women are regularly harassed by young men on urban Moroccan streets (Chafai 2021; Monqid 2011).
13. Before the COVID-19 pandemic, Marrakech received around two million visitors annually.
14. The United Nations understanding of poverty now also acknowledges that poverty is multidimensional and cannot be limited to a fixed set of financial assets. See also Zvan Elliott's (2015: 10–11) discussion of how poverty interrelates with gender.
15. See Maghraoui (2002) for an overview of how neoliberal economics and authoritarian politics have coevolved since Moroccan independence, while general levels of poverty have actually increased since the 1990s (Benjelloun 2002: 136).
16. Soussi cuisine is marked by several endemic ingredients. Saffron is grown on the mountains surrounding Taroudant and is unaffordable for most Moroccans, unless sourced through family connections. The argan tree only grows in the Moroccan south and the oil produced by cold-pressing its nuts has acquired global fame not only as a culinary ingredient but also as a beauty product. The Souss is also a major producer of tree fruits such as prunes and almonds. See Aylwin (1999) for a historical and symbolic analysis of some of these ingredients and dishes.
17. Gaul (2018) describes how Moroccans adopted gas burners much later than Egyptians, largely due to French colonial policies that sought to preserve Moroccan social and cultural structures.
18. According to the national population census of 2004, of the women born up to 1969, like Hajja, 52% of those born in Moroccan cities and 94% born in rural Morocco are illiterate (Sebti et al. 2009: 69). Of women born between 1969 and 1979, 33% of urban born and 81% of rural women are illiterate, like the generation of Fatimzahra and Rachida. Women born between 1979 and 1989, like Aicha, are only 18.5% illiterate if they were born in the city, compared to a shocking 64% in rural Morocco (ibid.); indeed, Aicha's younger sister-in-law Halima was barely able to read Aicha's cookbooks. For a critical discussion concerning rural women's literacy, see Zvan Elliot (2015).
19. *Tamazight* is mostly an oral language. Rifi *tamazight* is spoken in the northern Rif Mountains, *tamazight* in the Middle Atlas Mountains and *tashelhit* in the High Atlas, the Anti-Atlas Mountains and the Souss valley in the south of Morocco. The *tamazight* script *tifinagh* has been popularized by Amazigh activists since the 1960s and in 2004 became officially part of the school curriculum, but it is hardly used in everyday urban life.
20. Errazzouki (2014: 262) argues that working-class women's share of the labour force actually decreased from 30% in the 1980s to 11% in 2003. However, because low-income women often work in the informal economy, I doubt that these numbers accurately reflect women's participation in wage work.
21. In historically oriented accounts of Morocco, food takes on more central roles, e.g. in rituals and festive occasions (Aylwin 1999; Buitelaar 1993) or in reform policies and agriculture (Holden 2009; Swearingen 1987). Notable ethnographies of domestic food practices in other Muslim contexts are Barnes (2022); Maclagan (1994); and Naguib (2015).
22. Others have studied cooking, also mostly in the United States and Europe – see, for instance, Cairns and Johnston (2015); Caraher et al. (1999); and Kaufmann (2010). Since their approach is largely based on interviews and focused less on cooking as a practice and as knowledge, their research is comparatively less relevant.

23. Desmond (2006: 392) argues similarly: 'My body became a field note.'
24. I am not the only one to highlight the multisensory nature of ethnographic fieldwork. For instance, Pink (2009) proposes a more sensory approach to ethnography, albeit as a theory of place and place making that relies largely on the visual. Writing about Chinese foodies in Beijing, Xu (2019) speaks of 'participant sensation'.
25. Various ethnographies have since overcome the sensory ethnocentrism critiqued by Howes (1991), showing especially how hearing, smell, taste and touch are equally constitutive of our lived experience, in particular with regard to food (Sutton 2010).
26. In his ethnography of Chinese temple festivals, Chau widens 'sensory-interpretative' phenomenological ethnographies of bodily senses through a 'sensory-productive' understanding of a 'social sensorium, [whereby] the body and its actions themselves are key contributors to the production of a sensory event' (2008: 488).
27. Lave and Wenger (1991) were among the first to acknowledge the importance of the social learning environment, especially in everyday situations of learning.
28. Spittler (2001) provides good arguments for how casual conversations in combination with observation over a long period of time can lead to what he calls 'thick participation'.
29. Although keen photographers with their own smartphones, as Muslims my female research participants were wary of being photographed in their domestic attire, without a headscarf and outer garments. Out of respect, there are thus rarely recognizable people in these photographs, except when explicit consent was given.
30. Similar approaches to food can be found in Abbots (2017); Adapon (2008); Janeja (2010); Paxson (2013); van Daele (2013); Weiss (1996); and West (2013b). For ethnographic descriptions regarding the material environment more broadly, see Ingold (2011); Hernandez and Sutton (2003); and Sutton (2006).
31. Retsikas (2008) provides a self-reflexive analysis of the emergence and the effects of knowledge from the body during his fieldwork at a quranic school in Muslim East Java. Stoller (1989) more explicitly includes his own bodily suffering as part of his learning to become a Songhay sorcerer.
32. Like in the Moroccan village studied by Crawford (2008), faith and religion are so ingrained in everyday Marrakchi life that they are rarely verbalized or separated from other spheres of life and neither do I in this book.
33. See https://ich.unesco.org/en/RL/mediterranean-diet-00884 (retrieved 7 September 2023).

INTERLUDE 1

Kneading

I woke up from the rustling sound of tools in the kitchen, adjacent to my room. Like every morning, Aicha had started the day with the assembly of ingredients and tools for making bread. I immediately got up and sleepily staggered out of my room, only to find Aicha kneeling over the *qesriya* (a large earthenware plate) on the kitchen floor. She seemed to wait for me. 'You want to learn how to make bread?!' She pointed towards the *qesriya*: 'Ya-allah [go ahead]!' She smiled and I took her place behind it.

I immediately felt the water, the flour and the yeast in the making when I dipped my fingers into the warm hollow of yeast in the centre of the dough. Aicha poured water over the dough. I slowly and awkwardly began to mix the water and the flour with my right hand; with the left I did nothing, until Aicha handed me the kettle: it had proved unwieldy for her to pour water, as her movements did not match mine. I tried to replicate her gestures, but the dough behaved differently with me: it just grabbed my fingers and stuck to them, impairing my movement; my fingers seemed immobile. Aicha got impatient and took over again. She poured water generously (after she had earlier warned me not to add too much of it) and kneaded flour and water into a dough with a few quick movements. She then put aside the kettle and the real kneading began. Only then did she urge me to take over again.

I did, and felt small compared to the dough's thickness and resistance, its bounciness and stickiness. I drove my shyly formed fists into the giant heap of dough, but my strength only made it halfway. Aicha showed me how to do it: she pointed to the tips of her toes, demonstrating that she moved her weight up onto her feet and then drove her whole body weight down into the dough, her hands holding on to one another to form a unity against the resisting dough.

I took over once more, but felt incapable to channel all my strength into that one direction. I also could not replicate that double punch that Aicha performed: first driving the fist in, then flipping it 90° to also hit the dough with the wrists of both hands. After this punching, she showed me how to coordinate both hands in a smooth, rhythmic movement that punched and pulled the dough at the same time, as even as a kneading machine: with the right hand, you drive your fist in, while the thumb holds the fingers together; with the left hand, you grab the flattened dough; then you flip and drive the wrist of your right hand into the dough, while you flip the flattened dough over with your left hand, extracting your hand before the dough can grab it. Then the left hand performs the movement of punching and the other pulls the flattening dough, and so on.

Still, I could not coordinate my hands, and Aicha once again took over to demonstrate how her whole body contributed to sinking her hands into the dough in opposite but perfectly coordinated movements. Her breath accelerated rhythmically. How smooth and beautiful her movements were! But equally, how perfectly adapted to this movement her bodily constitution was; her neck-and-shoulder-complex betrayed these ten minutes of daily workout.

Three mornings later, I tried again. Aicha left the kitchen to sort lentils under the window in the hallway, leaving me alone in my engagement with the dough. This time I did manage to knead the dough through to the bottom; I employed my whole body to push into the dough and it worked much better. I also tried to form fists as I had seen Aicha do, but I only partly succeeded. I noticed how much weaker my left hand was and found myself almost exclusively using my right hand. I was just not able to replicate that movement with my left hand; it felt awkward, but I continued.

Suddenly, I heard Aicha emit a groaning sound. I looked up and saw a cheeky grin. Admittedly, I sounded like I was making love to the bread dough. As I paused to realize the intimacy of my engagement with this living mass, Aicha reprimanded me: 'It's not good to let it rest too long without kneading!' I continued to knead, increasingly exhausted, and asked her how I should know when to stop. Aicha mumbled: 'Well, when it feels ready.' She continued, pensively: 'How can I explain that?! You can feel it [*kathess*] . . . Anyway, the more you knead the dough, the softer the bread is.'

As I continued, now panting, I kept wondering aloud why the dough was so sticky on my fingers but not on hers. I ventured to say that my hands were much drier than hers. Aicha instantly replied that hers were as dry and finished up for me by assembling the sticky parts into one smooth mass, gently spreading vegetable oil on top, then carefully covering it with a plastic bag and a cotton towel to let the dough rest before shaping it into three loaves and bringing them to the public oven as she did every day.

CHAPTER 1

Taste Knowledge
Cooking with Six Senses

It was a hot afternoon during Ramadan in Aicha's employer's kitchen in Marrakech's medina. Together with her sister-in-law Halima, we prepared snacks for *al-ftour* (the meal breaking the daily fast after sunset). Aicha set up a pot of tea. Keen to help, I took a bundle of fresh mint from the fridge and asked: 'How much should I add?' Aicha took the bundle from me and picked the mint leaves herself. She had begun by saying '*sidi chouia* [add a little]', but quickly concluded: 'I have to do it myself, I need to touch it!' She added, pensively: 'You know, this is why the tea turns out with too much or too little sugar: I begin to make it, I know how much sugar I have got, but when Halima finishes it, like yesterday, she doesn't know how much sugar is in there and it turns out *messous* [tasteless, here: not sweet enough]'. She illustrated by lifting her palm cradling a piece of sugar: 'I have to feel with my hands [*khassni nhess b l-idiya*] how thick or heavy a piece is. Even if you show me a piece and ask if it's good, I cannot *feel* whether it is right or not.' Other Marrakchi cooks explained this feeling more enigmatically as 'according to taste ['*ala hsab dyel legout*]'.

Soon after, upon the whiff of a smell, Aicha pulled out a pizza from the gas-fired oven. She laughed when I asked her how long it had been baking: 'Ha, how should I know, I put it in and took it out again.' Just as she hardly tasted a drink or dish with her tongue to ensure that it would turn out well, she hardly measured time. She added: 'I don't cook things by time!' She still dished up *al-ftour* perfectly on time, to the minute: every evening, the moment of breaking the fast, which shifted by a few minutes every day following the lunar calendar, was awaited so impatiently that a delay in serving food would cause unnecessary tensions among everyone who had anticipated this moment since sunrise. Her sense of time was also noticeable in how she stated '*msha l-hal* [it's too late]' earlier that afternoon; she had not had the time to prepare pizza dough early enough for it to rise 'on time'. 'The bread dough occupied the *qesriya* [an earthenware plate used for dough kneading] for too long'. Instead, Aicha decided to use a portion of her bread dough for pizza and explained she cooks 'As long as it takes [*dakshi li khass*; literally: what it needs]'.

* * *

This vignette stands out from my fieldnotes because it represents a rare moment that verbalizes what is not usually verbalized: how a cook knows. This aspect of cooking knowledge remains underexplored. In this chapter I explore what constitutes cooking knowledge and, in doing so, show that taste and temporality are central to it. Conceiving of cooking knowledge as taste knowledge allows me to make sense of the related expressions 'according to taste' and 'as long as it takes', which refer to both individual and social dimensions of taste. While bodily taste perception is rarely verbalized, yet central to knowing cooking, taste as social evaluation is often conjured in the context of women's emancipation and serves as a moral compass in times of change.

A cook relies on taste to engage with and evaluate food as it turns into a dish, from raw ingredients into a meal that is ready to eat: when sourcing, processing, preparing and serving food, she might taste with her tongue, but, importantly, she will also smell, listen, look at and touch food. In other words, when recalling that feeling Aicha was referring to when she made tea, I also remember the smell of mint, the weight and texture of that piece of sugar, and the sound of bubbly boiling water in the kettle. Tasting food in the making through all senses and understanding cooking are one and the same process. By extension, an ethnographer's participation is hardly limited to visual perception or an isolated event. This synesthetic interaction of the five senses in everyday food practices is central to experiences of subjectivity and related to broader cultural, economic and political forces, as Sutton (2010) argues. Sutton proposes to treat taste as a starting point for anthropological analysis – a form of 'gustemology'. This notion is useful for studying taste not only as a bodily and multisensory form of knowing, but also as a broader set of values that inform everyday food preparation, and helps understanding how cooking knowledge is reproduced in the context of material and social change.

However, neglected in this concept is a sense of temporality, which I call a cook's 'sixth sense'. It involves both sensory perception and a more intuitive, extrasensory ability to understand the moral universe around food preparation. Engaging with food as it transforms for 'as long as it takes' requires attuning to its changing materiality within a given environment, including microclimate, kitchen technologies and those eating the meal, and thus also includes social dimensions of taste. Such a six-dimensional sense of taste only emerges in activity: many cooks only know what to do when they are doing it, as exemplified by Aicha's *al-ftour* preparations. Moreover, cooking 'as long as it takes' serves to define a good cook and, by extension, a good wife and mother. For low-income Marrakchis, it is not just about making food, it is about making *good* food. Thus, cultural values of food are also implicated in the temporality of cooking, especially in the context of material and social change.

The notion of taste knowledge highlights that there is much more to a domestic cook's knowledge than the mere act of preparing food. It is both an everyday practice and a cultural norm, it is perception and discernment, both individual and social practice, it unites and divides, and it engages humans and nonhumans. As such, taste knowledge is not static; it always links past, present and future experiences in an activity. As will become evident throughout this chapter, the notion of taste knowledge showcases how a phenomenological attention to intimate bodily sensations and their direct and indirect responses to material and social transformations allows us to understand broader cultural, economic and political processes, and how these in turn shape, and are shaped by, the work of low-income yet highly knowledgeable women.

I begin this chapter with the thick description of couscous preparation to demonstrate how bodily taste is multisensory. By engaging with the literature on taste as perception and as discernment, I then lay out how individual and social dimensions of cooking are joined in the concept of taste knowledge. In the second section I introduce the element of unpredictability that is part of taste knowledge through the presence or absence of *baraka* (God's blessing). Although a cook has no full control of food in the making and indeed collaborates with food and the material environment in an activity, *baraka* also affirms the powerful role of the cook and her knowledge. In the third section I move on to demonstrate how a phenomenologically inspired conception of taste knowledge also needs to account for temporality as a cook's sixth (at once individual and social) sense, significantly extending the notion of gustemology. Such an expanded notion of taste knowledge allows me to conceptualize the reproduction of cooking knowledge in material and social processes of change in Marrakech in the final section, especially in low-income households without access to health insurance and national social security.

How to Make Good Couscous

One crisp December morning, I returned from shopping in the nearby *suq* (market) and stepped into the warm kitchen.[1] Hajja sat on her cushion on the tiled floor. I handed her the heavy plastic bags. She quietly inspected what I had bought. Fatimzahra commented from a distance: 'That is not the couscous[2] Hajja wanted.' My heart sank. Hajja remained silent, took a few dry grains of couscous between her right thumb and index finger, rubbed them and then placed the grains in her palm to look at them: '*Zouin* [good, nice]!' I sighed with relief. Upon lifting the bag with the freshly slaughtered chicken, Hajja first grumbled that it felt too big. However, after rinsing it with water and rubbing salt and lemon inside and out, she concluded: 'This is a nice chicken.' She sat down on her cushion again and began to peel and then cut carrots, turnips and white cabbage into quarters over the floor; a small knife in her right and the vegetables in her left hand. Fatimzahra placed the water-filled bottom pot of the *couscoussière* (a two-layered pot – the larger bottom is used to prepare sauces, while the perforated top, the *keskas*, is used to steam couscous grains) on an individual LPG burner on the floor in front of her mother.[3]

As Hajja collected the quartered vegetables in a plastic bowl filled with water, Fatimzahra silently placed the pressure cooker between Hajja's feet on the floor and handed her the chicken. Hajja dropped the entire animal into the pot and added some vegetable oil. Without getting up, Hajja then reached into the deep shelf on her left for the spices, adding salt, ground black pepper, ground turmeric and lots of ground ginger. Upon this smell explosion, I remembered the clink-clonk sound of Hajja's rhythmic pounding of spices in her bronze *mehraz* (pestle and mortar) that had echoed musically in the courtyard and woken me up that morning. Less melodiously, Fatimzahra had then ground them fine in her Moulinex, a multifunctional electric kitchen processor named after the French brand.

Once satisfied with the turmeric-yellow colouring of the chicken and the pungent smell of ginger, Hajja took that small knife of hers in her right hand and cut a large onion over the pot: holding the onion in her left hand, she made vertical cuts while swiftly turning the onion with her left fingers. With a sweeping horizontal cut, she then severed the tiny pieces and shook them off onto the chicken. Hajja repeated these coordinated gestures of both her hands until she held only the stump of the onion and the chicken was covered in finely shredded pieces. She stirred everything and got up to place the pressure pot on the fire of the main gas hob. Sitting down again, she finally turned her attention to the couscous grains. She emptied the bag containing the grains that I had bought that morning into her beloved fifty-year-old *gsa'a* (a large plate used for preparing and serving couscous) made of walnut wood. Perceiving the quantity in the *gsa'a* as too little, she reached into the shelf next to her to see if there was more couscous. 'Ah, these are yellow; *al-'ayalat* (the women)', she exclaimed enigmatically as she added the visibly paler leftover grains to the *gsa'a* whilst pointing to the couscous I had brought. She enquired: 'Where did you buy this couscous? At Omar's?' 'Yes', I replied. 'It's yellow, because it's made by women in the countryside.' 'By hand?', I asked. 'Yes.' 'Is it different?' 'Yes, better.' Suddenly turning dismissive, Hajja added that women who work for wages do not know these things, indirectly referring to women like Aicha, as she often did when she wanted to demonstrate her superior knowledge: 'They study, they work, but they don't know this.'

As she talked, Hajja began to move her hands in circles to mix the two types of grains in the *gsa'a* (Figure 1.1). Fatimzahra placed a small pot with cold water next to her. Hajja lifted the pot with her right hand and poured some water into

Figure 1.1. Massaging couscous in a wooden *gsa'a*, Marrakech, 2012. © Katharina Graf

the curved palm of her left hand, jerking it up several times to ease the falling water's impact on the grains and to evenly distribute the smallest drops. When she had added enough water, she poured a handful of salt over the grains and began the 'massage'. She placed her hands at the top of the *gsa'a* and spread her fingers to pull like a plough through the couscous, forming miniature furrows. When her hands met at the bottom of the plate, she scooped and lifted both hands with couscous and rubbed her palms together until the grains had poured back into the plate. She repeated these gestures until her palms confirmed that the grains had absorbed enough water and that any clumps had dissolved.

Meanwhile, Fatimzahra made small incisions into the flank of the chicken with a large knife to see how it cooked. Hajja got up, looked at the chicken too, and was prompted to add more turmeric to give the chicken a yet deeper tinge of yellow. She sat down again and, with her joined palms, carefully scooped the first batch of couscous grains into the perforated top of the *keskas*. In that same moment – surprisingly well timed – the bubbly sound of boiling water became audible. Hajja immediately selected and dropped the carrot and turnip pieces into the pot opposite her knees on that separate LPG burner. She placed the *keskas* on top of that pot, closed the lid and sealed off the invisible gap between the bottom and top pots with a thick cotton ribbon so that the steam would penetrate the couscous grains more thoroughly.[4]

After what felt like an indefinite but brief amount of time to me, Hajja unwrapped the ribbon and took the *keskas* to tip the grains into the *gsa'a* between her feet. She repeated her massaging of the grains, now steaming hot, between her seemingly heat-insensitive palms, while adding more water and also olive oil. This time, however, she rubbed the grains between her palms much more gently, as if they had come to life and were sensitive to pressure. She finished her massage once the grains had an evenly shiny surface and scooped them back into the *keskas* for their second of three steaming rounds ...

Just before our lunch guests arrived, Hajja arranged the fluffy grains of couscous into a conic shape and carefully decorated the centre with chicken and vegetables, finishing her work by pouring the remaining sauce with a ladle onto the whole dish (Figure 1.2). As soon as I placed the large plate in the middle of a low table in the courtyard, the four guests and us dug our right fingers or our spoons into the shared dish, interrupted only by sipping buttermilk from our accompanying individual bowls.[5] When the last eater finished with the comment '*barak 'allahu feek* [God bless you]', Hajja knew her couscous had once more been delicious.

* * *

When I asked Hajja to explain how she prepared her couscous, I was told that like all Moroccan dishes, it is prepared 'according to taste'. Rather than using the Arabic term *madaq*, taste is called *legout*, derived from the French term *goût* for taste as perception and discernment. At times the phrase '*'ala hsab dyel legout*' referred to the individual taste of a cook and highlighted different cooking styles, while at other times it referred to a shared standard of taste and highlighted recognizable practices and rules (see Chapter 4). Beyond this expression, taste was rarely invoked verbally. Indeed, throughout my fieldwork, a dish was seldom described as delicious or tasty by cooks or eaters. If anything, on very rare and intimate occasions, a drink or dish was described as tasteless (*messous*), usually implying a lack of sugar or salt as in the opening vignette.[6] Moreover, tasting with the tongue (*iduq*) was much less relied upon than I assumed. The more experienced a cook, the less she seemed to taste with her tongue. If anything, a dish could be tasted shortly before serving to ascertain that everything had combined smoothly. As Aicha put it in that rare moment described at the beginning of this chapter, all of a cook's senses mattered to the success of a dish.

The anthropology of the senses has long been arguing that the senses work in collaboration and often synesthetically. This scholarship contributed to reinstating the so-called lower senses such as smell and touch to taste scholarship (Korsmeyer and Sutton 2011; Pink and Howes 2010). Speaking of tasting as a sensory method, Mann et al. vividly describe how 'there is already tasting going on while my food is still on the plate ... As the fingers move, the mouth anticipates ... fingers become involved in tasting even before they handle food on a plate: as they chop, as they knead, as they cook' (2011: 232, 233). Indeed, the etymology of taste, derived from the French *taster* and Italian *tastare*, also refers to feeling, handling and touching, and suggests a wider, multisensory connotation compared to the modern English word (Stoller 1989: 23), which chimes with the way Moroccans refer to taste.[7]

Taste Knowledge 35

Figure 1.2. Couscous served with *lben*, Marrakech, 2012. © Katharina Graf

Hajja's sensing body tasted the combination of spices when looking at and smelling the braising chicken, she tasted the couscous grains with her hands as she brought them to life between her moist palms, and she tasted the vegetables as she listened to the boiling water. Along the way, she assessed the transformations of the various ingredients into a meal, starting with feeling the weight of the freshly slaughtered chicken. Hajja corrected her assessment of its weight when she saw and felt the chicken between her fingers as she washed it. She added turmeric upon seeing and smelling the intensity of the spices. More subtly, she adjusted and synchronized several processes by combining her sense of the size of the chicken in the pot with the water set to boil in another and the amount of couscous grains steaming above it. Her sense of taste guided her throughout this process.

While the bodily senses of the expert cook join forces to produce a synesthetic perception of taste – to 'hear the smell' of food, as Kalymnians would say (Sutton 2014: 1) – and allow her to evaluate and adjust while engaging with food's transformations, the wider material and social environment also matters to the taste of a meal. 'According to taste' refers not only to a cook's synesthetic bodily sense of taste but also to the conditions of its emergence and the reception among eaters, and thus points to the broader material and social dimensions of taste. Halima, visiting from the Moroccan countryside, and I, the ethnographer visiting from abroad, were only partially embedded in Aicha's taste environment, which includes not only her husband and children, and her Marrakchi friends and neighbours, but also the raw ingredients and the material environment such as her kitchen, home and the local market. We were thus less attuned to what is considered the right amount of sugar in tea. By contrast, belonging to the same environment, Hajja and Fatimzahra were able to work jointly towards a certain taste of couscous, as I will detail below.

Seremetakis (1994a: 5) invites us to take seriously the Greek term for the senses, *aesthesis*, which means to feel, sense or understand good and bad, and which makes taste perception inherently evaluative; a method of discernment that is learned and shared, and thus social. As a bodily technique, taste as a method of discernment builds on both individual and shared experiences and reveals a form of habitus (Bourdieu 1977; Mauss 1973). At the same time, the question is not what marks 'good taste', including food quality or the acquired pleasure of tasting (Bourdieu 2010). Rather, I am interested in how taste informs cooking practices as bodily perception *and* as a culturally, economically and politically shaped ability to evaluate raw ingredients and food in the making. In Marrakech, taste knowledge cannot be reduced to good taste.

In the introduction to a special issue on the work of taste, Spackman and Lahne (2019) propose to regard sensing as a form of not only affective but also economic and political labour mobilized through the food system. The contributions by Tsigkas (2019), who describes tea production in Sri Lanka, and Kantor

(2019), who focuses on subsistence farming in Bihar, India, show respectively that practices of discernment can and should be disentangled from 'good taste' and the implicit social hierarchy of tastes. Cultivated perception is not only the preserve of professionals or high-class consumers, but also of people usually dismissed as unskilled labourers. Like the rural Indian farmers and cooks described by Kantor, Marrakchi cooks rely on their sensory perception to judge food and the broader material environment as they source, process, prepare and serve it to their families. Unable to grow their own food, this bodily engagement is informed by a long history of urban food insecurity and overall mistrust in national food policies (Graf 2018). For my research participants, who sourced unprocessed foods in largely unstandardized markets, the ability to discern, coupled with the sharing of information on price, provenance and quality with family members, friends and neighbours, was vital to ensuring food safety in everyday cooking (see Chapter 5). As evidenced by Hajja's multisensory engagement with couscous, sourcing and processing food – reflecting, by implication, a deep understanding of the Moroccan and global food system – are important processes to assess food's quality and safety and are thus fundamental to a cook's taste knowledge.

Baraka: Cook, Food and Environment

When a dish turns out well, like Hajja's couscous, it is considered to have *baraka*. However, *baraka* denotes not simply a blessed meal; it is also an acknowledgement that the outcome of every cooking endeavour – and the future more generally – is not entirely under the cook's control, but depends on divine favour. Indeed, whether or not humans intervene, food transforms (itself) in multiple ways and in resonance (or dissonance) with its environment. The notion of *baraka* points towards the agency of more than the cook in the making of a good meal. A growing body of anthropological work similarly argues that food can be considered an active collaborator in its transformation into a meal. The authors mentioned below describe the various ways in which not only the moods and roles of cooks and eaters interact with food as it transforms, but also temperatures, humidity, weather and the seasons, as well as the layout of the kitchen and home, including tools and technologies.[8] Their basic premise is that nonhuman things, including foods, can be considered agents through their affect and effect on humans and nonhumans. Janeja's (2010) research on Bengali food demonstrates the 'transactional agency' or 'collaborative performance' of food through joining sensuous ethnography with classic material studies and the work of objects in constituting social relations. Van Daele's (2013) auto-ethnographic encounter with cooking during fieldwork in Sri Lanka similarly explores the active role that nonhumans such as food, technologies or animals play in mediating and shaping social relations, including those of the foreign ethnographer (see also Fikry 2022). Yet, in pursuing their argument for conceiving of the materiality of food and the broader environment in the making of a meal, both authors eschew the important question of whether the cook has a special role in this assemblage.

While theorists like Bennett have a point in arguing against the 'narcissistic' idea that 'at the heart of any event or process lies a human agency' (2010: xvi and xiv), I adopt a human-centric and political economic perspective on materiality in order to understand 'how food's matter is *made* to matter by human practice and relations' (Abbots 2017: 23, emphasis in original). Cheesemaking provides a good example of what Abbot calls 'bounded vitalism' (ibid.).[9] The making of cheese brings the agency of the broader material and social environment to the fore, while also accounting for the sensory knowledge of the cook or artisan. For instance, West's cheesemakers verbalize their ability to engage with the broader 'ecology of production' (2013b: 331) as a *feeling* for milk, curd and cheese along their multiple transformative stages, and that resonate with Aicha's feeling described in the opening vignette. Paxson describes the cheesemaker's understanding of milk and curd as cross-sensory or synesthetic experience through 'allowing their sight, touch smell, and taste to register through one another' (2013: 131). According to her, experienced cheesemakers cultivate and train their sensory apparatus through 'sensory reason' to account for the interaction between the bodily senses 'sight, hearing, smell, taste, touch/tactility, *temporality*' (ibid. 136, emphasis added). By adopting the perspective of the artisan cheesemaker within broader ecologies of production, both West (2013b) and Paxson (2013) therefore differentiate the agency of the artisan from other agents in the cheesemaking assemblage.

This view chimes with the way Moroccans conjure *baraka* into successful events or routine practices, thus acknowledging the special role of the cook. Hajja's ability to make good couscous is intricately connected to the general Moroccan notion of *baraka*. *Baraka* is often translated as God's blessing or a supernatural power that reaches out into the world through a person, an animal, an object or a place (Geertz 1971: 44). Every devout Muslim seeks to acquire blessing during her lifetime to assure a good afterlife in heaven. However, as Geertz also suggests, in everyday life *baraka* has more profane meanings. Hajja's couscous is not simply blessed but also bodily satisfying, inducing wellbeing, luck and plenitude in those who partake of it, and Hajja is blessed for these effects in return. On a first reading, *baraka* thus reminds of the divine force that Bennett (2010: xx) makes an effort to discount as 'true' vibrancy. Indeed, according to Geertz, ascribing *baraka* is considered a theological question. However, my regular encounter with *baraka* in Marrakchi discourses and practices suggests that ascribing *baraka* in everyday life is a way to identify 'personal presence, force of character, [and] moral character' (Geertz 1971: 45) not in saints or kings, as Geertz argues, but in ordinary people and their actions. It is not necessarily a divine force. Rather, the notion of *baraka* acknowledges the special role of the cook in the making of a delicious meal, while also highlighting that her action is beyond her full control. Without *baraka*, a meal might be palatable, even good, but not fully delicious and satisfying. At the same time, *baraka* is elusive and unpredictable, like the outcome of every meal preparation.

The thick description of couscous preparations in the previous section drew out this whole complex of actors, including not only Hajja's, Fatimzahra's and my body, but also the couscous grains, the chicken, the vegetables and the spices, the knife, the *gsa'a* and the *couscoussière*, the LPG burner and the running water. It also illustrates that a cook's taste knowledge includes the ability to attune to a much larger network of actors and processes such as the urban infrastructure, Moroccan fields and regional ecologies, women's cooperatives and the factories that produce the couscous grains, the markets and shopkeepers distributing them, the bacteria inscribed in the decades-old wood of the *gsa'a*, the hands and mouths of the eaters, the courtyard table, the buttermilk and the many microbes living in and on them.[10] In this context, *baraka* highlights that it takes a good cook to make a good and satisfying couscous out of all this. And not just any cook. Hajja's taste orchestrates this event and it is she who is thanked by the guests for providing this delicious meal. It is Hajja's embodied taste, couched in a broader cultural appreciation for couscous, that invigorates and brings to life all other parts of this environment. In return, through the use of certain culturally valued ingredients or tools, such as handmade couscous grains or the wooden *gsa'a*, she heightens her chance of acquiring *baraka*. The use of less culturally valued ingredients or tools, such as industrially processed grains or the electric blender, reduces her chance. The more Hajja's body is willing to engage, the harder she tries, the more likely the dish turns out delicious and is blessed. Acquiring *baraka* requires an effort on the part of the cook; the cook is considered the driver and decisive actor in the assemblage of cook, food and environment. At the same time, *baraka* also accounts for the collaborative work of food and the environment in the making of a meal.

The Sense of Temporality

Then there is a moment when the meal is done, when cook, food and environment have done 'enough'. The word to describe this is *baraka* too. *Baraka* thus also points to the temporality of cooking. Aicha's and Hajja's attunement to food's transformations in a given environment conveys this sense of temporality, which joins the other senses to evaluate food as it transforms. A cook's taste knowledge therefore includes a sixth sense. Paxson hints at how time is also a matter of taste, for instance, depending on how 'fudgy' or 'cakelike' a cheese should be: 'As if time were a subjective rather than an objective tool' (2013: 145–46). Making cheese is 'not only knowing how to intervene in organic processes, but also knowing *when* to proceed from one intervention to the next. Gaining a feel for the curd engages a sense of temporality as much as tactility' (ibid. 146, emphasis added). However, Paxson stops short of analysing this subjective sense of temporality.

Phenomenological approaches to time are a useful starting point, promising to overcome the artificial boundary between bodily or 'task' and abstract or 'clock' time (Ingold 2011: 323). Merleau-Ponty states: 'I am not in space and time, nor do I conceive space and time; I belong to them, my body combines with them and includes them' (2001: 162). Munn further stresses that we and our practices are always in time, but also 'make time' through our acts (1992: 94). Speaking of landscapes or the environment, Ingold further argues that 'the rhythms of human activities *resonate* not only with those of other living things but also with a whole host of other rhythmic phenomena – the cycles of day and night, and of the seasons . . . And we resonate to the cycles of vegetative growth and decay . . . These *resonances* are embodied' (2011: 200, emphasis added). He concludes that the distinction between a bodily sense of time and an abstracted one holds only in theory (ibid. 332f).

Although Hodges (2008) criticizes that phenomenological accounts of time are severed from historical time or globalizing processes, this cannot be said of ethnographies of food, especially when shifting attention to temporality. In their attention to the production, distribution or consumption of 'fast' or 'slow' food, food anthropologists demonstrate historical sensitivity to local and global temporalities (e.g. Garth 2020; Mintz 2006; Wilk 2006). More concretely phenomenological, Abarca argues that temporality is inherent in every meal and describes how the beauty of a brief meal expresses a 'sense of history' through what she calls 'aesthetics of the moment' (2006: 104). Sutton similarly highlights that perception always involves a 'mixture of tenses and temporalities' (2014: 14, referring to Howes), of collective memory and imagination that contribute to embodied sensory experience, the basis of his gustemological approach.[11] These are important points, which I will develop in the next section, but there is still room for understanding *how* a cook engages practically with temporality. In order to fully grasp a cook's knowledge, it is equally important to attend to the multiple temporalities inherent in an activity, which in the context of material and social change necessarily relate the temporality of cooking to historical and global processes of transformation.

When sourcing, processing and cooking, a cook combines with and includes the transformative materiality of foods in a given environment through her six-dimensional taste knowledge (Figure 1.3). Her sense of temporality allows her to intervene (or not) at crucial moments in its transformation. Aicha's *al-ftour* preparations during Ramadan betray the experienced cook's resonance with food and the wider environment. Preparations usually started three hours before sunset and although Aicha denied cooking 'by time', under her lead the three of us served the meal to break the fast to the minute. For example, upon slapping

Figure 1.3. Combining with flour, yeast and water, Marrakech, 2012.
© Katharina Graf

the bread dough with her fingers to hear how the leavening worked and thereby assess the transformation of flour, water and yeast into bread, Aicha concluded that it was too late to start making another dough. Later, she smelled when the pizza had baked enough. While time is 'made' (Munn 1992: 94) in the activity, temporality is only partially controlled by the cook. Although the cook decides when to start an activity under various external constraints, once the ingredients combine, the activity assumes its very own temporality in conjunction with the environment – temperature, season, tools – and keeps requiring the cook's intervention at specific intervals under reliance on taste; and then at some point it is 'enough' (*baraka*).[12]

Marrakchi cooks explained further that foods transform in conjunction with much broader and less apparent processes, such as when an item was harvested, produced or processed, how it was transported or stored, and from where and how it reached a cook's kitchen. Being part of the same material environment, Aicha collaborated with the partially unpredictable workings of her bread dough, her tools and the kitchen space, and even the broader Moroccan food system (see Chapter 5), which on that day resulted in using a portion of it for making pizza in time for *al-ftour*. To a mere observer of routine food preparation, these multiple temporal dimensions of taste are hardly perceptible. When I tried to elicit a verbal commentary on an adjustment – for instance, when Hajja added more water to the couscous grains – she matter-of-factly stated 'it needs more', suggesting that food itself determined her adjustments, while, in fact, it was her six-dimensional taste knowledge of the grains in their wider material context that allowed her to perceive and act upon such needs as and when they emerged. It was only when I routinely joined in shopping, processing and preparing food that I started to participate and perceive these multiple temporalities of taste as well as their dissonances in times of change, as I will examine in the final section.

The Social Dimensions of Taste

In the context of technological change and women's emancipation, temporality also invokes social evaluation. While the multisensory and synesthetic engagement with food seems to suggest a highly bodily and individual form of knowledge, in this section I show how a cook's taste knowledge is negotiated with her family, neighbours and friends, and, consequently, includes an intersubjective dimension whereby individual experiences communicate with larger social processes.[13] In contrast to the bodily sense of temporality, this more social dimension of temporality and taste highlights the dissonances that are part and parcel of everyday cooking.

In the literature on food preparation and its reproduction, time is usually considered in relation to convenience. Women who work for a wage but are still in charge of domestic food work are assumed to have less time to prepare food and thus embrace time-saving kitchen technologies and convenience foods such as ready meals or processed foods (cf. Meah and Watson 2011). With some exceptions (Adapon 2008; Short 2006; Sutton 2014), the presumed lack of bodily and temporal investment in cooking is often associated with unhealthy diets, a simplification of domestic cooking and/or a loss of knowledge (Abarca 2006; Giard 1998; Mintz 2006; Pilcher 2002). Science and technology studies highlight that 'intelligent' kitchen technologies, seen as materializations of modernity, such as thermostats or microwaves that are reputed to 'do it all', in their manuals still warn cooks to check their dishes regularly, assuming they did not do that before (Silva 2000; see also Schwartz Cowan 1983). Such studies point to the ongoing importance of a bodily sense of temporality despite the advent of time-measuring or time-saving technologies. Indeed, technological change does not relate to material and social change in a simple, one-directional way (Wajcman 2015).

What foods, tools and techniques were kept, altered, adapted or given up in low-income Marrakech is not so much a matter of more or less time available, as Newcomb (2017) suggests for middle-class Fassis. Nor are such processes simply based on a desire for status or participation in modernity, as in Beni Mellal (Kapchan 1996), but rather on careful evaluation through bodily and social taste, which cannot fully be rendered in terms of convenience or modernity. While it is a fact that Moroccan women of all socioeconomic classes increasingly seek to study and/or earn a wage, and that concomitantly modern kitchen technologies and processed foods enter urban Moroccan homes, these changes do not necessarily translate into a loss of sensory knowledge or even of laboriously prepared homemade food – certainly not among the low-income women I conducted research with.

In his research on the Greek island of Kalymnos, Sutton (2014) shows how taste is embedded in a specific context of place and culture. Taste – for him especially the flavour of food – unlocks memories, expresses generational changes and bespeaks a form of 'existential quality' (ibid. 47) or what kind of person Kalymnians aspire to be in the context of modernization. Hajja's holding on to the *mehraz* coupled with Fatimzahra's Moulinex are similar expressions. Older cooks like Hajja adapted to so-called time-saving technologies in several ways, sometimes through another skilled body. Fatimzahra's movements were attuned to Hajja's in her interactions with materials: 'A somatic mode of attention means not only attention to and with one's own body, but includes attention to the bodies of others' (Csordas 1993: 139). Her attention was a form of practical mimesis 'based upon a bodily awareness of the other in oneself', which demonstrates not so much 'a reciprocity of viewpoints', but a *reciprocity of taste* based on 'similar kinaesthetic experiences . . . and a similar understanding of the activity' (Gieser 2008: 300, citing Jackson).

This reciprocity is based on embodiment of and action within a shared taste environment. For instance, whereas Hajja would have squeezed the hot flesh of the braising chicken between her fingers to feel its readiness, she also trusted Fatimzahra's mediated method of driving a knife into the flesh. Equally, Hajja used to grind each spice by hand with her *mehraz* and her rhythmic pounding gestures were testament to her bodily memory of that practice. However, during fieldwork she only precrushed spices and then handed them over for Fatimzahra to finish off the hardest work with the Moulinex, which cuts the spices (Figure 1.4). Although Hajja insisted on crushing rather than cutting spices to enhance their textures and flavours – similar to the Mexican *metate* (Abarca 2006: 73) – she trusted Fatimzahra's reciprocity of taste when the latter operated the electric blender to achieve a result without compromising Hajja's taste. More symbolically, in using the *mehraz* and the blender respectively, Hajja and Fatimzahra both also express who they are in the context of change.

Such technical and existential aspects of taste knowledge are related to domestic power relations and generational change. The use of electric appliances but also of cookbooks or online resources is the result of women's literacy and (partial) financial independence from men and/or senior family members and thus challenges the prevailing patriarchal system based on the dominance of men and seniors (see Chapter 3). Not only are fathers, brothers or husbands no longer

Figure 1.4. Electric blender, named after the brand Moulinex, Marrakech, 2012.
© Katharina Graf

the sole breadwinners, and lose decision-making power over household finances as a result, senior women, too, lose influence in the domestic context. As the older and more experienced cook, Hajja felt entitled to pass on most menial and tedious tasks such as cleaning and processing ingredients to Fatimzahra, who, in turn, could rely on technologies such as the blender to ease her potentially harder but less prestigious work. The use of the Moulinex shows how kitchen technologies contribute to this intergenerational shift of power by providing younger cooks with alternatives. As a result, knowledge flows no longer solely from older generations of cooks to younger ones, but also from younger cooks to older ones, making the sharing of taste increasingly reciprocal. New technologies and sources of knowledge thus translate not only into freedom from manual oppression in the kitchen (Kapchan 1996: 214), but also into a more equal exchange of taste knowledge across generations (see Chapters 2 and 3).

While certain tools and techniques such as processing cereals into couscous grains by hand were readily given up to save bodily effort and time, others were deemed essential to achieving good taste, such as massaging the grains by hand. Hajja knew well how to produce couscous grains from scratch, and preferred their taste, but she admitted that 'It was hard work'. She was glad that she could buy pre-processed couscous grains instead. Hajja acknowledged that younger women no longer knew how to do this or how to distinguish handmade from pre-processed couscous. At the same time, while these industrially produced couscous grains could be – and in non-Moroccan foodways usually are – soaked in boiling water and ready in five minutes, most Moroccan cooks still massage and steam their couscous grains as described above, a process that can take up to three hours. Wage-working but low-income women did not give up tools or techniques simply because they took time or because it was hard work. Although time-saving technologies such as pre-processed couscous grains or the pressure cooker are facilitating domestic food work, the temporal investment in food preparations is still widely considered a marker of good taste. Thus, while new technologies offer younger generations of cooks the choice to do otherwise and thereby change some practices, so far they have not altered what counts as good food in Morocco, as the following chapters will also show.

The example of couscous, the quintessential Moroccan dish, suggests that the expressions 'according to taste' and 'as long as it takes' are embedded in a cultural system of values and serve to pass not only bodily but also social judgement. While an experienced cook's ability to prepare good food was never doubted – a mother and wife simply 'has to be a good cook', Aicha once explained to me – a meal was only considered good if she also invested bodily effort and time in its preparation. 'As long as it takes' thus also points to the social evaluation of a meal and reflects some of the new challenges for younger generations of cooks. To give an illustration, one day, as I was eating lunch with Hajja and Fatimzahra, Aicha rang the door to greet her former neighbours. Aicha explained that she was bringing her daughter to the nearby preschool before going to work herself and, because she had not seen Hajja and Fatimzahra since she moved into a different neighbourhood, she briefly popped in to hear how they were doing. When Aicha left, Fatimzahra exclaimed briskly: 'It's only 1.30 pm! How can she be out at this time?!' Hajja answered contemptuously: 'Well, she certainly cannot have made a proper lunch!' I realized only months later, when spending a similar number of hours with Aicha sourcing, processing and preparing food, how this brief exchange conveyed not only (unfounded) doubts about Aicha's motherly care work but also a social evaluation of temporality in cooking, thus pointing to wage-working women's daily time constraints and struggles to be good mothers and wives.

Even so, while everyone struggled with different aspects of these changes, most low-income Marrakchi women I interviewed rejected time constraints as an excuse to simplify food preparations or use time-saving technologies if they compromised taste, even if they were pressed for time themselves. Instead, they tended to criticize women who did not attend to food's needs as it transformed, who did not cook 'as long as it takes'. By extension, not taking the time 'it takes' meant that they were not caring well for their families. Social status and women's self-proclaimed desire to be good wives and mothers continue to be associated with the preparation of time-intensive Moroccan meals such as couscous. This symbolic association has been observed across the food studies literature and links taste and the bodily sense of temporality to broader social values.

Sutton was told by a Kalymnian wage-working woman and domestic cook that 'even if a woman works full-time she will find time to cook . . . because doing cooking in a proper way, one that respects tradition, the senses, and health concerns, takes time' (2014: 171, 173; see also Adapon 2008: 20, 45). What counts as proper food is defined within the broader cultural context and often relates to women's identity in contexts of rapid change. Pilcher (2002) notes how the hard labour and time involved in making tortilla in the Mexican highlands gave women status and identity as well as respect and authority within the family and community. When the *metate*, a special grinding stone for hand-grinding corn flour, was gradually replaced by industrial mills women were reluctant to accept it, similar to how Hajja held on to the *mehraz* for pounding spices. Blend (2001) observes how in the Chicana literature the preparation of tortilla was imbued with symbolic significance through the time and effort put into its making; a synonym of love and care but also of a shared Mexican culture. Hence, its preparation is marked by a contradiction: hand-grinding corn flour for preparing tortilla is both a symbol of cultural resilience in the face of material and social change, while also asserting that time- and work-intensive food preparation is women's task; it empowers and simultaneously oppresses women.

This ambivalence is also implicit in Moroccan knowledge reproduction. Like tortilla, couscous expresses the tension between what is considered Moroccan (culinary) identity and the everyday constraints that younger generations of women face. In its preparation, the two temporal dimensions inherent in taste knowledge – bodily and social – come together most clearly. Couscous is not only the dish of the week that evokes Moroccan cuisine at large (Graf and Mescoli 2020; cf. MacDougall 2021) and preparing it 'makes' a Moroccan wife and mother (cf. Ingold 2011: 325); it also reveals a woman's sense of taste and her time constraints. Couscous is usually prepared by the oldest and most experienced cook in a family, typically for lunch on Friday, the Muslim day of rest. It is considered the most difficult of regular Moroccan dishes and it constitutes the pinnacle of a cook's knowledge.

Of the three cooks I worked with only Hajja regularly prepared couscous on Fridays. Aicha's mother-in-law initially sent a plate of couscous every Friday as if to express her more senior status despite – or because of – Aicha and family having moved out. Aicha explained that preparing couscous is considered so arduous and time-consuming because it requires a cook to be 'fully alert' – in continuous bodily engagement with food as it transforms – and thus difficult to manage by women who single-handedly manage all domestic chores:[14] unlike usual meal preparations, making couscous requires many small gestures and steps that do not leave time to pursue other domestic tasks in parallel, such as washing the laundry or changing nappies. Another major challenge in making couscous lies in handling the grains between steaming rounds and, according to Hajja, this was the reason why couscous required so much experience. While all the families I interviewed preferred eating couscous on Fridays, the time and effort it took were sometimes not reconcilable with their carefully calibrated daily routines, pointing to the constraints low-income wage-working women in particular experience.[15]

Wage work compromises low-income women's ability to invest 'the time it takes' and, by extension, to be good mothers and wives. Not only do these women have to manage wage work in often precarious employment situations without contracts and social insurance, and have less time for domestic work; they also carry out most domestic work and childcare alone, without recourse to other women's help as their predecessors in multigenerational households.[16] At the same time, in contrast to their middle-income counterparts, low-income women cannot afford to employ a domestic worker to do laborious and low-status chores such as cleaning the flat or processing raw ingredients (Montgomery 2019). Nor do they have access to convenience foods in supermarkets located in mostly unreachable middle- and upper-income suburbs (Newcomb 2017).

Although low-income women's economic capital does not directly translate into cultural capital as it does for middle-income women, it does not eliminate their desire to prepare good food for their family and thereby retain direct control over their health and wellbeing, as Aicha's case illustrates. Ever since she became a mother, Aicha strove to prepare proper Moroccan food such as making her own bread and serving a warm lunch to her husband and children every day. Her wage work allowed her to buy more expensive but healthy foods such as fruits and gradually also a fridge and a gas hob. Although it translated into more domestic work, moving out of her mother-in-law's house a few years later made Aicha her 'own boss' and take control of her busy schedule. Indeed, as soon as Aicha could arrange her part-time work around her domestic chores, she started making her own couscous, thereby establishing herself as a good wife and mother. Being the lead cook in her own home, Aicha achieved mature womanhood earlier than she would have in the multigenerational household (see Chapter 3). In this context, it is not surprising that although younger generations of urban women have more work and less time, they still strive to engage their multisensory taste in the laborious preparation of food. While these women unwittingly upheld, reproduced and shared those elements of their six-dimensional taste knowledge that were deemed essential to Moroccan foodways and to their social status as wives and mothers, in reproducing taste knowledge through new technologies and knowledge sources, in the longer term they will also contribute to changing the cultural values that sustain it, including who is considered a good cook and mother.

Conclusion: Food in the Making

So how does a cook know, especially in times of change? Taking seriously the expressions 'according to taste' and 'as long as it takes' and linking them through the notion of taste knowledge helps in understanding what constitutes a cook's knowledge. Taste knowledge captures the evanescence and incommensurability of practical ways of knowing, in particular the work of the senses and including temporality, while also speaking to a much broader system of cultural values in the context of material and social change. Based on a 'thickly textured' sensory exploration (Howes, in Pink and Howes 2010: 340) of couscous, the Moroccan dish par excellence, I demonstrated how a cook's bodily sense of taste goes well beyond taste on the tongue and encompasses all bodily senses, including a sixth sense of temporality. Although earlier studies showed that taste as an ability to discern is social and shared across bodies, including nonhuman agents such as food itself and the broader material environment, my analysis focused on *how* cooks engage with their material and social taste environment. Engagement with a given taste environment requires a cook's constant attunement to other bodies, things and processes. On the one hand, this makes taste knowledge and the making of a meal an unpredictable yet highly adaptive activity in which past, present and future experiences are carefully evaluated against changing technologies and new temporal constraints relating to education or wage work. On the other hand, this makes the reproduction of taste knowledge hard work that involves ambivalence and the subtle negotiations of social values.

Similar to Paxson's (2013: 49) argument that hard work itself produces value in food, such as taste, healthfulness or uniqueness, by working hard, domestic cooks and the meal acquire *baraka*. *Baraka* is not simply a supernatural force but a very tangible social value that marks a good cook's taste knowledge; it is only bestowed upon a cook if deserved and as judged by others. Thus, while multisensory taste knowledge – including a sense of temporality – is needed to get the taste right in every aspect of food in the making, it is only in combination with a cook's invested time and bodily effort that a meal is considered good by others. Conversely, not everyone's efforts are blessed. Referring back to couscous, my shopping efforts and Fatimzahra's assistance in the kitchen were not directly blessed by the eaters; rather, our contributions to making the meal delicious were subsumed under Hajja's taste knowledge and remained unseen and unvalued. *Baraka* thus also cements social hierarchies.

Overall, the notion of taste knowledge illustrates that by attending to intimate bodily sensations and their direct and indirect responses to material and social transformations, phenomenologically inspired research allows us to understand broader cultural values and how these shape (and are shaped by) the domestic work of low-income, yet highly knowledgeable women. By illustrating the multiple constraints these women face when preparing what they consider good food, this chapter also advocates for a less romanticized view of phenomenologically inspired conceptions of temporality as embedded in an activity and in harmonic resonance with the environment. The reproduction of taste knowledge and of families is hard work and requires a cook's skilful navigation and careful (re)shaping of deeply held social values. Making food therefore inevitably involves dissonance across multiple scales.

Notes

Some elements of this chapter have been substantially revised from Katharina Graf. 2022. 'Taste Knowledge: Couscous and the Cook's Six Senses', *Journal of the Royal Anthropological Institute* 28(2): 577–94.

1. Shopping food in the largely unstandardized Moroccan markets requires considerable knowledge (Graf 2015). Thus, usually the most experienced cook shops. However, because Hajja and Fatimzahra were limited in their mobility, they embraced the opportunity to teach me to shop in their stead.
2. The term 'couscous' denotes both the cereal grains and the final dish. Moroccans prepare it differently from non-Moroccans, for whom couscous is usually a quickly prepared side dish.
3. Older cooks in my research prepared food directly over the floor, sitting on a low stool or cushion, and younger cooks tended to work on a kitchen counter while standing. Still, the use of the floor or the kitchen counter is not always linked to generational preferences; it also depends on the task.
4. Sometimes bread dough is used to seal the two pots, for instance, when steaming meat for several hours.
5. Couscous is the only Moroccan dish I encountered that is regularly eaten with cutlery to ease eating the unruly grains. Older Moroccans usually use their hands to squish vegetables with grains to form small balls that can be popped into the mouth without making a mess.
6. In Moroccan homes there is usually no additional sugar or salt placed on the table. It is considered an insult to the cook to add either to the meal or drink.
7. See Mann and Mol (2019) for a critical engagement with the role of language and translation in conveying and analysing research on taste.
8. These studies are broadly inspired by the concept of networks and assemblages (Bennett 2010; Latour 2005).
9. In her ethnographic study of eating, Abbots rereads Bennett's notion of vitality as 'co-produced through the relations between eating bodies, discourse and things' (2017: 23). Rather than denying matter's agentic capacity, Abbots argues that it remains a dormant potentiality until it is 'invigorated through social and embodied human interaction' (ibid.). The distributed agency invoked by network and assemblage thinking is '*too* egalitarian' (ibid. 26, emphasis in original, referring to Bourdieu 2010), since not all actors in a network or assemblage are necessarily equal.
10. Not just couscous or cheese but also many other foods engage a vast ecology of production. This becomes tangible in Tsing's (2015) ethnographic account of the matsutake mushroom and its multisited embeddedness in capitalist forces such as global trade.

11. Abarca's (2006) and Sutton's (2014) take on temporality is informed by a broader argument about the aesthetic value of a meal and its relation to personal and collective memories, essentially debunking any division between aesthetic reason and bodily experience or between objective and subjective taste (cf. Shapin 2012). This argument paves the way for understanding temporality as both an individual and a shared sense of taste.
12. Likewise, food's transformation within an environment prompts a cook to begin a task. For instance, in summertime when it gets hot early, a cook begins to assemble and knead bread earlier in the morning to counter the faster working yeast.
13. MacDougall (2021) makes a similar argument based on research with domestic cooks in Amman, Jordan. See also the special issue edited by Jung and Sternsdorff Cisterna (2014) for ethnographic examples of the more social and political aspects of bodily sensing. Based on his research of Chinese festivals, Chau (2008) also argues that a collective sensorium can be socially 'produced' rather than just shared.
14. With respect to Greek cooking, Seremetakis wrote that 'the cook "has to be fully alert", because cooking is a sudden awakening of substance and the senses' (1994b: 27, emphasis in original).
15. For many wage-working women, its preparation was limited to Sundays. This represents a general temporal shift in Morocco towards a bureaucratic temporality or Western 'clock' time (Ingold 2011: 323) dictated by the operating hours of banks and governmental institutions. However, many low-income families such as Aicha's rely on employment in the informal economy, which follows the rhythm of daily prayers and culminates on Fridays. In Marrakech's popular neighbourhoods the temporal shift is therefore only partial and helps explain why lunch, especially on Fridays, remain(s) the most important meal of the day and week for many.
16. Also, men rarely carry out domestic work in low-income households. Elsewhere, I compare how Marrakchi women's double burden resembles that of many other women across the globe (Graf 2022b).

INTERLUDE 2

Cooking

Before I set out to explore cooking knowledge and its reproduction in Marrakech, I had read a great deal about apprenticeship and learning, both as an analytical and a methodological approach. I felt ready to study how young Marrakchi women learn to cook by learning it myself. Yet, my fieldnotes do not contain many descriptions of learning. I rarely observed a direct teaching situation, nor was I instructed much about how to cook while in the field (the situation captured in Interlude 1 being very much an exception). Towards the end of my fieldwork, I thus concluded that my material did not allow me to say anything new on that subject, and that learning to cook did not lend itself to ethnographic observation and description.

However, after fieldwork, family, friends and colleagues, curious to sample what some (only half-jokingly) called an 'extended cooking course', often asked me to prepare a couscous for them, the Moroccan dish par excellence. Initially I was embarrassed to confess that I had not prepared a single couscous during my fieldwork because, out of all Moroccan dishes, this one was considered too important to be left to inexperienced cooks like myself. But I was nonetheless willing to try. After all, I told myself, I knew what Marrakchi couscous was supposed to taste and look like, I had witnessed and contributed to its preparation and eaten it almost every Friday for one year. More out of sentimentality than practical consideration, I happened to have brought back with me a *keskas* (or *couscoussière*), a two-layered pot used by Marrakchi cooks to steam the couscous grains while simultaneously preparing the sauce.

When I started to prepare my first ever couscous by buying the necessary ingredients, I was not surprised to find myself knowing what to do. After all, I had shopped for couscous preparations many times and assisted in its preparation by Hajja, Rachida and other women on multiple occasions. I only had to adapt to my local food market context. But then, in the process of setting up my workspace in the kitchen, in preparing the meat and vegetables and in handling the couscous grains, I grew increasingly surprised at the extent of my knowledge: I knew what to do from beginning to end! My hands knew how to massage the olive oil into the couscous grains, my nose identified the right combination of spices and my tongue confirmed this, my ears told me when to lower the flame and when to add water, and, finally, my eyes gauged quantities and arranged the couscous on the plate just the way it should look according to my Marrakchi research participants. Beyond this multisensory and synesthetic bodily knowledge of making couscous, my equally embodied sense of temporality informed me when to add which ingredient and for how long to steam the grains; 'My body involuntarily knew what I consciously did not' (Seremetakis 1994a: 16). I had learned something after all.

CHAPTER 2

Participant Perception
Learning to Cook

In the Introduction I briefly presented the literature on cooking and knowledge, much of which refers casually to knowledge reproduction. With the exception of Sutton's work, this body of literature presumes that young women learn through observation and imitation of more experienced women, especially their mothers. The reproduction of this gendered food knowledge is described as the transmission of a more or less fixed body of knowledge from one person to another, which – especially in contexts with a history of domestic science as in France or North America – was accompanied by a shift from oral to textual reproduction in the form of written recipes and cookbooks (Cairns and Johnston 2015; Giard 1998; Kaufmann 2010; Trubek 2017). Remarkably, Short's British interview partners rarely set out to learn cooking; rather, they learned 'by chance' (2006: 37). In places with less emphasis on written words such as Mexico, learning is described as repeated observation and shared practice (Adapon 2008; see also Avakian and Haber 2005). But how do we learn cooking from cookbooks? How do we learn by chance? How do we learn by shared practice? Ironically, when I asked Marrakchi women how they had learned to cook, all invariably said that they had learned to cook from their mothers. Yet, none was able to explain to me how. These normally loquacious women, ready with explanations for nearly everything, lacked words to give me a satisfying answer.

Anthropologists studying knowledge reproduction among artisans of crafts other than cooking note similar challenges, as I will show. Rather than ask artisans how and what they know, as most scholars on cooking did, these anthropologists apprenticed themselves in order to understand from their own experience how a bodily craft is learned. Still, while these apprentice anthropologists had to disembody what they had learnt during fieldwork in order to think and write about it (Prentice 2008), I had to *re-embody* food preparation in order to fully grasp what I had learnt. As Interlude 2 illustrates, my cerebral approach and my involuntary visual bias had initially barred me from perceiving with all senses the emergence of my own understanding.[1] Only through engaging myself in preparing Moroccan food *after* fieldwork did I come to understand in how many different ways I had learned to cook – not only with my eyes but also with my hands, my nose, my ears, my tongue and my mouth – and how much of it had 'slipped past my mind's surveillance' (Giard 1998: 153) as I was learning. Based on this experience during and after fieldwork, the main argument of this chapter is that learning to cook as well as understanding learning require the attunement of all bodily senses through 'participant perception', including that of the ethnographer.

My own participant perception was arguably different from that of any Marrakchi woman or man. I sought to learn and, for most part of one year, spent my time deliberately participating in food preparation and reflecting about it. However, at the same time, I noticed, took part in or talked about specific situations when another learning cook prepared food, which, coupled with my own apprenticeship, gave me enough insight to compare our different experiences of learning and analyse the reproduction of cooking knowledge in this context. Aicha's daughters, one-year-old Rita and four-year-old Zahra at the time, though they would not qualify as apprentices in any formal sense, were learning something about Marrakchi cooking during my fieldwork. Before she was able to walk, Rita often played on the carpet next to the kitchen when Aicha prepared food. Especially when Aicha was kneeling on the floor to knead bread, Rita would stretch her hand to ask for a piece of dough to play with. She had seen her older sister doing so many times (Figure 2.1). Although Zahra did not spend much time with her mother in the small kitchen, she was often present when Aicha shopped at the market or processed vegetables and herbs in the living room.

Fifteen-year-old Ibtissam and twenty-year-old Zakia were at different stages in their apprenticeship. According to our many conversations after lunch, Ibtissam did not care to learn cooking. She preferred to help with simple tasks such as preparing tea or washing the dishes.[2] Yet Ibtissam knew more than she realized, as I noticed one day when she baked her first cake. Zakia was more advanced in her apprenticeship. She knew how to make bread but had not yet prepared a couscous, the pinnacle of Moroccan cooking (see Chapter 1). During my fieldwork, Zakia replaced Rachida when the latter was working long days outside the home. Although all experienced cooks I worked with could be considered experts, their continuous exposure to and engagement with new ingredients, technologies and media of and around food illustrate that cooks never stop learning. Thus, however incommensurate my own participant perception might have been during fieldwork, I had ample opportunities to contrast and compare my learning with that of other cooks and cooks-to-be at various stages in their learning and knowing.

The cases and moments of learning that I will describe in this chapter differ in two ways from learning in the more clearly circumscribed situations examined in apprenticeship studies. First, learning cooking in domestic contexts does not begin or end at a certain age or with a certain level of skill as apprenticeships in

Figure 2.1. Child's hand asking for dough in a *qesriya*, Marrakech, 2013.
© Katharina Graf

specialized crafts often do. Rather, as Aylwin (1999) confirms in her historical account of Moroccan cuisine, cooking knowledge is acquired through an entire lifetime.[3] Considering learning as the lifelong process of participant perception make it possible to identify learning situations that are hidden from direct observation. This leads to my second point – namely, that since cooking practices are not isolated from everyday domestic life, observation plays a marginal role in learning. A novice who participates in food preparation is likely to be charged with another task, often outside the confined space of the kitchen, and thus unable to attend to the experienced cooks' multiple small steps and gestures. Indeed, participant perception takes place irrespective of whether one wants to notice or not, for instance, when hearing the sizzling meat, feeling the texture of bread and stew when picking it up with the hands or when smelling a cake as it bakes in the oven.

Overall, this chapter is an attempt to find words for understanding and describing how we reproduce bodily ways of knowing such as cooking from one generation to the next. I identified three stages that build upon one another, which is reflected in the structure of the chapter. In the first section I explore how young girls and boys pick up a basic sense of taste through 'being there' from an early age and without which no formal learning takes place – what studies of apprenticeship consider to be learning through observation and imitation. As a result, many novices already know something when they begin to learn in the more conventional meaning of the term. In the next section I propose considering 'food as a guide'. Due to the way in which domestic food work is organized and set up in Morocco, novices learn to engage with food through gradually attuning their bodily movement and sensory perception to the transformative materialities of food. In the third section I describe how learning peaks when an advanced learner 'replaces' an experienced cook through a delayed form of multi-sensory imitation. Although mothers are not directly instructing their daughters, by asking them to cook in their absence and then eating and evaluating the result, experienced cooks set up learning situations that not only teach novices how to cook, but also instruct them in the broader moral values of making good food and of becoming a woman. These three elements of a novice's participant perception are embedded in an established division of labour and domestic hierarchy whereby senior women tend to have control over junior women's labour.

However, new technologies and media are altering this hierarchy. By introducing the main material changes that affect knowledge reproduction in urban Morocco in the final section, I demonstrate how younger cooks creatively engage new technologies and media to learn cooking, thereby reversing the flow of knowledge from younger to older cooks and altering formerly strict divisions of domestic labour. While discontent is rarely expressed verbally, inexperienced cooks manifest their struggle within clearly defined domestic hierarchies in manifold ways. As the negotiations and their places in the kitchen hierarchy evolve against a backdrop of acutely felt material and social change, most young women gradually acquire an ambivalent but strong sense of responsibility and moral obligation to cook for their (future) family. Although I point towards the negotiations of domestic hierarchies throughout this chapter, I will analyse how women of different generations experience and negotiate knowledge reproduction and power only in the next.

Being There: Knowing before Learning

One day in the summer of 2013, when Aicha's family and I had temporarily relocated to the *riad* of Aicha's employer, her daughter Zahra had a neighbour visiting her. The two four-year-old girls played catch-me-if-you-can, running in and out of the kitchen, where Aicha was preparing to knead bread. Zahra stopped to peep onto the countertop by standing on her tiptoes to peek into the *qesriya* (a large earthenware plate). She was not quite tall enough to see or reach anything, so she asked her mother if she could have a piece of bread dough to knead her own bread with her friend. Aicha explained that she had only just begun and told her to wait '*shi chouia* [a bit]' before the dough was ready. Zahra and her friend dashed off again. Roughly five minutes later, Zahra was back and claimed two small pieces of dough (Figure 2.1), which Aicha laughingly portioned off for them. Zahra took the pieces, sat down with her friend on the steps in front of the kitchen and both began to flatten the dough with their fingers.

* * *

This was not the first time that Zahra asked for bread dough, as was evident from her accurate sense of temporality. She not only remembered and interrupted her play outside the kitchen, she also returned at an interval that her mother had only vaguely defined. While Aicha readily accommodated her daughter's interest to participate in breadmaking, even if cursorily and playfully, Zahra's curiosity as well as her accurate sense of temporality betray her growing understanding of food preparation. Her activities suggest that she considered herself to be a part of her mother's routine food practices. She took for granted that both her and her friend helped to make bread. Although Zahra did not yet have any intention of learning to prepare food, her apprenticeship was already in full swing.

While this scene would scarcely qualify as a learning situation according to most concepts of learning, it forms a crucial aspect of Zahra's long-term initiation into cooking knowledge. Zahra was not, strictly speaking, present and attentively observing her mother prepare and knead bread, yet she was part of Aicha's activity and aware of the processes taking place through 'being there'[4]: Zahra adjusted her play to join her mother when she prepared the bread and even sought to participate with her friend in playfully making food. Indeed, both of Aicha's daughters were regularly present throughout the day, running or crawling and sometimes 'stealing' a food item for play or spontaneous consumption. Being there suggests that a girl or boy can know something before she or he chooses to learn; it is a precondition to learning in a more conventional sense.

Resonating with my own couscous preparation described in Interlude 2, it is often scholars' auto-ethnographic notes of their bodily experience that describe this element of learning – snippets like Seremetakis' 'involuntary' (1994a: 16) knowledge of how to pick and prepare greens in her family's garden in Greece. Giard (1998: 154) refused to learn cooking from her mother in mid-twentieth-century France and was surprised to remember the smells, colours and tastes of food when she tried to teach herself cooking through cookbooks as a university student. A recipe or a word were enough to re-activate the fragments of her embodied memory of food preparation. Adapon gives tangible clues about how she learned cooking during her research in Milpa Alta, Mexico, by: '*Absorb[ing]* culinary and gastronomic knowledge, *in* my body as well as in my mind' (2008: 2, emphasis added). For Adapon, watching was not enough; rather, she had to learn 'to feel the point of readiness when something was cooked "until it's done" or to discern how much water or broth to put into the rice pot until it was "enough"' (ibid. 2–3). Yet, she did not consider this to be proper learning because she 'did not have the benefit of growing up in a Mexican home' (ibid. 2) or of 'hanging out' (ibid. 12) like a boy turned professional chef in his mother's kitchen. She had not 'practised enough times to really *know* what to do' (ibid. 2, emphasis in original) or become '*attuned to* the subtleties . . . of Mexican cooking' (ibid. 12, emphasis added). For her, absorbing was not 'really know[ing]'; she emphasizes that the subtleties of Mexican cooking are only learnt as one grows up in a certain environment. Nevertheless, although she might not yet have acquired a fully developed taste knowledge (see Chapter 1), she knew something, including how Mexican cooks know before learning. Willingly or not, these authors had practised participant perception.

Being there includes a sensory attunement not only to food in the making but also to the broader material and social environment. In his study on artisanal cheesemaking, especially in the context of knowledge reproduction among family cheesemakers in France, West describes how: 'Everyone on the Bellonte farm. . .was "born into it", or "married into it".' He elaborates: 'Each spent time in the stable and in the cheese room long before they sought to learn, and long before others sought to teach them. *By the time they might have started learning, they seemingly already knew.* They rarely ever asked how to do something, and rarely were they explicitly told' (2013b: 330, emphasis added). Sutton, also quoting West's example, refers to this form of knowing before learning as 'co-presence' (2014: 17) due to the daily life that an expert cook and a novice share. But more so than the notion of co-presence, the term being there resonates with its phenomenological connotation of understanding as based on bodily experience, 'The forms that things are felt to take, the general sense of what it is possible to do with things, and the ways of being-in-the-world, derive from sensory interaction with the world' (Edwards, Gosden and Phillips 2006: 5).

Like the Bellontes, young Marrakchis learn by being there with their senses wide open to the world around them. The senses are not passive receptors of information, but already at an early age constitute a 'type of communication and creative channel between self and world' (Korsmeyer and Sutton 2011: 471). Marrakchi girls and boys learned when they walked with and listened to their mothers as they shopped, while playing in the house and smelling the foods their mothers cooked, and by picking up, feeling and eating it. I was rarely the only learner present when food was prepared, even if neither I nor my co-learners realized this at the time. Through their physical presence, Zahra and Rita learned how much time their mother spent in the kitchen every day and that their father came home when lunch was served. They learned about the daily, weekly and annual rhythms of food preparation. Like most children, they acquired a certain taste of and for food on which they were brought up, one that will always be associated with home and daily family life at a certain juncture of time and space. Through being there, Zahra and Rita already acquired a 'specialized knowledge' (Coy 1989) of markets and seasons, and as they did so, they entered a long-term multisensory rite of passage from girlhood into womanhood (see Chapter 3).

Boys and young, unmarried men were equally learning something. Whenever he was in Marrakech during my fieldwork, Aicha's younger brother Hassan was sent to buy last-minute ingredients and hung out around the kitchen whenever he was bored. Fatimzahra sometimes asked Boubaker, the twelve-year-old son of her neighbour and friend Saida, to help carry her shopping bags. Similarly, she was often helping her seven-year-old neighbour Omar with his homework in her kitchen while she baked a cake or biscuits. Whereas for Hassan, Boubaker and Omar, learning about food might end there, they have picked up many aspects of cooking knowledge through being there and lending a hand; they learned where to buy what kinds of foods, at what price and in what quantities or about the ingredients of a cake, tools and timing, and they tasted the final product. They also learned that as young men, their help is needed but that they are not required to cook themselves. Their apprenticeship often ended there. Their role in food preparation was already gendered and marked an important aspect of their growing into men (see Chapter 3).

Considering being there as the first element of learning does not suggest a learner's 'participation' in the strict sense of the term (Portisch 2010). She or he is rather sensing along in Merleau-Ponty's (2001) understanding that we cannot separate our experience of the world from the world. Being-in-the-world is always a being in a particular world (Stoller 1989). Young girls and boys are situated from an early age in a social learning situation and this situation affords them the possibility to learn (Lave and Wenger 1991). Being there takes place whether or not a girl or boy seeks to learn and knowledge is reproduced before the decision to learn is made. Following West (2013b) further, I thus want to stress how being there is not a passive form of learning that, just because it does not involve deliberate observation or imitation, does not qualify as enskilment (Ingold 2011). Being there refers to the fundamental importance of growing up and playfully engaging with a very particular material and social world, which at the same time is the only place from whence the world can be known. By accounting for knowing before learning through being there, these examples also make the case for going beyond observation towards understanding the contribution of all bodily senses, including a sense of temporality, to learning. To further account for this form of silent and partially invisible yet 'tasteful' (Stoller 1989) learning, I propose adopting a multisensory and materialist understanding of Ingold's (2001) 'education of attention' in the following section.

Learning with and from Food

Early on during my fieldwork with them, Ibtissam declared that she neither knew how to cook nor cared to learn. Nevertheless, one afternoon in March 2013, I observed how she baked her first cake. Ibtissam and I were alone in the

60   *Food and Families in the Making*

Figure 2.2. Mixing batter by hand, Marrakech, 2012. © Katharina Graf

kitchen; she was washing dishes as she always did after lunch. I sat on a small stool next to the sink, observing and chatting with her. When she had finished the dishes, she began to pull out the ingredients for the cake from the storage underneath the countertop. She did not use a recipe, nor did she watch a video on YouTube, as her older sister often did before she prepared a dish for the first time. As Ibtissam shuffled here and there, pulling out containers of flour, sugar and vegetable oil, she suddenly shouted out loud: 'One glass of sugar, right? And how much oil?' Rachida shouted back from the upstairs salon that she needed the same amount of oil. All ingredients were now placed on top of the counter, including an empty tea glass for measuring.[5] Ibtissam then took the electric blender from the shelf and, somewhat clumsily, put several ingredients directly inside: four eggs, one glass of sugar, one of vegetable oil and a small portion of natural yoghurt. She plugged the blender in, switched it on and blended everything for a little while. Then she poured the liquid mass into a plastic bowl, added one small package of baking yeast, another of vanilla sugar and three tablespoons of flour, using the spoon to fold it in. Her movements were similar to Zakia's. She smiled at me and suddenly asked if she should use her hand, although she had already decided that she would: with her left hand, she held the bowl. Upon diving in with her right hand, she immediately realized she needed more flour.

Not ever having felt the batter before, Ibtissam's gestures were somewhat helpless: she had seen others prepare cakes so often, as she told me, but clearly she could not associate a feeling with the gestures yet. The liquidity of the batter seemed always the same to the uninvolved eye (Figure 2.2). At one point, she went upstairs with the bowl to ask Zakia if the consistency was fine, who, after briefly sticking her fingers into the batter told her: 'Not yet.' Ibtissam went back into the kitchen and carefully added more flour. Then she also made me touch the batter and I told her to add yet more flour. When she decided not to add any more, she said, 'I should remember this feeling' – that is, remember the feeling of the consistency and reaction of the batter to her mixing and squeezing it between her fingers. Later, when Ibtissam took the cake out of the oven, her mother remarked that it was a little too dry because it had remained in the oven for too long. Ibtissam replied that she had smelled the cake was ready but did not believe it could be after so short a time. She did not trust her sense of smell yet.

* * *

This was the first cake that Ibtissam prepared from start to finish and she took pride in preparing it largely without help – evidently she knew much more about baking than she cared to admit, despite her rejection of learning cooking.[6] She had previously only helped to process foods, such as sorting and cleaning herbs and rice or lentils, starting from the age of thirteen or fourteen.[7] Before making the cake, Ibtissam explained that she had often seen her mother and sister prepare cakes, as if to say that she should know how to do it. In line with what studies of food and knowledge reproduction claim, there was an implicit assumption amongst Marrakchi cooks that *seeing* how a specific dish was prepared was enough to replicate it. Rachida told me several times that: 'Once you have seen how I do it, you will be able to do this yourself.' While this suggests that Rachida and other cooks give observation a high rank in learning to cook, at least discursively, and that observation is part of learning, it falls strikingly short of explaining why Ibtissam struggled nonetheless. My doubts were confirmed when Ibtissam dived into the batter with her fingers. Her perplexity manifested itself in her face and in her unrhythmic right hand's movements. It seemed as though her visual image of the batter and the gesture of stirring it, which she had seen so many times, had no corresponding feeling of food's transformation in her fingers yet. Carefully adding spoon after spoon of flour while stirring the batter with her fingers, she tried to approximate not only the right consistency of the batter but also the *feeling* of the right consistency. As she engaged her body in making this cake, by squeezing the soft mixture with her fingers whilst moving her whole hand clockwise in the bowl, she learned to respond to the batter's changing consistency.

By taking seriously Ibtissam's expression that she should 'remember that feeling' when the batter had achieved the right consistency and texture – and extending the previous chapter's argument – I follow more materialist understandings of food. Importantly, at this particular juncture of her apprenticeship, when she engaged with food for the first time by herself, Ibtissam was not simply learning by doing; she was learning from and with food. In new, intimate bodily engagements such as these, when the electric tool is discarded in favour of the hands to feel the changing texture, food instructs the novice cook through its transformative materiality. Although Ibtissam's deft preparatory steps, some of her gestures of mixing and even her confusion as she engaged with the cake in the making of it suggest that she had already acquired a few bodily techniques (Mauss 1973) – enough, at least, to realize the lack of coordination and of rhythm when she combined the ingredients into a batter with her hands – the vignette also illustrates that as part of the process of acquiring a bodily practice (Bourdieu 1977), Ibtissam still had to learn how the batter should feel when it reaches the right combination of ingredients. She had seen her mother and sister prepare this cake, she had smelled it as it was baking in the oven, she had heard the sounds it made when mixed with a blender and by hand, she had tasted the final dish and held it in her hand; she knew something before learning. What she had not yet learned was the ability to judge food's transformative capacities in the making. On that day, Ibtissam advanced from learning through being there to the next stage of her apprenticeship: food now became her main guide.[8]

Ingold argues that the 'growth of knowledge in the life history of a person is a result not of information transmission but of guided rediscovery' (2001: 115). Guided refers to the imitative copying of an experienced practitioner (see the following section) and rediscovery suggests that each novice discovers knowledge anew. For Ingold, the 'education of attention' therefore includes both imitation and improvisation, both teacher and learner. While for Ingold guidance is provided by an experienced human practitioner who sets up learning situations within a specific environment, I witnessed how food invited Ibtissam to attune her bodily senses and thus became her guide: 'The novice watches, feels, [smells, tastes] or listens to the movements of the expert [i.e. food] and seeks through repeated trials to bring [her] own bodily movements into line with those of [her] attention so as to achieve the kind of rhythmic adjustment of perception and action that lies at the heart of fluent performance' (ibid. 115). Wacquant's (2004) auto-ethnography of learning to box is useful for considering these more collaborative bodily dimensions of learning. According to him: 'The gist of pugilistic knowledge is transmitted outside of [the trainer's] explicit intervention, through a "silent and practical communication, from body to body"' (ibid. 113, citing Bourdieu). While Wacquant notes the collective dimensions of learning to box, whereby other boxers serve as a visual model for the learner, I include food and the bodily sensation of its transformation in this 'collective pedagogy' (ibid. 99).

Teaching is therefore not limited to a human expert making something present to and setting up situations for a person; it extends the collective pedagogy to include nonhuman guidance and captures food's contribution to setting up a learning situation. Ibtissam called on her sister's and my embodied knowledge to hone her feeling of food, but, at this stage in her apprenticeship, only food could truly guide her towards the right combination. Once she felt the transformation of the batter and entered into silent communication with it, she took note of how she should remember that particular feeling of the batter's thickness in response to her gestures. Her experience of learning to bake this cake was similar to the French cheesemakers: 'Working with the curd, they learned from the curd itself' (West 2013b: 332).[9] By engaging with food as it does things and attuning her bodily perception to this transformation, a novice learns to prepare food. In other words, a cook has to learn to 'bring out each ingredient's best qualities. Knowing how to develop the flavour of a food depends on an interest in understanding it and how it reacts with other foods' (Adapon 2008: 18).

At the same time, as the previous chapter has argued, each future preparation will be dynamic and thus slightly different from the previous one, requiring the bodily attunement to food's ever-changing capacities. Depending on the qualities and quantities of the ingredients used, the tools at hand, the weather and temperatures, but also her own mood and patience, and many more variables, Ibtissam will enter into a bodily 'dialogue with [her] environment' (Portisch 2010: S77) through her growing multisensory perception of food's transformations. The fluency of her performance will grow with her ability to take account of these diverse dimensions and respond to the unpredictable materiality of food. Food's transformative materiality marks not only an element of unpredictability in every cooking endeavour, but also requires every novice to find her own strategy to engage with it, every time anew. This example highlights how cooking skills cannot simply be transmitted from one generation to the next, 'but are regrown in each, incorporated into the modus operandi of the developing human organism through training and experience in the performance of particular tasks' (Ingold 2011: 5) and in a particular material and social taste environment. By attuning bodily to what food does as it is transformed and transforms itself, a Marrakchi cook-to-be learns to consult food before she can enter the final stage of her apprenticeship.

Learning through Replacement

On another day in March 2013, I had the occasion to observe Zakia making lunch by herself. Rachida was out at work and Ibtissam was at Saturday school. Although Zakia was a little exhausted from her week at university, she began to make bread as soon as I arrived at 10 am. After combining soft and hard wheat flours, water, yeast and salt in a dough, she began to move her hands just like Rachida and other expert breadmakers. While kneading, Zakia explained that the dough needs to be really well kneaded: 'To make good bread.' However, midway through, she realized that she had no *nukhala* (bran) or any other flour left and started picking flour out from the half-mixed dough to reserve it for shaping the loaves later on. She used a large spoon to fish out some remaining dry parts of both *gemh* (durum wheat) and *fors* (soft wheat) flour. She also did not pour warm water onto the yeast, as I later saw Rachida doing it, but used cold water despite the chilly spring temperatures. With her fists deep into the dough, Zakia concluded that she was much slower at kneading. Still, she was confident about all the rest: 'I make bread just like my mother.'

When it was time to bring the bread to the public oven, we noticed that Zakia's loaves stuck to the cloth covering them. She had not coated the loaves with enough flour when she placed them on the baking tray for resting. While she managed to peel off the two uppermost loaves, slightly deforming them as she did so, she could not detach the lower three loaves and, frustrated, scraped them off and put the dough in a plastic bag and into the bin. Zakia emphasized that she would put the dough out on the roof terrace for the birds later; she would not throw it away. Zakia then messaged Ibtissam to buy three loaves on her way home. She confessed to me that this had never happened before: 'It was as if this was the first time I made bread.' We hurried out of the house to bring the two saved loaves to the public oven and buy fresh ingredients for lunch. Upon our return from the nearby *suiqa* (small market), Zakia proceeded to make a *tajine* (stew) just in time for everyone's return for lunch.

After lunch, keen observer that she is, Rachida discovered the discarded dough in the plastic bag as she came into the kitchen to wash herself for her prayer. Instead of praying, Rachida decided to reknead the loaves, afraid of wasting the precious produce. With her face still wet and her scarf on the head, she made bread out of the ruined dough. She added more flour, which she found in a plastic box under the countertop, a package of dry yeast, some vegetable oil, warmed water and then started to knead the dough with fast, strong movements. Ibtissam joked by saying that this bread would not be edible, to which Rachida responded matter-of-factly: 'It will be exactly like all other breads I make.' Ibtissam was not convinced and kept chuckling. Rachida was a little bit angry with Zakia for having discarded the dough as if it was no longer good. As she thrust herself into the dough, Rachida exclaimed with a reproachful voice that she does not waste food.

* * *

In his study on the transmission of cooking knowledge, Sutton describes how a Kalymnian mother instructs and corrects her daughter from the sidelines, thereby teaching her 'All the tricks and adjustments one must make for things to come out right' (2014: 119). Mother-to-daughter instruction in Marrakchi food preparation is more indirect than on the Greek island. Rather than being instructed one to one by more experienced cooks, Marrakchi cooks-to-be learn through *replacing* the lead cook for the preparation of a dish or entire meal in their absence. Replacement is based on a delayed form of multisensory imitation that rests on participant perception, similar to how I was able to reproduce couscous for the first time after fieldwork (see Interlude 2). Thus, although Zakia had not intentionally observed her mother before she prepared her own bread – and then imitated her mother's movements under her instruction as Kalymnian cooks and apprentices of other crafts are doing (cf. Ingold 2001; Marchand 2009; Sutton 2014; Wacquant 2004) – Zakia had perceived her mother's bread and lunch in the making many times when she helped to process and clean foods.[10] Zakia was developing a 'reciprocity of taste' (see Chapter 1). She had heard, smelled, touched, tasted and seen her mother's food preparations, and drew on that bodily experience to prepare lunch in Rachida's absence. Zakia's copying of gestures and movements was the result of having spent her entire life in the vicinity of her mother and other cooking family members, eventually joining in preparing food through separate tasks such as processing vegetables or baking.

Although Rachida and the other experienced cooks I worked with rarely showed or pointed out crucial aspects of a crafting process, as Ingold (2001) or Sutton (2014) describe, they were nonetheless crucial in setting up adequate learning situations. By asking Ibtissam to bake a cake and Zakia to prepare lunch in her stead, Rachida afforded both of them an adequate possibility to learn. Moreover, Zakia was not let off easily with her failed bread loaves. Instead, Rachida demonstrated the importance of a detailed knowledge of and engagement with her taste environment (see Chapter 1). In this case, Rachida's role of instructor is retrospect; she knew where to find more flour when Zakia had thought there was none. If Zakia had controlled all food containers before beginning to prepare the bread dough, she would have been better prepared to deal with her forgetting to put bran aside for shaping the dough into loaves. Although Rachida did not point out her tricks and adjustments as Zakia was preparing the bread, like Kalymnian mothers do, she used her own preparation of the discarded dough as a delayed form of illustration.

Learning through replacement is based on trial and error, similar to learning with and from food, but the stakes are higher. Since the learning cook is replacing the lead cook, the food she prepares is part of the daily provision of food to family members and/or visitors and thus should be reliably good. The replacing novice assumes partial responsibility for the outcome of the meal and is being judged according to socially shared standards of good food (see Chapter 1). As such, learning through replacement is not only about delayed imitation of a set of gestures and practices but also about learning to become a woman (see Chapter 3). Whereas from Zakia's point of view, she had simply misjudged the proportions of the ingredients and the transformation of food itself – and took responsibility for this mistake by sending Ibtissam to buy bread – from Rachida's perspective, she had erred in a much more profound way: by discarding the bread loaves in the bin, Zakia had shown disrespect towards bread itself, the symbol of all foods and of God's benevolence. As the spiritual symbol of all food, bread cannot be wasted. In doing so, Zakia rejected the primary gift of God (*al-ni'ama*) and committed a sacrilege. Rachida thus taught Zakia the spiritual value of bread by postponing her prayers and rekneading the bread loaves herself rather than risk losing the dough as it kept transforming under the influence of yeast, moisture and heat.

Similarly, while Zakia became frustrated and angry with the sticky dough to such an extent that she would place the dough in the bin, Rachida taught Zakia the key values of patience and perseverance in a woman's everyday life.[11] These values are at the core of Moroccan understandings of womanhood, for a good cook is primarily a patient (*sebbar*) and persevering cook who takes 'the time it takes' and makes a bodily effort to prepare good food for the family. In other words, through their participant perception in the social space of the kitchen and home, young women in low-income families also incorporate the expectation to cook as mothers and with it absorb a widely shared sense of responsibility and morality.[12]

Although conflicts or disagreements rarely erupted openly during my fieldwork, precisely because of the constant invocation of women's strength and value lying in patience and perseverance, Zakia's failed bread loaves could be read as a symbol of her frustration and discontent.[13] While her mother's lesson was manifested in rekneading that dough, Zakia's opinion was materialized in the sticky and misshapen bread dough that had ended in the bin. Zakia was exhausted from her previous week at university and, though less outspoken about it than her younger sister Ibtissam, she did not particularly look forward to kneading bread for her own future family. When speaking about her ambitions for the future on another occasion, Zakia confessed to me that the one thing she would definitely not prepare by hand, once she was married, was bread. She would rather buy it than go through the physical ordeal of kneading it every morning. Yet, when revisiting her family in September 2023, two years after her marriage and two months after the birth of her first child, I was not surprised to find that Zakia now regularly prepared her own bread. Aicha's change of behaviour when she became a mother (not when she married!) is similarly indicative of the importance that homemade foods achieve for the reproduction of the family, starting with homemade bread. However, even if not outright acknowledged by my research participants, younger cooks' reliance on new technologies and media did alter the underlying generational hierarchies, and the division of labour implicit in these three elements of knowledge reproduction, in more open and long-lasting ways, as the final section will illustrate.

Technologies and Media: Reversing Intergenerational Learning

On a hot Ramadan afternoon in 2013, it was Zakia's task to prepare the daily *al-ftour* snacks to break the daytime fasting, because Rachida expected to return

Figure 2.3. Making pizza, Marrakech, 2013. © Katharina Graf

late from work. Zakia decided to make pizza, her favourite Ramadan dish (see Figure 2.3). She was keen on new ideas and began searching for and skim-watching several YouTube videos on her smartphone, all of which featured experienced middle-aged Moroccan female cooks.[14] While watching with her sister, we discussed how to adapt the presented recipe – for instance, which toppings we preferred, what herbs or what flour to use. Once decided, Zakia sent Ibtissam to buy the missing pizza toppings in the nearby street market, before she and I went into the kitchen to begin preparations. Without consulting her phone again, Zakia set up her ingredients visibly on the countertop like the women in the video and in televised cookery shows (see also Ibtissam's cake preparations). This set-up differs from the usual style of food preparation I observed by more experienced cooks who readied ingredients just when they were needed.

However, when Zakia began to mix the pizza dough ingredients with both hands, she abandoned the script and style of the videos, her gestures now resembling those used when preparing Moroccan flatbread (see Interlude 1). As her slight body worked hard to knead the heavy dough in the unrelenting summer heat, she explained to me that she makes homemade pizza (*pizza dyel dar*), like all Moroccans make pizza, either with *kefta* (minced meat) or with canned tuna. However, inspired by one of the YouTube videos, she decided to make her pizzas smaller than usual and to add grilled peppers as a topping. Once the dough had proven, she rolled it out with a wooden stick resembling a former broom stick, quite unlike the rolling pin used in the videos. Just like the YouTube experts,

Zakia tried to cut out individual portions of dough with a turned soup bowl, but soon realized this did not work. The dough stuck to the bowl and got misshapen. Zakia scanned the kitchen for an alternative, until her eyes identified the plastic lid of a jar. It worked and she proceeded, placing the round loaves directly on two baking trays for a brief moment of baking in the gas oven. While she instructed Ibtissam to carefully attend to the loaves in the fickle oven upstairs, Zakia brought the tomato sauce and other toppings in individual bowls upstairs and put them next to the oven. But what a disappointment when Zakia pulled the pizza out of the gas oven: Ibtissam had not pinched the dough with a fork and it had risen too much! Zakia hissed: 'You also watched the videos, why didn't you make holes with a fork like them?!' However, she swiftly proceeded to add tomato sauce and toppings on each pizza with a large spoon and her hands, successfully flattening the puffy rounds after all. Her preparations continued thus, sometimes imitating the expert in a video, sometimes relying on her bodily experience and imitating her mother's gestures.

* * *

In contrast to North America or Europe, where domestic cooking among low-income households has been influenced by material changes for eighty to a hundred years (Counihan 2004; Giard 1998; Schwartz Cowan 1983), affordable domestic technologies and media entered low-income urban Moroccan homes ten to twenty years ago and only gradually. Marrakech's medina was being equipped with electricity and running water from the late 1990s onwards, largely following the growing influx of tourists (Ernst 2013; Wilbaux 2001) and only in the 2000s in the more popular (*cha'abi*) neighbourhoods such as Rachida's. As a result, electric appliances like fridges or blenders as well as so-called traditional media like television, now ubiquitous across low-income Morocco, are still a fairly recent addition in many low-income urban kitchens and homes.[15]

This material change within Moroccan cities coincides with social change, in particular the spread of girl's schooling and growing rates of literacy. Older cooks, especially in low-income urban households, born in rural Morocco before the 1980s rarely read a cookbook, employed metric measures or used the internet to source new recipes during my fieldwork. When cooks-to-be like Zakia and Ibtissam came of age in the early 2010s, smartphones and a mobile internet connection were just becoming accessible. During my fieldwork, both girls owned a smartphone and usually had access to mobile internet via prepaid phonecards.[16] While digital technologies and social media were immediately popular among Marrakchi youth, more outdated media such as radio or books were not popular. The latter were simply not relevant for low-income Marrakchis teens and tweens, creating a curious media gap between younger generations of educated youth and older ones, like Aicha and Fatimzahra, who used not only their smartphone but also cookbooks and televised cookery shows to attune their taste knowledge. At the same time, the middle-aged lay experts in Zakia's YouTube videos demonstrate that although illiteracy prevents many older and experienced cooks like Hajja or Rachida from access to textual media such as cookbooks or online blogs, the spread of digital media with more multisensory content such as online videos, photos or voice messages is equally popular with older users and thus prevents simplistic conclusions about correlations between age, literacy and technology use.[17]

While education and especially women's emancipation have led other Morocco and gender scholars to conclude that cooking is no longer social and therefore its reproduction is at risk (Kapchan 1996; Newcomb 2017), I made different observations. This section demonstrates how young women of low-income background harnessed new technologies and media to make food that is considered easier and faster than traditional Moroccan dishes. As a result, young women – willingly or not – alter not only food preparation but also domestic hierarchies. Taste knowledge now also flows from younger cooks to older cooks. Importantly, new technologies and media such as the smartphone and YouTube channels do not lead to a simplification of cooking knowledge as these scholars and many public commentaries suggest; rather, they widen younger cooks' possibilities and sources of knowledge.[18]

The vignette shows that Zakia had already acquired enough experience to transfer and productively combine several YouTube recipes with those she knew herself and in engagement with the specific material environment of kitchen, oven and market. For experienced apprentices like Zakia, new sources of knowledge complement existing ones and come to play a major role only once the learning cook has passed through all the three described stages of participant perception. To make the pizza dough, Zakia relied on her substantial experience of breadmaking and coupled these with the ideas gleaned from YouTube to shape the dough into much smaller and thinner loaves. She flexibly employed available objects such as the broom stick and the plastic lid to account for the nontransferability of the video experts' suggestions. The vignette describes the subtle adaptations and creative solutions advanced learners like Zakia come up with, from choosing to applying new inspirations to her existing knowledge. By contrast, Ibtissam had not yet acquired enough experience with the unpredictable heating of their oven, nor did she know yet that dough always needed to be pricked to prevent it from bubbling up. The uptake and success of new technologies and media thus depend on a significant level of experience on the part of domestic cooks.

Through employing her smartphone and social media to make food, Zakia not only widens her sources of knowledge beyond her immediate material and social environment, but also participates in decision making and planning in food preparation, a task usually in the hands of the senior lead cook (Chapter 3). Traditional and new technologies and media such as cookbooks, television shows and social media allow literate young women to experiment with new forms of social learning and gain experience independent of their mothers or mothers-in-law. Importantly, these new learning situations are still based on experts, but are decoupled from domestic hierarchies and existing social relations. The cooks sharing their recipes via YouTube videos or WhatsApp chats were predominantly middle-aged women who cooked in their private kitchens and, judging by their gestures and verbal commentaries, had considerable experience. While these women resembled Rachida and other senior domestic cooks in Zakia's social environment, they were also strangers for Zakia and her family. Therefore, the knowledge of these cooks could be consulted independently of normal rules of social interaction, especially regarding deference to seniors, which are shaped by strong webs of rights and obligations (Maher 1974; Newcomb 2009). Practically speaking, a video could be watched multiple times or stopped short if it did not match Zakia's expectations, a recipe via chat could be altered and adapted without requiring explanation or argument on Zakia's part, or one video or recipe could be compared to another without offending anyone. In short, Zakia remained free to choose, adapt or reject ideas and expertise without having to confirm or challenge these women's social status at the same time.

New technologies and media like the smartphone and social media in particular thus contribute not only to new forms of taste knowledge but also to altering the generational hierarchies of domestic work, whereby decision making, planning and preparing a meal are firmly in the hands of the lead cook, usually the oldest female family member.[19] While I will explore a more conflictive situation emerging from this role reversal in Chapter 3, in this case the effects on domestic labour division were more subtle. As a wage-working woman and – at the time of my fieldwork – sole breadwinner of the family, Rachida needed her daughters to help with domestic work more than other mothers. Thus, although Rachida outwardly sought to appear as a proper domestic Moroccan cook and generally rejected what she considered 'fast' or 'European' food such as pizza, she was not opposed to Zakia's new recipes.[20] Indeed, her daughter's interest in European foods and YouTube recipes was welcomed. Zakia preferred European dishes because 'they are easier and take much less time' to prepare. While she consulted her mother about small details such as which ingredients or tools to use or where to find them in their kitchen, Zakia planned and carried out the preparations largely independently of her mother. By drawing her mother and other senior women of the neighbourhood into detailed conversations about these dishes after a shared meal, Zakia managed to partially reverse the age-based association with expertise and control. Through reflecting on her experience and sharing her newly gained knowledge with other experts, Zakia not only took ownership of her cooking, but also approached the status of an expert and temporarily became these women's social equal.

It would be too simplistic to relate Zakia's advancement in the domestic hierarchy solely to her formal education. Although Rachida was partially illiterate and has never studied or acquired a professional skill like her daughters, deference to seniors, which was (and still is) an important cultural value in both rural and urban Morocco, trumps education. Zvan Elliott (2015) demonstrates persuasively how especially women from low-income backgrounds achieve seniority not through education and a successful professional career, but through marriage and becoming a mother. Thus, while giving Ibtissam and Zakia scope for trying new recipes and taking control of dishes that they liked, Rachida also insisted on her daughters' awareness that a Moroccan girl needed to cook 'like a Moroccan [*bhal shi maghribiya*]' if she wanted to marry and become a woman. In everyday practice this subtle negotiation resulted in a mutually beneficial situation whereby Rachida could count on her daughters' help in the kitchen and they had their mother's support trying to prepare dishes that they liked, but that were not considered Moroccan or 'good' by Moroccan standards (see Chapter 4). From a more long-term perspective, and recollecting the argument in the previous section, senior women like Rachida thus managed to reproduce not only Moroccan taste knowledge and cultural values such as female patience and perseverance, but also the notion that complete womanhood is only achieved in the figure of the lead cook and mother.

Conclusion: Cooks in the Making

Learning cooking is so thoroughly embedded in everyday life in low-income Marrakech that it easily remains hidden from view, as it was initially from my own. It was only through *re-embodying* Marrakchi taste knowledge *after* fieldwork that I realized how I had learned and was able to understand how others were learning cooking. Cooks-to-be and the ethnographer learn through bodily attunement to the material and social environment of the domestic cook, a continuous process of learning that I called 'participant perception'. In the absence of direct observation or verbal instruction, which results from cooking being a routine part of everyday family life rather than a more clearly demarcated apprenticeship in a specialized craft, other senses gain importance in imparting an understanding of taste knowledge. This chapter has illustrated that young Marrakchis and I learned a lot simply from smelling, hearing, touching, feeling and eating food as we provisioned, processed, cooked, baked and/or served it alongside experienced domestic cooks.

Participant perception comprises three distinct stages, which build on one another and engage women and men differently. I described the first stage of learning as 'being there' or as knowing before learning. Being there implies that most girls and boys learn something about food already in the womb as they absorb tastes and movements. Without deliberate attention to food, as they grow up, they note what foods are served, how, when, by and to whom through all their bodily senses simply by participating in everyday routines around food. The next stage of participant perception resembles more closely what apprenticeship scholars would consider learning. Cooks-to-be, usually girls, are tasked to prepare small side dishes or bake a snack and, in engaging with the transformative materiality of food, learn with and from food itself. Through feeling the texture of ingredients as they combine and change with the hands and body, a novice is guided by food. Once she has attuned her bodily senses to food, a young cook learns through replacing an experienced cook. This final stage of participant perception is marked by casual observation and delayed imitation, since a young cook replaces the lead cook only when the latter is absent. In deciding on the right moment and the right tasks, expert cooks afford younger cooks the possibility to grow their taste knowledge and simultaneously ascertain the reproduction of the underlying spiritual and cultural values pertaining to domestic cooking and womanhood.

All three stages of participant perception were dominated by experienced cooks. To some extent, knowledge is thus reproduced or regrown based on the previous generation's taste knowledge. However, this chapter also demonstrated that knowledge flows are reversed through the use of new technologies and media such as the smartphone and social media apps. Thanks to their (digital) literacy and desire for different tastes, my younger research participants incorporated new sources of knowledge in their cooking, often including so-called 'European' foods like pizza or pasta. In doing so, they widened their family's taste knowledge and altered domestic hierarchies of labour. At the same time, the example of Zakia's pizza preparations shows that by welcoming these new practices, older generations of cooks like Rachida also managed to reproduce the expectation that a woman cooks for her family and only in doing so achieves socially sanctioned womanhood. That said, in reproducing or regrowing their taste knowledge, each cook also partakes in shaping the practices and discourses that mark material and social change in Morocco more broadly. Thus, through the incorporation of a variety of old and new technologies and media, domestic cooks of all ages ever so subtly alter, re-create or challenge conceptions not only of Moroccan foodways but also of what it means to be a woman in contemporary urban Morocco, as the next chapter goes on to show.

Notes

1. Wacquant (2004: 117–18) similarly argues that bodily learning remains imperceptible to those who do not know in practice and that the more a novice learns, the more she or he is able to perceive.
2. Dishwashing is methodologically speaking an interesting task, because it marks the boundaries between family and visitor. In Rachida's household, where I did not live, I was never allowed to wash the dishes, despite offering to do so many times. I was considered a guest,

albeit with a special status of familiarity. In Fatimzahra's and Aicha's households I took the role of dishwasher from the beginning and soon it was expected from me, marking my integration in the domestic division of food work.
3. This is also shown in the study of 'kitchen life' in Britain (Wills et al. 2013).
4. This expression is reminiscent of Geertz's (1988) notion of the anthropologist as 'being there' during fieldwork, of having penetrated and being penetrated by another form of life in a certain place at a certain time. While this certainly applies to my own fieldwork experience, including the way I communicate my having been there, I expressly apply this notion also to those I worked with.
5. Tea glasses were a common measuring tool in baking, possibly adopted from cookery shows on television.
6. This attitude was echoed by many young women I talked to and is not unique to Morocco (e.g. Sauvegrain 2009). Indeed, it was acceptable for an unmarried woman in urban Morocco not to learn how to cook while she studied or worked. At the same time, it was largely indisputable that upon marriage – a fate that many women took for granted, whether they continue to work or not – a woman will cook.
7. For girls of low-income families in contemporary urban Morocco who go to secondary school like Ibtissam, this is an early age for initiation into food work compared to the daughters of middle-income families, who start baking and cooking only when marriage looms, if at all (Newcomb 2017). By contrast, rural girls tend to help from around seven years of age (Crawford 2008; Montgomery 2019).
8. This second stage of learning separates girls and boys most markedly. Within the domestic setting of the family, few boys would be asked or allowed to engage bodily with food. It is only in circumstances when boys or men live without women – for instance, when migrating for education or work – that they prepare food.
9. Paxson refers to this form of learning as 'synesthetic reason' (2013: 131) and Sutton proposes calling this process of constant bodily adjustment and use of one's bodily senses to evaluate what food does as 'somatic intersubjectivity' (2014: 116, 122, citing Patel).
10. Zakia's temporally delayed imitation is akin to what Lave calls 'successive approximation' (2011: 75), which includes erring and self-correcting.
11. These values resonate with concepts of 'Muslim' womanhood elsewhere in the region. For a critical comparative analysis, see Abu-Lughod (2002) and Mahmood (2005).
12. Most apprenticeships involve a simultaneous absorption of a 'moral universe' (Marchand 2009).
13. See Stoller (1989: 19–22) for an evocative example of the weapons of the weak, whereby a bad-tasting sauce expresses a junior woman's discontent with her position of powerlessness within her polygamous family.
14. Media studies scholar Lewis calls this form of sharing advise via online platforms 'ordinary expertise' (2018: 215). A growing scholarly debate discusses how so-called how-to videos and instructions by amateurs on blogs or social media challenge the status and role of professionals and experts (Lewis and Phillipov 2018).
15. For a discussion on the reception of and engagement with television among low-income Casaouis, see Ossman (1994) and Sabry (2005).
16. Low-income Marrakchis of all ages routinely compared televised commercials and marketing offers of the major phone companies, switching between several sim cards to get the most free minutes and gigabyte allowance for their money. When running out of credit,

they sometimes temporarily connected to a neighbour's WLAN or used a public Wi-Fi hotspot.
17. The situation is different in rural settings, where Amazigh and oral communication dominate, barring especially low-literate women from using smartphones (Dodson, Sterling and Bennett 2013). The Moroccan context thus contrasts in more than one way with the linear 'domestication of technology' theory advocated by media scholars (e.g. Burgess and Green 2018; Kirkwood 2018).
18. See Murcott (2019) for a critical discussion of the interrelations between commonsense assumptions around food and eating and scholarly engagement with these.
19. These technologies also alter gendered relations as my conversations with cooking men illustrate. Online videos and blogs allowed especially men who live apart from their natal families to hone their taste knowledge through easy recourse to experts other than their mothers or sisters and without them knowing.
20. For my research participants, 'European' food was synonymous with fast food (see Chapter 4).

INTERLUDE 3

Brewing

A few days before her mother's return from the *haj* pilgrimage to Mecca in mid-November 2012, Fatimzahra and I began to prepare *haluwat* (a generic term for sweets) of all kinds. Fartimzahra ground spices and roasted seeds, I sieved fine flour, she mixed the ingredients for cake batters and cookie doughs, I shaped them and placed them on trays, and she attended to each batch in the large gas oven across the *riad*'s courtyard. We worked well into the night before Hajja's return. Although we cooperated quietly and spoke few words, the atmosphere was festive and loaded with excitement. Little did I know that these long days in the kitchen were only the beginning of weeks spent labouring to serve food and drink to Hajja's entire extended family as well as neighbours and friends who visited to celebrate her safe return from Mecca and pay their respects. As time wore on, my feelings shifted from an ethnographer's joy at the many occasions to participate in food preparation to sheer exhaustion from working round the clock.

It was a sunny afternoon in early December and we had just sent the son of Hajja's brother and his family of five out of doors to go for a walk in the medina after having served them a lavish lunch. Fatimzahra and I were clearing the table and tidying up the kitchen when the doorbell rang. Hajja called from her bedroom to inquire who it was and Fatimzahra went to open the door. Yet more visitors! My heart sank – I had hoped for a few hours of break to take notes. Fatimzahra retreated to the kitchen and quietly panicked, breathing hard, holding back her tears from sheer fatigue. Hajja rushed to prepare another room for the new guests. In a concentrated effort to calm herself, Fatimzahra instructed me to buy milk, bread and *msemen* (layered pancakes) in the *suiqa* (small market along the road), while she devoted herself to the task of readying tea and coffee pots, glasses and trays. Following a desperate impetus to save time, I asked Fatimzahra whether I should buy ingredients for dinner as well. Hajja overheard me as she entered the kitchen to help prepare *kaskrut* (afternoon snack) for the new arrivals and silenced me with a gesture of her hand to signal that this was not the moment to be thinking of dinner. And so I went out with only Fatimzahra's instructions, swallowing my frustration and trying to ignore the certainty that two hours later I would have to go grocery shop again, this time following Hajja's instructions.

Upon my return some twenty minutes later, the guests had installed themselves in the second salon – doubling as their guest room for the days they would stay with us – while Fatimzahra put the finishing touches to the multiple snacks and drinks she wanted to offer. As the host, Hajja sat down with her guests in the salon. While arranging the *msemen* on a tray, Fatimzahra asked me to make tea. Evidently, she had forgotten to prepare it. I was puzzled and protested that I had never prepared tea for guests before. She insisted and I complied. I put water to boil on the hob, measured the gunpowder tea in my hand and added it to the *berrad* (a plump silver tea pot). I then picked mint leaves from the bundle in the fridge as I had seen Fatimzahra do so many times before. After pouring the boiling water into the *berrad*, I let it brew for a minute or two, then gently stirred it in circles and poured the dark green water directly into the sink. I stuffed the mint leaves into the *berrad*, added more boiling water and turned on the gas to boil it further. Upon switching off the hob and closing the lid a few minutes later, Fatimzahra and I began carrying everything to the salon across the courtyard. For a split second, I rejoiced in the accomplishment and looked forward to retreating to my room to rest.

Yet, as we balanced the second round of foods and drinks on our trays, Fatimzahra told me to also serve the tea. I gasped; this was decidedly her task! But by the time I could have responded, we had already arrived in the salon. The chance to object had passed and I swallowed my thoughts, as I had done so many times throughout these weeks. I took the seat behind the low table on the side upon which the tea was to be served. Hajja left the salon to plan dinner, Fatimzahra went into the kitchen to prepare another round of snacks for the first group of visitors, who would soon come back from their walk. I was left alone with the three guests, trying to regain my composure and serve tea the way it should be done. They immediately started asking me questions, laughing heartily about my funny *darija*, while acknowledging how well I mastered to crown each glass of tea with the desired foam. I submitted to my role and entertained our guests until they, too, decided to go for a walk in the medina. As I cleared the table and the doorbell rang again, this time announcing the return of the first group of guests, I had a sense of déjà-vu. . .

CHAPTER 3

Culinary Connectivity
Negotiating Womanhood and Family Meals

One June morning in her kitchen, Aicha asked me to prepare our daily bread. Working the dough, which always seemed so subtle and elastic under Aicha's hands but was sticky and dense for me, I suddenly understood what it meant to knead it every day. Bodily knowledge, certainly, but also so much strength! I realized then that while Aicha shaped the dough, it shaped her too. In this sweaty moment of failure, I remembered how different Aicha's body was when I first met her back in 2007 compared to now. Aicha's strong wide shoulders and her brawny body betrayed her new status; she had become a wife and mother by kneading bread.

At night on that same day I joined Aicha while she was fileting sardines for next day's lunch on the breezy rooftop terrace of her flat. She rhetorically enquired: 'You know what Ismail told me on my way home?' Ismail was the young shop assistant and a cousin of her husband, and he usually picked up the lunches Aicha prepared for him and another shop assistant every day. I was curious: 'No, what did he tell you?' Aicha could not decide whether to laugh or to cry when she replied: 'They found a blonde hair in the bread while eating lunch.' I blushed and looked up, expecting her to scold me in her direct manner. She saw my face: 'Don't worry, they were not disgusted, they thought it was funny and called it "Katie's bread". But Ismail also told me that he does not like any other bread than mine. You know, they really want their bread, my bread.'

I was still embarrassed the next day and did not know what to say when Ismail picked up lunch and – with an enigmatic smile – also told me of that hair of mine. Much later I stumbled upon the poem 'breadmaking' by the thirteenth-century Persian poet Rumi: 'You remember breadmaking! This is how your desire tangles with a desired one' (1995: 183–85). I understood that my intentions had inadvertently entangled with someone I neither desired nor felt attached to.

Breadmaking is not only a metaphor for love, passion and spirituality as in Rumi's poem. While metaphorically the man in the poem kneads dough and makes love to the woman, in Marrakech, it is women who make bread and thus 'make love' to their family in everyday life. Marrakchi women knead and shape bread with their strong, loving and skilled hands, and through the act of kneading also shape their bodies, their conjugal relationships and their families; in short, they shape themselves, their family and their culture.[1] And bread shapes them in turn. Since bread symbolically – and often materially – stands in for food in general, the daily preparation of food can be understood to also make the self and the family. My hair in the bread raises the central question of *who* cooks and for whom.

* * *

In patrilocal and multigenerational households young women do not usually manage daily food preparation. Newly married women move in with their husband's family and come under the control of their mother-in-law. Women like Fatimzahra who do not marry usually keep living with and remain under their own mother's management and have even less control over domestic matters. The elements that determine authority and task allocation within a multigenerational household depend on seniority and the relation to the head of the household.[2] More prestigious tasks such as cooking or provisioning food are reserved for the wife of the male household head; in the case of his death, this is often a senior woman.[3] Younger women get low-status and menial tasks such as processing ingredients, serving meals and cleaning up. In multigenerational households today, the woman in charge of cooking is still in charge of managing domestic labour and, through it, also manages the household's social relations. This is the case for both male and female relations.[4] In this context, I found that it is not gender equality that younger women strive to achieve, but emancipation from senior women's domestic dominance.

The explanations for this relate to idealized notions of womanhood and the family.[5] Within a marriage, a strong emphasis was placed on children. Both Marrakchi men and women considered themselves – and were considered by others – a mature adult once they had their first child. Becoming a wife is thus only a partial transition to mature womanhood, which is reached upon becoming the mother, ideally of a boy (cf. Zvan Elliott 2015), and, as I will illustrate, by doing what mothers are expected to do: cooking and caring for their family (cf. Bordo 1993; Butler 1993). Aicha's case is illustrative here. I have often quizzed her on the many changes that had taken place since I had last seen her, 'Before we married, Hassan and I smoked and drank [alcohol], he cooked sometimes or we went out for eating, we had fun! When we married, he still prepared *tajines* for us now and then and we often ate *fih zenqa* [street food]. But when Zahra was born, that was over. I want to cook for the girls; I have to be a good and respectable mother.'

Until a young mother manages domestic food work, she does not take control of making her self and her family. To explore these processes, I first describe contemporary gender relations and how they are changing with respect to food work. I explore why women continue to cook and see to the daily reproduction of the family, even when working for a wage, and why men are not stepping up to help their wives. I then demonstrate how education and an independent income have earned low-income urban women bargaining power within the family. This, in turn, allows them to convince their husbands to move into a smaller household, centred on the conjugal family, where they assume full control over all domestic matters and thus emancipate themselves from senior women's control. Rather than change gender relations, this move alters the power relations between young and old cooks, as I show in the second section.

In the third section I describe how, as a consequence, domestic cooking is increasingly managed and undertaken by only one cook. Ironically, in striving to continue to make good food for their husband and children, young cooks were reinforcing the ideal of mature womanhood as the caring and cooking wife and mother, and thus worked even harder than previous generations of women. Although new kitchen technologies and media as well as widening social relations significantly enlarge the knowledge resources and practical possibilities of younger generations of cooks, as the previous chapter highlighted, these new sociomaterial relations entangle young cooks in new, largely hidden webs of power. The final section brings together these multiple layers through the notion of 'culinary connectivity'. Considering the crafting of womanhood and of the family as culinary connectivity allows me to analyse not only why young low-income Moroccan women continue to view food preparation as a key practice that defines their womanhood and their family, but also points to the larger political economy of domestic cooking. The making of the self and of the family is no longer conceived within the bounds of patriarchy based on gendered dominance, but on the relational processes of *becoming through* food in the wider context of poverty and structural uncertainty.[6]

Men and Food

When I entered the kitchen on a hot afternoon in the middle of Ramadan, I noticed two earthenware *tanjiya* (a slow-cooked meat stew) urns in the corner by the door. I asked Aicha whether Hassan intended to make a *tanjiya* tonight. She replied: 'Yes, his friend Younes wanted to taste it before he goes back North.' Around 6 pm, just before Aicha, Halima and I began our preparations for *al-ftour* (the meal breaking the fast), Hassan came into the kitchen with a heavy plastic bag. Aicha immediately asked him how much he had paid for the meat, but his answer was evasive: 'I don't know, Younes paid for it.' Aicha and I looked at each other and we were thinking the same thing: he must know how much Younes paid, since he took him to the butcher and advised him on the quantities and cuts. Clearly, Aicha suspected them of having paid too much and Hassan knew it too.

Meanwhile, Hassan emptied the plastic bags: several large chunks of meat, four garlic cloves, two *msiyr* (preserved lemons) and a small plastic bag of *smen* (clarified butter). He placed everything next to the *tanjiya* urns and asked Aicha where she kept the cumin. Instead of telling him, Aicha turned to get it herself and also handed him a plate. Hassan instantly went to the task of preparing the dish (Figure 3.1). He generously poured ground cumin onto the plate and whisked every piece of meat in it. Some meat pieces were too big and he cut them in half with a knife that Aicha handed him. Aicha stood next to him, closely observing what he was doing. She was hugely entertained that her husband was preparing food, giggling and commenting on how clumsily he cut the meat. My presence with a camera and a notebook only furthered his perceptible unease. Hassan's gestures, though displaying skill and a sense for what he was doing, betrayed his nervousness. He rushed. Aicha soon realized that her cheerful way of mocking him stressed him and began to change her tone to include him in her chatter. He relaxed a little. She asked him whether he could also get *monada* (lemonade) to serve with the meat. He replied: 'No. I prepare the food, you buy the drinks.' Aicha laughed out loud and said: 'OK, you're the cook today and I'm the one with the money!'

Hours later, when we had finished the midnight meal and carried everything back into the kitchen, Aicha asked me: 'Why did you not eat more meat?' 'Because it was *messouss* [tasteless; here, it lacked salt] and I don't like to eat so much meat at once.' Younes meanwhile brought more dirty dishes and listened to our conversation. Aicha readily agreed that it wasn't tasty and as she stored away the meat into plastic containers, one of which was for Younes for his trip home the next night, she elaborated: 'It was *khaib, khaib bzef* [really bad]! I would have added *beldi* olive oil and more *msiyr* for more taste. The meat that Hassan bought was not good.' I nodded and Aicha went on: 'And it wasn't cooked long enough, it wasn't soft. I would have brought it much earlier to the *mul al-farnadshi* [a man operating the oven of a hammam, where *tanjiyas* are slow-cooked].'

* * *

This vignette points towards the diminishing importance of men in the reproduction of everyday family life and speaks to broader social changes with respect to gender relations. Whereas women are gaining decision-making power thanks to their income, husbands lose influence in domestic matters. Hassan's *tanjiya* preparations materialize and symbolize these changing power relations. In the following, I will unpack this scene to demonstrate why, because of these changes, gendered relations were not considered the most problematic domestic issue by my female research participants.

Figure 3.1. Placing meat in the *tanjiya*, a Marrakchi speciality prepared by men, Marrakech, 2013. © Katharina Graf

The setting in this vignette differed from how *tanjiya* is usually processed and consumed. According to Mohamed el Haouz, a Marrakchi ethnobotanist who once invited me to shop, prepare and eat a truly delicious *tanjiya*, it is made for a day out with family and friends. A *tanjiya* is prepared directly on the side of the butcher's counter, in public, with ingredients bought directly on the spot. It is made one day in advance to cook overnight in the oven of a hammam and is picked up on the way to the gardens, always transported in its name-giving cooking container. Typical *tanjiya* preparations resemble meat grilling in North America or Europe, which is similarly masculinized and strongly associated with leisure and outdoor cooking, clearly demarcating it from feminized routine food preparation in the kitchen (Sobal 2005).

In the above scene Aicha and Hassan deviate from these procedures in symbolically meaningful ways. First, Hassan prepared the *tanjiya* in Aicha's kitchen and as a dinner for family and friends. Preparing food in the kitchen for a domestic meal is not usually something that a married man would do, as I was told by women and men alike.[7] Hassan trespassed into what is univocally considered female space and practice, explaining his jittery gestures and his haste. Aicha not only physically limited Hassan's movements in the kitchen by handing him everything he needed, she also displayed her superior taste knowledge by commenting, in Younes' presence, how bad the *tanjiya* was and how she would have prepared it, even though she had never made one herself. Further, Hassan argued that since he prepared the food, Aicha should buy the lemonade. Buying relatively costly drinks like lemonade is a treat for the family by 'the one with the money' – usually the male breadwinner – to express his love and care for the family (cf. Naguib 2015). Hassan stressed this ideal of complementarity by suggesting that since *he* prepared dinner, it was Aicha's turn to treat the family and guests to lemonade. Yet, whereas for Hassan this temporary role reversal caused laughter among us, for Aicha this was not so very different from other days when she used her income to buy treats for their children, especially drinks, snacks and seasonal fruits.

According to my female and male research participants, men's most important role in domestic matters was providing their wives with *siyar* (literally 'to spend money', chopmoney).[8] In return, a woman was expected to take care of the household. This complementarity in the reproduction of the family resonates across cultural contexts, whereby cooking in particular stands for nurture and remains deeply associated with women's caring role within the household.[9] As main breadwinners, Marrakchi men were generally not expected to help in the household or with childcare, a model that exists across classes in Morocco. For instance, when meeting a group of educated, working women from mid- and upper-income backgrounds in Rabat – some of whom I knew from going to Cadi Ayyad University in Marrakech together in 2007 – we talked about women's roles in a marriage. My friend Zainab explained: 'Men expect contradictory women.

They want us to be highly educated and modern, for instance by dressing in Western fashion and also in our opinions and attitudes. But they also want us to be traditional, to wear the veil and accommodate our husband's wishes, including cooking for him and caring for our children.' All five women concluded that these expectations were unlikely to change, as 'culture' was deemed too strong.[10] Similarly, not a single man I interviewed suggested that his (future) wife might work to supplement the household income. They described their ideal wife as one who cooks and cares for the family full-time. This holds true even as urban families are shrinking.[11]

However, in practice this complementarity was rarely upheld. Low-income women's wage work substantially increased the family income. Often, it constituted the sole income. For instance, Aicha and Rachida bought fruits for their daughters on a daily basis, since they considered them healthy, despite their relatively high cost. Equally, when I asked Aicha after a long and tiring day what exactly she would like her husband to do to help with food and housework, she vehemently replied 'Nothing!' and concluded that he would not know what to do and that it would only 'mess up [*fih al-shlada*]' her routines. Apart from providing *siyar*, my interviews with men of all income groups confirmed that Marrakchi men were rarely involved in domestic chores involving food preparation, even when their wives had a full-time paid job. Only when a woman required a product that could not be sourced or processed nearby or that was difficult to handle did she send her husband, brother or son (cf. Graf 2015). Women controlled what they received and did not refrain from sending the shopper back if he did not buy what she wanted. Moreover, as suggested in the vignette, many Marrakchi women I interviewed suspected men of paying too much for food and/or being unable to identify good-quality foods.[12]

Marrakchi men's tenuous engagement with food in domestic settings is directly related to men's changing role in Moroccan society. Without a reasonably stable job, no young Moroccan man could expect to marry, as Conway-Long shows in his study on the effects of social change on Moroccan men. He describes Moroccan men's decreasing contribution to family affairs as a 'zero-sum-logic' (2006: 149), whereby women gain financial and political bargaining power within the family and men lose power. Zvan Elliott depicts the struggles of low-income women *and* men to find wage work and to care for themselves and their family within a patriarchal but liberalizing state with an interview with an Islamist activist: 'The root problem lies in the fact that Morocco is an undemocratic country, where one institution reigns supreme. Consequently, not only women but men, too, suffer from injustice, poverty, and disenfranchisement' (2015: 90).[13]

The implications of a man's inability to provide were particularly evident with regard to Rachida's husband Mohamed. Rachida often told me: 'I have no husband. A husband helps his wife [with *siyar*], mine doesn't.' During our long days in the kitchen, she often recalled how he drank alcohol and sometimes hit her when they were newly married. After Zakia's birth, she wanted to divorce him, but her parents convinced her not to and so she stayed with him and eventually had Ibtissam.[14] When Mohamed then lost his respectable job as an artisan jeweller, Rachida had no choice but to earn and manage the family's income. Her sister Meriem, who was only five years older than Zakia, moved in with them while Ibtissam was a baby to help Rachida with the household. Mohamed no longer had a role within the household and, consequently, Rachida discursively denied his existence as a husband and person. During one of my shorter research visits in 2017, Rachida and her daughters lived in a rented apartment in another part of the city to avoid Mohamed's drinking problem and his related bursts of abuse.[15] However, giving in to her daughters' pleading in their father's favour, the three women moved back in with Mohamed after approximately one year.[16]

Aicha's financial management also illustrates this problematic shift of domestic power. As a member of an informal women's saving group (*jama'a daret*), Aicha regularly paid a small sum of money into a shared pot of money and each month a different woman had access to that pot. Aicha used the money thus saved to buy large things 'for herself', such as her sporting machine to lose weight after the birth of her second daughter but also her oven-stove and her fridge-freezer. When they moved into their own flat in 2012, Aicha's money from the *jama'a* paid for furniture, while Hassan paid the deposit and the rent. Upon Aicha's suggestion, Hassan joined the saving group during my fieldwork, even though it was run by and for women. This way, Aicha argued, they could save more money for their newly established household. In combination with the *siyar* she received from Hassan since moving out of his mother's home and the small rent I paid for my room, Aicha was in control of the household's finances. While discursively Hassan was still the breadwinner and was required to cover all regular expenditures, in practice both Aicha's income and her management of most of their finances were vital to their small budget. Hassan's import in the reproduction of the family decreased even further with the onset of the COVID-19 pandemic in the spring of 2020, when both Aicha and Hassan lost their jobs in the tourist economy. Upon my enquiry via WhatsApp, Aicha described Hassan's role as husband and father as acutely curtailed: 'Without his work and income he suffers depression, he has no reason to get up in the morning. He sees his children every day but he cannot do them any good [i.e. has no money to buy them things].'

Through wage work and their everyday practices of food preparation, low-income Marrakchi women increase their contingencies, whereas men have decreasing room for manoeuvre for claiming their complementary roles within the family. Although urban women across income groups work for a wage (see also Kapchan 1996: 212ff; Montgomery 2019; Newcomb 2017: 41ff; Sadiqi and Ennaji 2006), low-income women's wages alter the family's financial management more profoundly. They pose a direct challenge to the patriarchal ideal of men as breadwinners in practice, if not (yet) in discourse.[17] At the same time, most lead cooks carefully guard the domestic as a female space and physically limit men's movement therein. In combination with women taking over financial management, this not only leaves low-income men without a clearly defined role in the daily work of reproducing the family, it also means more work for their wives, whose wages are not enough to buy help.

Still, although the women I worked with were acutely aware of the double burden this shift entailed for them, as well as the frustration and marginalization it caused among their husbands, patriarchal gender relations were not actually considered problematic by these women and men. Rather, low-income women were keen to escape the generational hierarchy among women. The picture that emerges in the following section shows that it is not gendered emancipation, which low-income Marrakchi women seek through wage work and financial independence, but freedom from dominance based on seniority. As one of the culturally most valued domestic tasks, the preparation of food is central to younger women's efforts to emancipate.

Seniority and Power

We were peeling fresh peas one summer evening on Aicha's breezy roof terrace. While contemplating the peaceful moment, Aicha told me how living with Hassan's mother Habiba and her relatives had been unbearable for her:

> They treated me like a *femme de ménage* [Aicha used the French term for maid], I was told to do this and do that. Hassan gave *siyar* to his mother, but not to me! That's why Habiba wanted us to live with them: for the money! Zahra [Aicha's daughter] was small but I never stopped working. Of course, they didn't like that I had my job and often told me to quit it. So that I become their servant all day long?! No, oh, no! After one year [of living with the in-laws], I told Hassan that I wanted my own kitchen, at least that! I wanted to cook for my family, be my own boss. Imagine, I had to eat Habiba's food every day! Hassan didn't like it, but he agreed and got me a kitchen. But they still treated me like a maid and expected me to do all the dirty work. Oh, I hated it!'

In October 2012, two years after she got her own kitchen and a few months after the birth of her second daughter, Aicha, her husband and their daughters moved out of Habiba's household. Hassan had found and rented the small flat where I later stayed with them. Aicha concluded our conversation by expressing how happy she was to be mistress of her own household: 'Now I can do whatever I want!' Managing her own household, Aicha emphasized, did not mean there was less work to do; on the contrary, she worked much harder, but at least she was in full control.

*   *   *

While many food scholars have rightly argued that cooking reveals the power dynamics in a family, their focus has often been on the gendered dimensions of these negotiations (Bowen, Brenton and Elliott 2019; Cairns and Johnston 2015; DeVault 1991; Lupton 1996) or on those between parents and their children (Boni 2023; O'Connell and Brannen 2016). However, this vignette highlights that gender or children were not considered the most problematic determinants of such negotiations. Rather, women and men perceived older women as problematic; the Moroccan proverb 'Women become the devil with age and men become saints' (Mernissi 1987: 138) is suggestive of this opinion. Aicha's desire to move into her own flat, where she was in full control of her domestic work and leisure, was widespread within the Marrakchi and Beni Mellali families I interviewed. As the previous chapter also illustrated, younger women's education, wage work and independent income offer a way out of an often oppressive domestic hierarchy based on seniority.

Unmarried Fatimzahra is a case in point. Except when Hajja carried out the month-long pilgrimage to Mecca (*al-haj*), during which Fatimzahra temporarily became the lead cook in the household, their division of domestic and food work was strongly hierarchized. Hajja managed the household finances and food stock, she planned, directed and evaluated food provisioning and processing, and carried out the actual cooking for lunch, the most important meal of the day. Fatimzahra was usually in charge of shopping, making bread and condiments such as juices and salads for lunch. For *kaskrut* (afternoon snack), she had more decision-making power, making tea but also planning and preparing snacks to serve with it. During my stay with them, I initially shared and gradually took over shopping, serving meals, washing up, running errands and 'Playing the fool to amuse the company' from Fatimzahra (Maher 1974: 122). When Fatimzahra asked me to prepare tea in her stead (see Interlude 3), the promotion was due more to the circumstances of having to prepare large amounts of food for many guests than to my advancement in the domestic hierarchy of food work.

As third cook, responsible for the least esteemed and most tedious tasks of food preparation, I was expected to be on call anytime and thus least able to determine my time. In busy periods like these I was barely able to use the toilet when I needed to or to go to sleep before everything was clean and ready for another day of hosting and serving guests. I repeatedly lived through the constraints and frustrations that marked younger cooks' experience of domestic work in multigenerational households. Indeed, Fatimzahra often agonized about her status as second cook without the ability to determine food preparation and her domestic life in general. Though usually patient and devoted to easing her mother's life, Fatimzahra lost her temper several times after Hajja's return. As we shopped, cooked and served the many guests almost incessantly over the course of six weeks, her and my lower-status roles became more apparent than usual.[18] Being past the age of marriage and with only a small income, Fatimzahra had no choice but to accept her mother's dominance.

Aicha was more fortunate. Her income enabled her to convince her husband to move out of his mother's house and become lead cook in her own household. Although Hassan, too, preferred to have his 'peace of mind' in his own home, Aicha told me, equally he did not want to upset his mother. Since mothers are strong figures across the region and, especially for men, constitute a lifelong reference in terms of decision making, practices, emotions and tastes (see also Borneman 2007; Conway-Long 2006; Naguib 2015), they are also major competitors of young wives like Aicha, and not only emotionally. When explaining the benefits of moving out, Aicha reminded me that Hassan had paid his mother *siyar* as is customary in multigenerational households: 'Now he doesn't have to anymore, so we save that money for us.' More importantly, moving out of the patrilocal household allowed Aicha to determine not only everyday meals but also her social relations and thus her self, as I will explore in the next section.

Although Aicha was proud of her ability to financially support her family, including her parents in the countryside, she considered her domestic and especially her food work as more important than her wage work. Her motivation was, similar to urban women of the previous generation, to be an 'excellent housekeeper, a virtuous wife and a devoted mother' (Davis 1983: 65). As a young woman who had come to Marrakech in search for a job, Aicha had enjoyed the freedom to eat and cook what and when she liked, favouring 'European' fast food like pizza and sandwiches. Yet, she did not question the fact that once she became a mother, she would cook for her family. She attached value and pride to the fact that she cooked for her own family and stressed that this shift from pizza, jeans and short hair to *tajine* (a stew), *jellaba* (a long overgarment with a hood) and *hijab* (headscarf) had only taken place when she became a mother, not when she married. For Aicha, as for most women I talked to, this shifting sense of self towards the ideal of the cooking wife and mother following the life cycle was not as ambivalent as it was for the wives and mothers described by scholars working in Europe, America or Australia.

Across societies, food sharing is vital to notions of feminine care and familial affection. According to Lupton (1996), the role of the mother as the arbiter of familial care and love through offering food and nourishment emerged with industrialization and the notion of romantic love. Womanhood became synonymous with motherhood and food preparation was considered an altruistic act, not one of work. Food is prepared with the eaters in mind, their preferences and needs, and serves to maintain and manipulate social relations, as my hair in the bread illustrated. The more work is invested in its preparation, the higher the symbolic value of a meal (see Chapter 1). However, North American mothers are torn between the responsibility of preparing food for their families, and thus caring for them, and of earning an income as paid workers, which prevents them from taking the time needed to prepare what they consider good food (e.g. Bowen, Brenton and Elliott 2019; Cairns and Johnston 2015; Trubek 2017). Even though fathers increasingly help to cook, mothers still consider it their responsibility. This ambivalence is the result of shifting social values. Collier (1997) and Counihan (2004) trace how wage work, and the growing importance of monetary income in Spain and Italy respectively, contributed to shifting women and men's primary site of identification away from domestic work and the home as a key determinant of personhood. With industrialization, wage work and the public sphere were increasingly valued over domestic work and the home, just like Newcomb (2009, 2017) describes for middle-income Fassis.

Although wage work and the shift towards the conjugal family similarly reinforces the ideal of womanhood as caring wife and mother, low-income Marrakchi women were less ambivalent about this change. In fact, through moving out of the patrilocal household and assuming full control over domestic work, these women realize their ideal of womanhood much earlier than their predecessors. Since these women's daily food work has been and continues to be valued highly, its central role in family and social life as well as moral personhood is still widely recognized, as it is also among other low- and middle-income communities (Abarca 2006; Counihan 2009; Sutton 2014). The home, and the daily practices of reproducing the family within it, remains the primary site of identification for low-income women in Marrakech. Indeed, as part of their apprenticeship in cooking (see Chapter 2), young women learned early on that one day it will be their time to cook for their family. Few women I talked to – regardless of their socioeconomic background – questioned this, though they were aware of the double burden that this entailed for them, much like their Euro-American counterparts. The crucial shift from one generation to the next is whom they cook with and how they hone their cooking knowledge once they cook without others.

Cooking with(out) Others: New Sociomaterial Relations

Just before Ramadan Aicha wanted to prepare *amlou* (almond-oil-honey spread): 'Because Hassan likes to eat it for *al-shor* [the meal before sunrise].' Since Aicha had never made it herself, she asked her mother-in-law. She phoned Habiba to fix the time to meet and prepare *amlou*. Habiba told her that it has to be made with the *raha taqlidiya* (hand-operated grinding stone) and that it takes time to grind the almonds. When hanging up, Aicha sighed: 'We could have blended

Figure 3.2. Grinding almonds and oil with the *raha* to make *amlou*, Marrakech, 2013. © Katharina Graf

the almonds in less than half an hour with my neighbour's Moulinex, instead we will spend the whole night at Habiba's. But I want *amlou beldi* [here: handmade amlou]. Hassan will be happy to eat it for *al-shor*.' A few evenings later, Aicha, her daughters and I went to Habiba's house, Aicha's former residence. Aicha had roasted almonds just before leaving, as instructed on the phone. On our way, we bought one litre of vegetable oil, also following Habiba's instructions. Argan oil, which is normally used, was too expensive for Aicha and she reasoned that she would have had difficulties finding real argan oil in Marrakech's markets in any case.

As soon as we entered the house, Habiba took the bag of almonds from Aicha and lifted it to her right ear. She explained: 'I want to hear whether you roasted them enough.' She was satisfied by what she heard. While we unpacked everything else in the salon, Habiba's sister-in-law Amina, who is part of the same household, sat down behind the *raha* and prepared herself to grind the almonds with the vegetable oil (Figure 3.2). Aicha offered to grind the almonds in order to learn how to do it, but Amina refused: 'You don't learn how to use the *raha* in one evening! It takes years of experience to feel the *raha* and move your arm just at the right speed. Crush the almonds in the *mehraz* [pestle and mortar] for me, will you?' Aicha submitted to Amina's experience and two hours later we left Habiba's house with a dense velvety paste. Habiba had advised Aicha to add thyme or orange flower honey before serving *amlou*. However, in an effort to save money, Aicha eventually decided to sweeten the mixture with sugar instead. She felt that by grinding the almonds with the *raha*, she had done what it takes to make the *amlou* that would please her husband.

* * *

This vignette brings together a number of themes in this book. It shows not only how material and social changes such as new kitchen technologies are incorporated into taste knowledge and how living in a smaller household contributes to altering its reproduction; it also describes the new sociomaterial relations younger generations of cooks must negotiate if they want to hone and improve their taste knowledge. Aicha's ambition to learn making *amlou* illustrates that: 'The cultural reference point for each of us [Moroccans] is the taste of the maternal cuisine' (Hal 1996: 34, my translation). The Moroccan professional cook and anthropologist Hal concludes that upon marriage, Moroccan women undergo a culinary 're-learning [*réapprentissage*] with the mother-in-law' (ibid.). The vignette shows how the desire and often also the need to learn new recipes, and improve and expand one's taste knowledge, emerges from and feeds back into a changing social and economic context of cooking. This may be in response to the likes and dislikes of husband and children, the health of a family member or oneself, changing household finances and/or special occasions. How, when and what a cook in contemporary Marrakech learns is thus the result of manifold situated negotiations in a dynamic material and social environment, and bespeaks the inherently creative and dynamic reproduction of taste knowledge.

In order to prepare *amlou* and thus re-create the taste of her husband's maternal cuisine and declared favourite Ramadan food, Aicha accepted her in-laws' expertise. Although it can be bought ready-made, Soussis like Hassan prefer the taste of *amlou beldi*. A speciality of the Souss Mountains, *amlou* combines ingredients and tastes such as almonds, argan oil and honey that are unique to that region. As befits *beldi* products, the tools and techniques of producing and making it are as important as the ingredients. From Habiba's perspective, it was especially the tool and the skill to grind the almonds that determined the beldiness of *amlou*. Anticipating the definitions of Chapter 4 that food is considered *beldi* based on a situated understanding of taste, provenance and/or context of production and distribution, it is interesting to note that Habiba dismissed argan oil, which is endemic to the Souss, as an important ingredient of *amlou beldi*. Instead, she stressed her and Amina's bodily way of operating the *raha*; a tool that, she emphasized, was no longer produced. In other words, Habiba emphasized their expertise and gatekeeper role in the preparation of *amlou beldi*, while downplaying all other elements that equally determine its beldiness, and that Aicha could potentially provision through other means. Indeed, Habiba's definition of *amlou beldi* was informed by the continuously strenuous relationship between her and Aicha.

Habiba's insistence to use the *raha* and Amina's refusal to allow Aicha to try grinding the almonds herself were motivated not so much by their arguably greater taste knowledge, but by their desire to reassert their control over Aicha after she had moved out. However, through access to new technologies like the blender, more affordable industrial ingredients like sugar and vegetable oil, or by asking friends and neighbours for recipes or kitchen tools, young women like Aicha get help from other sources and are no longer dependent on their female relatives' knowledge. Aicha's preparations for the first Ramadan she managed and hosted herself included a range of material and social sources of knowledge and tools that far exceeded those of her senior female relatives. At the same time, this example illustrates the difficult position in which younger cooks find themselves once they no longer live in the same household and learn alongside senior family members. Although Aicha had full managing control as a newly minted cook in her own kitchen and household, she did not have the necessary experience to prepare all typical Ramadan dishes herself. Yet, while this shrinking of urban households led Kapchan (1996) and Newcomb (2017) to conclude that cooking is no longer social and its intergenerational reproduction is therefore at risk, I reach a different conclusion.

Aicha's position of negotiation was strengthened by a multitude of new sociomaterial relations. First, Aicha could have used other tools to make *amlou*. By stressing the possibility of using the Moulinex to blend the almonds instead of grinding them in the *raha*, Aicha highlighted the choice she was able to make. Of course, recollecting the argument in Chapter 1, food's materiality and a tool's idiosyncrasies also enter these negotiations. Grinding almonds with oil in the *raha* yields a product of a very specific taste and texture, different from the blender, which chops the almonds without releasing the nuts' own oil. Equally, each tool requires a different bodily engagement of the cook. For instance, the *raha* is not sold but handed down from one generation to the next, thus limiting the ability to learn how to turn the handle and feel the crushing of almonds. By contrast, the blender requires electricity and a cook's ability to interpret and operate its buttons, thus conjuring a whole new range of material relations and skills (see also Schwartz Cowan 1983; Silva 2000). While new technologies like the electric blender cannot and do not fully replace traditional tools like the *raha*, by offering an alternative choice, they nevertheless enable young cooks to reject their seniors' techniques.

Second, like Zakia in Chapter 2, Aicha was able to choose whose expertise to rely on to learn a new recipe. Not being a born-and-bred Soussiya like Habiba and Amina, Aicha's taste knowledge necessarily differed. Since *amlou* is a *beldi* specialty of the Souss, and Habiba embodied the taste of the Souss, Aicha's ignorance of its preparation was not due to a lack of experience, but a result of her embodiment of a different taste knowledge, marked by her own natal region (see Chapters 1 and 4). In other words, although Aicha's taste knowledge was arguably

Figure 3.3. Learning to mix ingredients for *sellou*, a Ramadan sweet, Marrakech, 2013. © Katharina Graf

not as developed as Habiba's, Aicha could not have known this recipe and thus did not show herself unworthy of the position of a lead cook. For situations that did reveal her incomplete taste knowledge, Aicha relied on other, more friendly relations, marked not by unequal relations of power, but by a reciprocal exchange of knowledge and food. For instance, she asked our mutual friend Fatimzahra what ingredients she needed to make *sellou*, a sweet snack. Fatimzahra, whose *sellou* was reputed throughout the neighbourhood, proposed to grocery shop together to ensure Aicha bought the best suitable ingredients from trustworthy shopkeepers. For the processing and assembly of these ingredients, Aicha asked advice from Rqia, another expert cook and the mother of her neighbour and friend Hind, who helped Aicha without imposing her authority as a senior cook (Figure 3.3). Aicha returned the favour by bringing a plate of *sellou* to Fatimzahra and Rqia during Ramadan.

Rachida and her daughters' food preparations included similar new sociomaterial relations. Chapter 2 described in detail how although Rachida relied on her daughters' help to run the household, with roles assigned by age and esteem of tasks, Zakia's and Ibtissam's (digital) literacy altered their position of negotiation vis-à-vis their mother. Being able to read recipes in *fusha* and use media like the internet, their access to alternative sources of knowledge surpassed those of their mother. As a result of her daughters' education, Rachida's food work was organized and negotiated differently from more typical multigenerational households. Without access to supermarkets to buy convenience foods or enough income to buy help like her middle-income counterparts (Newcomb 2017: 120; Montgomery 2019), Rachida needed help from her daughters and other women. Yet, rather than assume full dominance as senior women in multigenerational families often did, Rachida granted her daughters more freedom with food work, enabling them to object or express preferences that daughters like Fatimzahra or daughters-in-law like Aicha could not.

While the shrinking of families does change how women cook in everyday life and challenges the traditional division of domestic labour, these examples show how the knowledge to cook as well as key cultural values around it are being reproduced on new terms. Aicha chose to prepare *amlou* and largely determined the conditions of its preparation even as she asked her mother-in-law for help. Younger generations of cooks like her or Zakia harness new sociomaterial relations via new kitchen appliances, cookbooks and a growing choice of ingredients as well as friends or neighbours to achieve more power in the domestic division of labour. As the lead cook in her own household, Aicha in particular was in a significantly improved situation to negotiate the sharing of experience and related positions of power. Since establishing her own household, Aicha's position of negotiation was that of a decision maker and Habiba, a managing householder like Aicha, was her social equal.

Thanks to these new sociomaterial relations, younger generations of women gain more power in intrafamilial negotiations around domestic work and life, and achieve what they consider mature womanhood much earlier than previous generations of women. Even though few girls I talked to embraced a future as cooks, domestic work and especially cooking were not rejected as a main practice of identification. On the contrary, by putting emphasis on homemaking good food just like their predecessors, younger generations of women (un)wittingly reproduce traditional social values around women as hardworking and caring wives and mothers. Thus, although emancipating from power based on seniority and challenging who possesses cooking expertise, young Marrakchi wives and mothers continue to invest time and bodily effort into making good food for their families and, as a result, work much harder than previous generations of low-income women. What motivates them to do so?

Making Meals, the Self and the Family

Joseph's (1999) concept of relationality, whereby selves are defined as shaped in relation to others, helps us to understand young Marrakchi women's desire to cook for their family in spite of new kitchen technologies and their wage work. Centred on her ethnographic research with urban Lebanese Muslims, Joseph argues that a society that values the family over the individual person and in which a person achieves meaning in the context of the family or community has different ways of determining personhood.[19] This observation is not unique to the Arab region. For instance, Kondo argues that Japanese women's mature selfhood is achieved in accommodating the needs of others: 'Persons seemed to be constituted in and through social relations and obligations to others. Selves and society did not seem to be separate entities; rather, the boundaries were blurred' (1990: 22). Importantly, Joseph (1999) looks beyond gender to include other social relations and factors that determine personhood in the Middle East and North Africa.[20]

Joseph (1999) emphasizes the temporally limited dimensions of being, which resonates with the situatedness of *beldi* foods and people that I will discuss in Chapter 4. From this perspective, becoming is a lifelong process that includes contradictions and conflicts. Selves are shaped not only by larger societal and cultural values but also by changing material situations as well as a person's life cycle, as Aicha's case illustrates. According to Joseph, relational being does not preclude individual or collective agency; by contrast, relationality seeks to highlight other forms of agency than that of the individual subject. Thus, relationality and individualism, though seemingly contradictory, often coexist. Joseph's notion of 'patriarchal connectivity' accounts for this seeming inequality within the families she studied, whereby men and mothers or mothers-in-law have more say and control in familial decision-making than young or unmarried women. Connectivity is defined as 'Relationships in which a person's boundaries are relatively fluid so that persons feel a part of significant others' (ibid. 12). Persons do not experience themselves as bounded, but rather through 'reading each other's minds' (ibid.) and attending to their likes and dislikes.

With respect to food, Carsten demonstrates in her research on Langkawi Island that family or kinship is a process of becoming that is to a large extent based on feeding, both as receiving and as giving nourishment. She concludes that: 'Boundaries between people and what they consume – food – ... may be less clear than we tend to assume' (Carsten 1995: 225). More recent ethnographies of Southern Asia confirm that food is collaborative in the production of social life, especially in how cooks and eaters relate to each other through adapting to the different tastes and preferences of family members, friends or, indeed, the ethnographer (Janeja 2010; van Daele 2013). Conversely, not cooking for others or serving what is considered *bad* food can be considered an act of resistance (Stoller 1989). Indeed, this happened routinely whenever Habiba visited Aicha in her new home 'only to see the children', as she would hasten to add upon each visit. Hurt that Habiba 'did not come to see me too', Aicha served foods that she herself declared as bad but that she served nonetheless, since 'Habiba does not deserve any better'.

Applying Joseph's concept to cooking implies that the more a woman is in control of domestic food work, the more she also realizes herself. Connectivity means anticipating what one's eaters would like to eat and learning how to plan and prepare new foods such as *amlou*. The serving and ingesting of food made by the hands of the loving cook is a means of extending the self materially and – at least partially – becoming the other. When a dish is met with success, it therefore not only reinforces the bonds between the cook and her audience, it also materializes the cook's connectivity to her family and friends.[21] In the case of my hair in the bread, such involuntary bonding can cause some embarrassment. At the same time, Marrakchi cooks carefully negotiated their own preferences with those of others. For instance, Aicha used others' likes and needs to convince her husband, whom she described as a 'picky' eater, to prepare certain foods. Equally, during the month of her mother's *haj* when she was in full control of all domestic work, Fatimzahra considered the days she was fasting as good occasions to prepare and serve foods such as fish that she did not like to eat.

Joseph (1999) argues further that patriarchal connectivity does not necessarily bespeak inequality, though it often mobilizes kinship to legitimize and institutionalize domination based on gender and seniority. However, with the shrinking of households described above, relational connectivity undergoes a significant shift away from being determined by patriarchal dominance towards what I call 'culinary connectivity'. The establishment of an independent household, based on a multitude of new sociomaterial relations, allows young Marrakchi women not only to escape dominance based on seniority and gender. For them, as for Joseph's interlocutors: 'Maturity is signaled [sic] in part by the successful enactment of a myriad of connective relationships' (Joseph 1999: 12). In contrast to Joseph's patriarchal connectivity, which necessarily understands maturity in terms of seniority, the notion of culinary connectivity is decoupled from age – and to some extent even from experience.

Culinary connectivity highlights the important symbolic and material role that domestic food preparation plays in entangling selves and others. The lead cook not only decides what to provision and how to store it or how to process ingredients and cook meals, but also allocates portions of cooked food: since most Moroccan meals are eaten from a shared plate, the lead cook usually dissects the more precious parts with her fingers, served in the centre of the plate, and places them in front of each eater according to their status and presumed needs. Husbands or older sons as well as guests tend to get the bigger and better pieces. Meat in particular is carefully portioned and allocated because it is usually scarce in low-income households. The lead cook feeds highly valued foods to highly valued family members and friends. Within culturally determined bounds, she also determines what counts as highly valued foods and people in the first place and thus ever so subtly crafts, negotiates and challenges her and each family member's social roles and statuses.

At the same time, culinary connectivity points towards the struggles and constraints that Marrakchi cooks experience in the context of poverty and general vulnerability. If a marketed product such as food is central to making meals and the family, then the inability to provide the *right* kind of food (see Chapter 4) curtails a cook's culinary connectivity and limits her ability of reproducing her self and her family through culturally meaningful practices. A cook's limited culinary connectivity, in turn, limits her chances of provisioning good food through nonmonetary channels such as friends or relatives (cf. Garth 2020). In fact, my research on bread confirmed that a person with limited relational connections – rather than merely a low income – is what my research participants described as poor or *meskin* (cf. Graf 2018).

Furthermore, especially the new sociomaterial relations that younger cooks rely on to develop and improve their taste knowledge – via electric kitchen appliances, television, smartphones and social media – entangle them in new, often hidden relations of power. Domestic appliances like blenders or televisions constitute a major investment often financed through informal women's saving groups (*jama'a daret*); electricity is required to power them; a mobile internet connection requires a smartphone and the acquisition of free minutes and gigabytes – money that many of my research participants did not always and regularly have. Electricity is cut off surprisingly soon after missing one of the monthly payment deadlines, which, at the time of my fieldwork, had to be made in person in a local branch. Without offers for cheap mobile data bundles, my research participants had to wait several days, sometimes weeks, before being able to purchase a new one. As described above, to take control of her cooking, Aicha relied on products from anonymous profit-making companies, thoroughly enmeshing her in a capitalizing but not democratizing society (Maghraoui 2002). Indeed, both Errazzouki (2014) and Zvan Elliott (2015) highlight the persistence of patriarchal paternalism in their critical examination of the effects of recent economic and women's rights policies on Moroccan working-class and unmarried, rural women respectively. A young cook's dependency shifts away from senior women and the multigenerational household, and enmeshes her in the more invisible and no less patriarchal economic relations of the free market. The crafting of culinary connectivity in contemporary Marrakech is thus increasingly dependent on precarious wage work and informal resources, which are notoriously scarce and unreliable for women of low-income backgrounds.

Conclusion: Families in the Making

Starting with my hair in Aicha's bread, this chapter explored how and why the domestic preparation of food is central to low-income Marrakchi women's sense of the self and of the family. I showed that while many women and men across income groups continue to adhere to the ideal of gendered complementarity – whereby Moroccan men are discursively construed as breadwinners and women as family cooks – in everyday practice young wives and mothers of low-income backgrounds are increasingly complementing and often replacing men as primary breadwinners. Importantly, rather than challenge gendered relations of power, these women's wage work and their growing literacy were harnessed to challenge the dominance exerted by senior women and to negotiate the reproduction of cooking knowledge and of the family on new terms. More experienced senior cooks were still called on for help, but thanks to the use of new kitchen technologies and other sources of knowledge such as cookbooks and social media, coupled with their friends' help, this is now done on the young cook's terms. As a result, younger generations of low-income Marrakchi women achieve the ideal of mature womanhood much earlier than their predecessors.

Yet, this chapter also illustrated that although new sociomaterial relations enable younger women to determine how to cook, care for and relate to others, what it means to be a wife and mother in low-income Marrakech has not yet fundamentally changed. In fact, younger generations of cooks have to work more to live up to idealized notions of womanhood and the family, which are still defined through the preparation of elaborate homemade family meals. By accounting for the use of new technologies and social media and how they are harnessed to reproduce these notions of womanhood and the family in everyday food preparation, the concept of culinary connectivity allowed me to analyse how these transformations result in the ambivalent reproduction of existing ideas of womanhood and the family. Through taking control of their daily cooking, young Marrakchi cooks materially and symbolically shape themselves and their families; they are enacting their culinary connectivity.

At the same time, culinary connectivity points towards new, largely hidden relations of power in a capitalist economy and thus also accounts for the political economic dimensions of womanhood and the family meal in contemporary Moroccan society. The engagement with electronic kitchen appliances and social media creates new dependencies with unpredictable consequences for low-income households such as Aicha's. This became particularly evident during the COVID-19 pandemic. Having renounced the power and protection of Hassan's mother and the extended family by moving out of the multigenerational household, Aicha and Hassan have become more dependent on their wage work and income, yet without gaining access to insurance or social security like their middle- and upper-income counterparts. Losing their incomes as they did since the onset of the COVID-19 pandemic in the spring of 2020 risked losing not only the financial but also the material and social basis of their everyday life. Having entangled my desires with Aicha's during many months of cooking and eating together, it was obvious to me that I would at least partially make up for their lost incomes until better days. Aicha's poetic remark one summer night during Ramadan 2013 that 'Money is short lived, it disappears; what stays are human relations' proves no more apt now than it did then. In other words, until the state does not provide (the environment for creating) mechanisms of inclusion for its neediest citizens, low-income Marrakchi women have no choice but to carefully craft a multitude of culinary connections.

Notes

Some elements of this chapter have been substantially revised from Katharina Graf. 2022. 'Cooking with(out) Others? Changing Kitchen Technologies and Family Values in Marrakech'. *Journal of North African Studies*, online early view.

1. See also Jansen's (2001) account on bread preparation and wine consumption in Algeria, which express and reproduce conflicting bodily and cultural identities.
2. Compared to collaborative cooking for festive occasions (Buitelaar 1993), everyday cooking is task divided and resembles a professional kitchen with separate work stations (Papacharalampous 2019).
3. In rural Morocco it is not unusual for women to marry young – even underage – to men up to thirty years older (cf. Zvan Elliott 2015). As a result, these women are often widowed relatively early on in their lives, like Hajja or Aicha's mother-in-law Habiba.
4. Since Muslim hospitality is based on eating together and exchanging food, cooks also control men's socializing in domestic contexts (Maclagan 1994; Conway-Long 2006).
5. Of course, different notions of womanhood and the family coexist in Morocco. Not all women aspire to achieve this particular ideal of womanhood, nor is it static and unchanging. I rather depict and analyse what I found to be a dominant trope of womanhood.
6. While the family is an important analytical focus in other regional ethnographies (e.g. Fikry 2022; Joseph 2018; Meneley 1983; vom Bruck 1998), in Morocco the anthropological gaze tends to focus on women and gender (Cairoli 2011; Kapchan 1996; Newcomb 2009; Salime 2018; Zvan Elliott 2015). Montgomery's (2019) work on female domestic workers and their female employers in Rabat is an exception.
7. Conversations with male friends from university and interviews with male chefs revealed that although many Moroccan men know how to cook, they would not do so in their mothers' or their wives' kitchens.
8. Chopmoney, a term coined in Ghana, is money for the daily provision of food that women receive from their husbands (Clark 2014).
9. Gendered complementarity relating to domestic work has been described for other Arab contexts (e.g. Fikry 2022; Maclagan 1994; Naguib 2015) and for various societies in North and Central America (e.g. Adapon 2008; Cairns and Johnston 2015; Counihan 2009; Garth 2020), Southeast Asia (e.g. Carsten 1995) and Europe (e.g. Counihan 2004).
10. This echoes Zvan Elliott's (2015) argument that education does not automatically empower women in the context of patriarchy, despite decades of women's rights politics and international development in Morocco.
11. Scholars confirm a shift away from multigenerational towards conjugal households across urban Morocco (Chekroun 1993; Sebti et al. 2009). In addition, the conjugal family itself has shrunk due to women's education and a rising age when women marry. In Marrakech the average number of children born per woman was 2.07 in 2004 and the average age of marriage of women living in the medina was twenty-eight in the same year (Sebti et al. 2009: 103–4). Although not very common, younger generations of rural

wives also seek to move out of their in-law's house and establish a separate household (Zvan Elliott 2015).

12. This stands in contrast to rural Morocco or other urban Arab contexts, where men tend to be responsible for the weekly shopping and provisioning of food.
13. See Carney (2015) and Garth (2020) for nuanced accounts of the gendered effects of economic liberalization and a retreating welfare state on domestic food work in the US and Cuba respectively.
14. Although women are legally entitled to divorce since the reform of the family code (*mudawana*) in 2004, the attached social stigma and the practicalities of divorcing often prevent low-income women from pursuing a divorce (cf. Zvan Elliott 2015).
15. In my experience, Mohamed was a kind man with the habitus of a forgetful and harmless old man roaming the neighbourhood for small moments of entertainment. It was only during the rare moments when he drank alcohol that he became 'a different man', his daughters explained to me. He died in the spring of 2023.
16. Before moving out, Rachida had applied for a government grant to rebuild and refurbish the family house. It was also the success of getting this grant that contributed to the decision to move back in with her husband.
17. In rural Morocco, where multigenerational households are still widespread, married women tend not to pursue wage work and adult single 'girls' tend to give their income to their fathers or other male household heads (Zvan Elliott 2015).
18. Moroccan women are expected to be patient and persevering no matter what the circumstances, especially those in a subservient position such as Fatimzahra. It is thus not common to witness a woman losing her temper. Rather, as I show throughout the book and as other anthropologists of the region show (e.g. Abu-Lughod 2002; Mahmood 2005), expressions of discontent or resistance take much more subtle forms in Marrakchi homes.
19. Relationality resembles Eickelman's (1985) argument that Moroccan kinship is actively crafted based on the contextual and spatially determined notions of *qaraba* (closeness) and *asabiya* (group feeling).
20. For instance, vom Bruck (1998) points out that age and status are important markers of social and spatial relations in patriarchal societies.
21. Writing about *baladi* bread in Cairo, Barnes and Taher (2019) argue similarly that provisioning bread is not only about provisioning but also a practice of caring for and making relations with people, things and the state.

INTERLUDE 4

Provisioning

On a Sunday in early December 2012, I left the house around 10 am for the Mellah *suq* (market). The air was still cold from the night, but where individual rays of sun penetrated the medina alleys, it was warm. We had family guests from Taroudant, Hajja's hometown, and Hajja had decided to make chicken couscous even though it was not a Friday. This was the first time I was sent alone on such an important grocery shopping errand. Hajja had only instructed me to get 'couscous vegetables', assuming I knew by now which vegetables go into couscous. Fatimzahra, by contrast, described the chicken I was to get in more detail: 'Buy a *farush* [cockerel]! Make sure the shopkeeper does not give you a *djaja* [hen]! Tell him that if he does, you'll send it straight back. You'll recognize the *farush* by its red head decoration and its yellow feet.' She stressed every word and had a fierce look when explaining this to me, assuming not only that I did not know how to identify a cockerel, but also that the shopkeeper would try to trick me.

I reached the covered section of the market, the *marché couvert* of the Mellah *suq*, and went straight to the chicken seller. Fatimzahra's worries were unfounded; he recognized me from previous visits and enquired about Fatimzahra and her family. Once this customary exchange of news was over, I queried the price of chicken. 'Miatayn-wa-Tmanin [280]'; his reply was good news. Not only was the price comparatively low, but his choice of using riyal rather than dirham as currency – though only implicit in the number '280' – indicated my acceptance in the market space.[1] I asked the vendor to show me a nice *farush*. He pulled a recalcitrant white chicken by its legs from the cage behind him and placed the terrified animal in front of me, saying: 'This is the nicest I've got' (Figure 4.1). I nodded in agreement as he placed the chicken on the scale in front of me: 2.6 kg. 'But what about the coloured ones, there, in the other cage? They are livelier than this one', I asked spontaneously and pointed at another cage. I did not recollect having seen these tall chickens in his shop before (Figure 4.1). 'These are *beldi*, they are real nice! Not as fatty as the normal ones. They are more expensive.' I asked how much they cost: 900 riyal, 45 dirham per kilogram – three times as much!

Figure 4.1. Shop selling live *rumi* and *beldi* chicken, Marrakech, 2012.
© Katharina Graf

The white cockerel protested loudly when the man took him off the scale and handed him to the butcher across the passage. I was now convinced that I had gotten a good one; according to Fatimzahra, a noisy chicken was healthy and tasty. I waited next to the chicken seller's scale while listening to the butcher processing the cockerel: the sudden end of its complaints when he cut the head off, the raging sound of the machine that tore off the feathers, the sharp knock of the heavy knife that cut off the feet. Less than five minutes later, the butcher handed me the dead chicken, the body still warm and supple in the white plastic bag.

I left the *marché couvert* for the stalls along the adjacent street to buy couscous vegetables: carrots, turnips, courgettes, pumpkin, white cabbage, tomatoes, onions and hot chili peppers. While enquiring about prices – which had risen slightly compared to previous days – I touched, smelled and looked at each single vegetable to select what I deemed best. I collected each type of vegetable in a small basket. By now I had developed a feeling for estimating the weight of the produce I needed. I continued towards Omar's shop to buy 1 kg of couscous grains. He recommended the loose variety and I trusted the choice of this friendly man from the Souss, whom I knew since my earliest shopping trips with Hajja in 2007.

My return seemed endless, for the heavy plastic bags cut into my hands and seemed to prolong the distance to the house. Upon entering the door, I was surprised by the silence. 'Our guests have gone to Jemaa el-fna until lunch', Fatimzahra told me as I entered the kitchen and sat down next to Hajja. As I sipped the tea Fatimzahra had just prepared, she asked me the price of each vegetable. She was surprised to hear how expensive they were: 'Did you buy the vegetables in the *marché couvert*?' I reassured her that I bought them from the outside stalls – after all, I had accompanied Fatimzahra often enough to know that she only bought vegetables from the open-air stalls, which were much cheaper than those inside the covered section. Fatimzahra concluded that it must be the season that had driven up prices: 'It snowed in the mountains, so they cannot transport as many vegetables as usual. And there is probably *'idraab* [strike], too. These days transport businesses are often on strike.'[2]

Meanwhile, Fatimzahra had begun to tear the white chunks of fat off the chicken's skin. This reminded me to ask why a *djaja* is not as good as a *farush*. Fatimzahra explained: '*Djaja* are smaller and the meat shrinks when you cook it'. Hajja added '*al-mra diema saiba* [women are always difficult]' and exploded in laughter. When she had caught her breath again, she concluded with a cheeky smile: 'We prefer men.' As she continued to empty the plastic bag containing the vegetables, she grinned with pleasure and told Fatimzahra that I had even thought of buying chili peppers. Both looked at me with satisfaction; for once, I had done everything right.

Notes

1. 100 riyal = 500 francs = 5 dirham. After months of painstaking learning of *darija* numbers, currencies and their conversion rates, I was able to quickly convert 280 riyal/kg into 14 dirham/kg in order to pay the seller.
2. National expenses towards supporting the subsidy system – which also includes soft wheat and sugar – peaked at 6.6% of GDP during my fieldwork. The government therefore announced cuts to gasoline subsidies, against the popular expectation that businesses and citizens had a right to cheap gasoline. Indeed, in 2014 gasoline subsidies were eliminated step by step (Verme, El-Massnaoui and Araar 2014).

CHAPTER 4

Beldi Foodways
Situating Food Quality

Writing with ethnographic detail about a middle-income family in the Moroccan city of Fes, Newcomb declares 'the end of the Mediterranean diet' (2017: 101). As a result of globalization, she writes, individualistic eating, '[w]here children's tastes are catered to and everyone has something different to eat' is on the rise, '[t]he Moroccan diet has become less healthy', is more determined by packaged foods and a 'fast-food diet has become the order of the day' (ibid. 104). She links these changing consumption practices to new understandings of time, family and gender, whereby: 'Women's self-definition changes from affiliation with the private to the public sphere' (ibid.). The result of these changes is captured in the notion of '[t]he citizen-consumer who asserts her identity through the products she buys' and replaces '[t]he woman for whom long hours in the kitchen were a crucial part of female self-definition' (ibid. 105). Newcomb concludes: 'Traditional cuisine is increasingly associated with ceremonial occasions or holidays ... Convenience, productivity, individuality, and new regimes of timekeeping have displaced cuisine as central to citizenship' (ibid. 123–24).

These observations will sound familiar to many food scholars. They resemble changes in food consumption practices across middle- and upper-income Europe and other highly industrialized contexts. However, they do not chime with my research with low-income families in Marrakech and might even surprise those who have been to Marrakech and experienced the omnipresence of food and food-related activity all over the city (see Preface). Looking beyond urban middle- and upper-income families in Morocco's coastal cities to include the everyday food practices of low-income, recently urbanized Marrakchis paints a very different picture of change and with different implications for the future of domestic cooking. Indeed, I found that Moroccan foodways (*al-makla al-maghribiya*) continue to play an important role in everyday life. Understanding why these women continued to cook every day despite a growing range of alternatives is not only a question of cultural values as described in the previous chapter; it also requires attending to the whole range of practices, discourses and networks that matter to provisioning, processing, preparing, serving and eating what is considered good Moroccan food. To do so, this chapter will situate domestic food work in the broader Moroccan food system and thereby introduce the broader political economic dimensions of cooking.

The main motivation to invest time and money into provisioning, processing, preparing and serving food is to provide not just any food but *good* (*tayyib*) food for the family. Benkheira (2000) argues that for Muslim societies, a food is considered licit if it is good (*tayyib*) and gives pleasure to the senses (*tyb*). In Northern Africa *tyyeb* also means cooking itself and *t'ab* refers to cooked, ripe, mature or edible food. These words share the root t-y-b and are thus semantically related. In other words, a carefully homecooked meal is considered good food and I extend this observation to show that carefully sourcing, selecting, processing and presenting food also makes it good. Overall, this chapter argues that low-income Marrakchi cooks are – and collectively always have been, as the next chapter will show – concerned about the quality of the foods they eat, including where it comes from, how it has been processed and how it tastes. This is why they continue to make homemade food, often against all the odds.

Following the popular index of quality based on *beldi* (of/from the country), the specific practices, discourses and networks of low-income urban Moroccans around good food can be described as '*beldi* foodways'. Importantly, *beldi* foodways are neither urban nor rural; rather, they connect the two just as many low-income Marrakchis continue to cultivate their roots in rural Morocco. Although there is a widely shared Moroccan way of cooking, as I will show later on in the chapter, *beldi* indexes regional or homemade food and advocates a situated understanding of food and eating practices. *Beldi* foodways shift the attention away from a narrow focus on food consumption and diet towards understanding domestic cooks as *producers* of good food and families.[1] From such a perspective, there is no static domestic Moroccan – even less a Mediterranean – diet that can be 'lost'. It also shows that what many low-income Moroccans lack is not an understanding of what is described as healthy food, but healthy food itself.[2]

Offering good food to the family begins with the knowledgeable provisioning and processing of food, as I will show in the first section. Most low-income Moroccans provision food on a daily basis in their local *hanut* (small corner shop), the shops and stalls along their local high street (*zenqa*), in the *suiqa* (small market) or, once or twice weekly, in the *suq* (market).[3] Except for the *hanut*, which besides bread sells mostly pre-packaged foods such as milk, yoghurt and small snacks and drinks, the foods on offer in the *suiqa* and the *suq* are largely unpackaged (see Figure 4.2). Raw ingredients are generally preferred over processed foods, because my research participants want to 'know what's in the food'. While Newcomb

Figure 4.2. Corner shop (*hanut*) selling daily needs items, Marrakech, 2013. © Katharina Graf

(2017) decries the falling apart of the Central Market of Fes and the rise of the supermarket visited weekly by car, later on in the chapter she acknowledges not only that the Central Market is still in use and favoured over supermarkets due to its fresh, unprocessed food products (see also Amine and Lazzaoui 2010), but also observes that 'some lower- and middle-class Moroccans still favor the traditional shopping experience' (Newcomb 2017: 121) for reasons that I will detail in the first section. Importantly, especially in the context of urbanization and a globalizing food market, what food is considered good in Marrakech depends on the personal trajectory and situated emplacement of each urban cook, as I will explain through the Moroccan index of *beldi* and *rumi* in the subsequent section. As a standard of quality, *beldi* is crucial to understanding the individual practices of domestic cooks and how these relate to more widely shared understandings of Moroccan cooking, in particular regarding lunch preparations, as I will elaborate upon in the third section.

In the final section on dinner and convenience foods, I will argue furthermore that *beldi* foodways also point towards the broader social, economic, political and ecological factors of everyday food preparation. The notion of the 'citizen-consumer' obscures how low-income, wage-working women struggle to live up to the widely shared ideal of making good food for the family due to financial constraints. Although it is undeniable that Moroccans are increasingly overweight and obese (Mokhtar et al. 2001) – equalling many European and the American averages (FAO et al. 2020) – it is not possible to reduce this development to a changing diet, even less to consumers' ignorance about nutrition and health. Vague concepts such as the Mediterranean diet and its purported decline due to various processes of globalization risk misapprehending and misrepresenting how the many material and social changes that take place across Morocco are dependent on income and location. For a middle- or upper-income Moroccan woman – by definition nearly always urban-based – it is not unusual not to cook. On the contrary, she has likely outsourced the tedious aspects of domestic work to less privileged women (Montgomery 2019). Accounts focused on diet and consumption often remain impervious to the broader political economy of food and its bearing on low-income people's everyday foodways. Indeed, most of my research participants were acutely aware of the correlations between what they eat and their physical wellbeing, and thus were particularly critical of industrially produced and pre-processed foods. In response, as the previous chapters have also highlighted, they continue to invest time and effort into homemaking good food despite their limited temporal and financial resources. At the same time, their low income often prevented them from purchasing foods that tend to be widely considered good, such as fresh fish, fresh fruits or extra virgin olive oil.

Provisioning Good Food

On an ordinary morning, Fatimzahra and I headed to Omar's shop in the *suq* to buy spices, coffee, couscous grains and other dry goods. It was after 10 am and his small shop was busy. Yet, compared to the buzz of the street, it appeared calm. Similar to most shops of this kind, his consisted of one large room filled up to the ceiling with packaged and unpackaged dry goods, which also spilled into the street outside and characterized many Marrakchi markets. Upon entering, Fatimzahra greeted Omar with a nod and went straight to the back of the shop to sit down on a little stool. Like most shopkeepers, Omar kept track of who entered his shop and, in strict order, addressed each customer. Fatimzahra knew that it was her turn when either he or one of his assistants offered service. Until then, she talked to other customers about prices and qualities of food or inspected those of the products that were displayed openly (see Figure 4.3). She took a root of ginger (*skinjebir*), lifted it to her nose, broke it in two, peeled a small piece off and placed it on her tongue, then tossed it around with her tongue to taste it and assess its texture. She picked several pieces and placed them aside while picking the fibrous pieces from her mouth. She repeated this process with aniseeds (*n'effe*), this time comparing two different varieties, one bright green and long, the other small and green-brownish; according to the handwritten sign, the latter cost a third more than the former.

At this moment, Omar's teenage son turned towards her and asked: 'What do you want today, Madame?' The seeds still in her palm, she asked him whether the more expensive aniseeds were from Morocco (*n'effe beldi*). When he confirmed, she asked to get '*Mya d-riyal* [hundred riyal, equalling 5 dirham]', a common measure for buying spices. He filled a plastic bag with a small scoop and placed it on an electric scale, added a little, then closed it in an elegant twisting gesture and placed this one, and each following bag of spices that she ordered, on the side. As Fatimzahra sent him into each corner of the shop, she asked him about the price or provenance of a product, occasionally touching, smelling, tasting or looking closely at an item that had changed since she had shopped here the week before. When Omar's son did not know the answer, Omar himself was quick to tell Fatimzahra what she wanted to know. Although Omar was always busy billing other customers or selling precious products such as argan oil or saffron from behind his counter, he caught every exchange, phrase or question in his shop.

Once Fatimzahra had checked off each item on her mental shopping list, she went to the counter. Omar's son began to lift each bag or item visibly for us, calling out each item's price from his memory before placing it in a larger plastic bag. As he listed each item, Omar wrote the prices on a sheet of paper and typed them into his calculator. At the same time, Fatimzahra asked Omar about his family and the ongoing olive harvest in the Souss, their shared native *bled* (country or hometown). Omar's soft and friendly voice contrasted with the sharp calls of the hawkers outside his shop. The brief exchange of news ended when he gave her the final price in riyal. Fatimzahra quickly converted the sum in her head into the dirhams she owed him. After a good half-hour of resting,

Figure 4.3. Spices and herbs on sale in the *suq* (market), Marrakech, 2012. © Katharina Graf

choosing, waiting, chatting and paying, we left the shop with our grocery and went home.

* * *

This vignette describes an ordinary shopping scene in one of Marrakech's many *swaq* (markets, plural of *suq*). In the absence of institutional standards for many food products, looking at, touching, feeling, smelling and tasting the fruits, vegetables or spices on offer in this haptic environment were usually the first steps in the process of provisioning food.[4] Since the prices of these products were rarely signposted, as they are, for instance, in butcher shops, the first question every shopper asked concerned the daily price of a product (see Interlude 4).[5] Low-income shoppers are well informed about market fluctuations due to seasonal climate and rainfall, transportation routes and diversions, policy reforms or import quotas thanks to listening to the radio, social media and talking to each other, as well as exchanging news with farmers, shopkeepers and bakers (see also Zirari 2020a). By asking the prices from several shops and stalls, they ascertain the daily price before buying a product. Whereas daytime food prices were considered to be rather predictable, quality was not and required the shopper to carefully choose her products through multisensory engagement. As a result of relatively short regional supply chains (Codron et al. 2004), most fresh food products on sale across Moroccan markets are not packaged, labelled or portioned. In this context, provisioning and making good food begins with knowing the broader food market (see Chapter 5).[6] The more knowledge and control a Marrakchi cook has, the more food becomes good, thus defying the disembodied and abstracted standards of food that are increasingly normative in our thoroughly globalized food system.[7]

In his classic piece on the Moroccan *suq*, Geertz (1979) introduces the 'bazaar economy', a marketing system that is responsive to this lack of institutional structures and scarcity of information. He identifies two main procedures employed by shoppers to find and guard information about price and quality. 'Clientelism' establishes relations of trust between shopper and vendor, whereas 'bargaining' is based either on extensive comparison of prices across many vendors or on a clinical approach to ask a lot of information from few vendors. According to Geertz, bazaars – but even thoroughly globalized markets such as Tokyo's seafood market (Bestor 2001) – are determined by an 'information game', where information is the key resource: 'In the *suq* the flow of words and the flow of values are not two things: they are aspects of the same thing' (Geertz 1979: 199). While for Geertz it is paradoxical how 'comprehensive ignorance promotes local knowledge' (ibid. 230), I consider this a logical conclusion: individual shoppers *have to* be highly knowledgeable and informed in an otherwise flexible and often unpredictable local, regional and global market context. Although information is differently distributed in these markets, certainly vis-à-vis supermarkets, it is no less accessible or transparent than in consumer markets where labels convey information about price, provenance and quality of standardized and packaged products. Indeed, in a context where illiteracy is still widespread, the written word and small printed labels are more exclusive forms of information than talking to vendors.[8]

As the above vignette exemplifies, domestic cooks rely on several practices to ascertain food quality. First, they engage all their bodily senses to assess food quality. They establish relations of trust with shopkeepers. Furthermore, many draw on family connections in the rural hinterlands, coupled with their understanding of regional ecologies, to gain direct access to locally grown foods. By processing these raw products through cleaning, sorting, trimming, portioning and storing, domestic cooks further ensure that food is good for their family (Graf 2015). For instance, a residue of pesticide or fertilizer (*duwa*; literally medicine) on fruits or vegetables is identified through sight, smell and touch. If it is unavoidable, the skin of apples, tomatoes or peppers is peeled off, even though the skin is known to contain many important micronutrients and fibres. Spices are generally tested for quality through chewing on them before they are ground. Grains for homemade flour are split with the fingernails or crushed between the teeth after they have been visually inspected. Through their multisensory bodily engagement and in regular exchange with other shoppers or sellers, most of my research participants were able to tell whether the grains have been irrigated or not, whether fertilizer has been used, whether it has been a wet or a dry year and so on.

Spiritual and ethical considerations also underlie these provisioning and processing practices. First, shoppers and shopkeepers constantly invoked the spirituality or *baraka* of food. Food has to be treated with respect, including animals. Bread or bread-like foods in particular are not thrown out, but are redirected to feeding other creatures. Thus, only respectfully treated food can be fully good food.[9] Second, good food also refers to food security and the ability to share food with those who have less. This explains the strong emphasis on commensality and the cultural emphasis on sharing food in everyday life. These ethics also explain the ongoing existence of a social contract based on the popular expectation that the state provides food to its poorest citizens in an environment historically marked by frequent droughts and food shortages (see Chapter 5).

In this context, it is not the institutionalized certification and labelling of food quality that a Marrakchi shopper trusts; rather, it is her own bodily and ethical practices of provisioning and processing that make food good and explain why experienced cooks are responsible for shopping in Marrakech. In other words, chiming with the definition of taste knowledge in Chapter 1, only food which can be known through bodily engagement can be considered good food. From this perspective, categories of near/safe/good and far/risky/bad foods are experienced and embodied rather than externally determined; the expertise lies with the cook who through repeated experience develops her own bodily standards to judge food and thus rejects national or global standards.[10] Rather than considering these practices as new behaviour in response to industrializing and capitalizing food production and retail (Goodman, DuPuis and Goodman 2012), Marrakchi practices of provisioning and processing are an established and necessary way of ensuring one's family has access to and ingests what is deemed to be good food. This case poses an interesting counternarrative to the worldwide proliferation of food standards and labels in the broader context of globalizing supply chains and supermarket driven retailing, including its alternatives in Islamic (e.g. Bergeaud-Blackler, Fischer and Lever 2016; Fischer 2008) or Western market contexts (e.g. Grasseni et al. 2014; Trubek 2008; West 2013a).

Beldi Foods in the City

For low-income Moroccans, markers of food quality relate to taste, provenance, context of production, health and wellbeing, safety and food security. Quality is named and indexed through the vernacular concept of *beldi* and *rumi*. For a first definition, the Moroccan term *beldi* means 'of/from the country' (adjective of *al-balad* or *bled* in *darija*) and *rumi* means 'foreign' (adjective of *al-rum*, Rome, from/of Rome – i.e. Christian). I encountered the term *beldi* for the first time when helping Hajja to select foods that she wanted to take on her pilgrimage to Mecca. She deliberately packed *beldi* foods on this one-month trip abroad, filling an entire suitcase with preserved lemons, olives and homemade snacks such as *sellou*. In the following weeks I noticed how many foods, things or people were in fact considered *beldi*, but it took a couple of months of fieldwork before I encountered the paired term *rumi*. *Beldi*, much more so than *rumi*, harbours emotional meanings and values, and hence was used in more nuanced ways than *rumi* in everyday practices of indexing food (and people).

According to the ethnobotanist Mohamed El Haouz, *beldi* and *rumi* index food quality based on three dimensions: provenance, taste, and context of production and distribution.[11] Provenance or origin of a food relates to the terms more literally, since *beldi* refers to one's own hometown or region. Thus, produce that is sourced from one's home region is referred to as *beldi*, whereas foods grown outside of that region are referred to as *rumi* even if still grown in Morocco. For instance, from the perspective of a Marrakchi cook, *beldi* broad beans are grown in the Haouz, the agricultural hinterlands of Marrakech, and *rumi* beans are grown in any other region or abroad. Furthermore, *beldi* denotes a strong flavour and *rumi* a weak flavour. For instance, *beldi* cumin is considered strong and intense in flavour, whereas *rumi* cumin is associated with a less strong, more average flavour. Often cumin that is named *beldi* is grown in Morocco, while *rumi* cumin tends to be imported. Third, *beldi* denotes artisanal production and a short supply chain and *rumi* denotes an industrial and mass-produced product and often a longer supply chain. For instance, *beldi* chicken is an artisanal, small-scale farmed animal, which can be identified by its multicoloured feathers and a skinny, tall body. Rumi chicken, by contrast, is an industrially produced animal that is white, stout and rather fat (See Interlude 4, Figure 4.1).

According to Rachik (1997) and other Morocco scholars, this index exists throughout Morocco and is not limited to food; it also refers to other things and to humans. In fact, the pair is used throughout the Middle East and North Africa for similar classifications of local-foreign or traditional-modern, for instance, as *baladi-rumi* in Palestine (Meneley 2014) or *baladi-afrangi* in Egypt (Early 1993; Naguib 2015). Food anthropologists have found examples from across the globe detailing how people differentiate processes of food production, distribution and consumption according to similar taste-place concepts.[12] However, as fieldwork progressed, I noted that this pair as a 'theory is neat only in the hands of a symbolic anthropologist' (Early 1993: 62) and defies any attempt of simplification. Not only are these terms charged with ambivalence and contradictions – *beldi* in particular oscillates between changing valuations and imageries of the rural person, place or object as backward and uncivilized, but also as traditional, unspoiled and authentic. They also acquire differing, sometimes contradictory meanings with respect to food. They are not in opposition to one another, nor do they have a fixed meaning. What foods are considered *beldi* depends not only on an urban or rural perspective but also on each person's past and present life context.[13] It is because of this ambivalence and its situated meaning that *beldi* is such a useful analytical concept to understand food quality and situate the many different ways in which things and people are considered 'Moroccan'.

Beldi vegetables and fruits of (typically small-scale) production are marked by their diverse, even unsightly shapes and tend to be smaller than *rumi* varieties, which as a consequence of their industrial production are larger and uniform in appearance. *Beldi* products were often raw and unwashed, and therefore required more processing work than more standardized *rumi* products – though the latter were considered to just hide 'dirt' in the form of pesticides or fertilizers, and thus were also subjected to careful processing. Products that had no *beldi* equivalent such as rice or pasta were not named *rumi*, although they were largely imported or produced industrially. In fact, *rumi* products were more commonly referred to by their country of origin – for instance, Canadian lentils or Egyptian cumin. Imported foods were generally associated with industrial and mass production and were considered to be of lower quality.

However, neither of the terms refers to just good or just bad quality, because they cannot be disembodied. In the context of emigration to the city, their multiple meanings vary with each spatial and bodily context over time, sometimes contradicting one another.[14] Thus, although *beldi* could to some extent be said to embody a specific 'taste of place' (Trubek 2008), it does so in a highly situated and bodily way that sounds more like 'my, your or her taste of place'. For instance, for Aicha, a piece of meat from a ram grown and butchered in her hometown embodied a 'taste of the *bled* [*fih legout dyel bled*]', which she considered better and tastier than the meat of unknown provenance that was on offer in Marrakech. This meat only became *beldi* for Aicha in the context of migrating to Marrakech. Her visiting mother described this same piece of meat as just 'meat', since the meat she consumed in the *bled* was reared locally (cf. Simenel 2010). By contrast, for Aicha's husband the meat of his family's hometown in the Souss was *beldi*. Thus, this piece of meat was *beldi* only for Aicha and as such contained the taste and texture of *her* past, linking her to her rural origins, and reflecting her relation to Marrakech in the present. In this case, *beldi* is not simply an abstractable taste of place that can be marketed at a higher value; it is the taste of Aicha's *bled*, imbued with her bodily memories of the past, of childhood and of life in the *bled* (cf. Meneley 2014; Seremetakis 1994b).

Another example illustrates how the situatedness of *beldi* also shifts temporarily as a result of bodily displacement. One afternoon in Rachida's house, we were eating *kaskrut* (a teatime snack) with Meriem, Rachida's visiting youngest sister. Rachida invited me to taste the olives and pointed out how strong they tasted: 'They are *beldi*, you can taste the salt, right? They are much saltier than those they sell here.' She continued: 'My [other] sister, the one near Ourika, has preserved them.' Rachida smiled with pleasure as she placed one in her mouth. Suddenly, Meriem said in her soft voice: 'No, these are not *beldi*.' When I enquired, she relativized her statement by adding: 'Well, maybe they are *beldi* here in Marrakech but for me *beldi* olives are those our mother makes at home.' For Meriem, the visitor, these olives were not *beldi* even though it was also her sister who had processed them. Still, Meriem could understand why these olives were *beldi* for Rachida. By softening her initial statement, Meriem acknowledged Rachida's but also her own temporary bodily emplacement in Rachida's food environment and its consequences for labelling these olives *beldi*. Moreover, she suggested that Rachida's notion of *beldi* olives widened over time, since she, too, must have once considered their mother's olives as quintessentially *beldi*, certainly in her youth in the *bled*. Rachida did not comment, so I can only assume that for her, as a rural migrant living in Marrakech, there are multiple *beldis*. This subtle hierarchy within particular *beldi* products points to the multiple emplacements that especially rural migrants like Rachida and Aicha literally and metaphorically embody when they source, process and ingest food that they deem good for their families.

More pragmatically, one's geographical origin determined the ability to differentiate between *beldi* and *rumi*, or, by extension, between pure and impure. During a tour of their small museum in Taliouine, I interviewed a member of the regional cooperative selling 'real saffron [*sa'fran al-horr*]' produced in the surrounding Anti-Atlas Mountains of the Souss. She assumed that only Soussis were able to distinguish real from impure saffron. Marrakchi markets are known to sell adulterated saffron to their many *rumi* (here meaning non-Soussi) customers. Although the cooperative labelled their products and sold the whole saffron thread in high-quality packaging, according to her, this was not enough to gain consumer trust within Moroccan markets. Indeed, the way in which my research participants consume saffron is illustrative. As a native Soussiya, Hajja had a detailed knowledge of where, when and how real saffron was harvested and sold. She only stocked up when she visited her family in the Souss valley in the winter season. Aicha, by contrast, was not sure whether she could identify *sa'fran al-horr*, as her natal family had never used it for cooking. She admitted that she did not really taste the difference between fraught and real saffron, and, as a result, was not overly concerned with its purity.

Here, the differences between my research participants' family foodways described in the introduction came into play. Hajja's detailed and all-encompassing knowledge of Moroccan cuisine betrayed her long life as the wife of a once well-to-do urban Marrakchi notable (*sharif*). When her husband was still alive and they were wealthy, she often prepared lavish multiple course meals for his guests, for which she sourced speciality food products such as saffron, argan oil and honey from her native Souss. Her taste knowledge of these high-value products still expressed itself in the meals I ate during my fieldwork, even though she had to rely on her maternal family's generosity to provide these. Aicha and Rachida did not grow up with tastes such as saffron or argan oil; these were simply not available in their *bled* and too valuable to afford. As a result, they had not acquired the respective taste knowledge (see Chapter 1).

More generally, a cook's memories of past efforts involved in food processing were bound up with these terms. For instance, homemade couscous grains – which nowadays are only handmade in some rural areas – are associated with hard work and patience. Older cooks like Hajja remembered the toil too vividly to wish to process couscous grains by hand again. Most urban cooks preferred to use the *rumi* version, which is industrially produced, often by transnational firms. Among my younger research participants, who had never processed wheat into couscous grains by hand, I noted a tendency of nostalgic reverence for *beldi* couscous. Yet, as they had no bodily memory of making couscous by hand, they perceived no difference in quality or taste and did not refer to the industrially produced couscous grains as *rumi*, unless I specifically asked them. Identifying a product as *beldi* is thus also closely tied to the multisensory memory of a cook's taste, and notions of *beldi* and *rumi* shift over the space and time of each cook's life trajectory and knowledge reproduction.

Finally, in the context of poverty and health, it is important to emphasize that most *beldi* products on sale in urban open-air markets were more expensive than their *rumi* variants. While buying *n'effe beldi* is an affordable and regular treat for Fatimzahra, buying *beldi* chicken at three times the price of its *rumi* relative is unaffordable for most low-income Marrakchis (see Interlude 4). Similar to the industrially processed couscous grains that are now ubiquitous in urban homes, the distinction between *beldi* and *rumi* is not invoked when a cook could not afford to source better food. Instead of suggesting a notion of false consciousness, I propose considering this a kind of 'post-rationalization' (Khouri-Dagher 1996: 120), whereby cooks turn a constraint into a choice: for the low-income women I worked with, *beldi* chicken was rejected not because it was too expensive, but because it was considered to be of lower quality, less meaty and less tasty than the *rumi* chicken that they could afford.

Taken together, provisioning, processing and indexing good food as *beldi* or *rumi* are highly contextual processes that acquire meaning only in the situated confluence of body, space and time which defy abstraction and marketization. This is why *beldi* foodways also situate the low-income cook and her family within Morocco. Establishing which foods count as *beldi* inevitably establishes where you are coming from and where and who you are in relation to others and to the world. In choosing and indexing food according to the historically and geographically emplaced concept of *beldi* and *rumi*, individual cooks and their families re-create connections between their present lives in urban Morocco, their past in the agricultural countryside and their future from one generation to the next. When and how these terms are used in everyday food provisioning is thus also indicative of how cooks and their families relate to others. Therefore, these practices are not simply a symbol *of* these relations (Douglas and Isherwood 1978; Miller 1995) but also practices that *create* them (see Chapter 3). In provisioning and processing what they consider to be good food, low-income Marrakchis make sense of and each take a small but undeniable part in local, regional and global processes of food production, distribution, exchange and consumption (see Chapter 5).

Although *beldi* and *rumi* highlight the situatedness of foods and of cooks, most Moroccans agree on a number of important basic elements that mark Moroccan foodways. These were never more evident than during lunch preparation, the most important meal of the day for my Marrakchi research participants.

Lunch: Cooking the Moroccan Way

I arrived at Rachida's house on a Wednesday morning in February 2013. She did not work outside the house that day. Upon entering the door, I was already halfway in her kitchen and witness of her breadmaking. When Rachida finished kneading, she brewed mint tea, toasted bread from the previous day and served breakfast with *beldi* butter and *beldi* olives in the salon upstairs. Upon returning to the kitchen, she lifted the cloth covering the bread dough, slapped it and, hearing the 'right' sound, she concluded: '*Khemrt* [it has risen].' She immediately partitioned the dough, flattened the loaves and stacked them on a wooden tray. Rachida then donned her black *abaya* (a loose, black overgarment that covers the whole body) and her black *hijab* (a scarf covering the head and neck) and tucked the tray under her arm. We left the house to bring her bread to the *ferran* (public oven) and shop ingredients for lunch in the *suiqa*. On our way, Rachida mentioned that we were already quite late with lunch preparations. Indeed, the time window for eating lunch together was small: Zakia returned from university at 1 pm, but Ibtissam's lunch break at school was between noon and 2 pm. 'At least Ibtissam can clean up the kitchen and hang the laundry before lunch', Rachida hoped. Once we reached the *suiqa*, we entered the public oven and Rachida placed her loaves in the queue in front of the *ferran* proper, instructing the *mul al-ferran* (baker) to let the loaves rest some more before baking them.

Upon our return, Ibtissam had indeed cleaned up the kitchen and was hanging the laundry on the roof. Rachida quickly took off her outdoor clothes and began lunch preparations, once more noting: '*Msha al-hal* [it's getting late].' With skilled movements she gutted and cleaned the entire chicken we had bought with salt, vinegar and running water in the sink, and proceeded to make a lemon sauce to rub the chicken with. Her gestures handling the chicken and her movement to and fro between the storage, the fridge and the spice shelf were so fast that I barely kept up with noting down her gestures. She had begun to add spices, but I did not see which ones, so I enquired: 'Which spices did you put in?' She replied, 'Everything [*koulhou*].' I had heard this answer so many times already that I provocatively asked: 'You didn't put *themira* [sweet paprika], did you?!' Rachida interrupted her rapid gestures, turned around and looked intently at me: 'Of course not! You never combine *themira* with chicken!' 'So what did you put?', I insisted. Rachida gave in and listed '*kharkum* [turmeric], *skinjebir* [ginger] and *sa'fran* [here: colouring saffron], they go together'.[15] She did not mention that she also put salt and ground black pepper; that went without saying. At that moment, Zakia came home, the tray with the baked bread under her arm. As soon as she had taken off her *hijab* and changed clothes, she began to help with lunch preparations to be able to eat together before Ibtissam had to return to school.

* * *

This vignette raises several elements that mark typically Moroccan ways of cooking and eating, both in Morocco and in the Moroccan diaspora (cf. Hal 1996; Mescoli 2016, 2020; Wolfert 1973).[16] Thus, while practices of provisioning and processing food are situated and context-specific, cooking and eating food follow widely shared patterns. This section describes what defines Moroccan cooking and eating, including a specific range of utensils and tools, regular ingredients and combinations of meat, vegetables and spices, predictable processes of cooking, similar gestures and techniques of the body and shared practices of commensality.

The most recognizable tool in daily food preparation is the *tajine*, a thick earthenware saucepan with a conical or convex lid, depending on the regional origin of the cook (see Figure 4.4). For instance, in Marrakech and the Haouz, a conical lid is typical, whereas Aicha used a convex lid, as is common in the Middle Atlas region. A *tajine* is used to prepare stews of the same name that consist of meat and/or vegetables and are slow-cooked over charcoal or gas. *Tajines* are always served with bread to scoop the food. A recent addition to – if not a replacement of – the *tajine* is the pressure cooker. Most cooks I encountered preferred to use their seasoned *tajines* – only Rachida regularly prepared her stews in a pressure cooker to 'speed up the cooking', but she still referred to the resulting dish as a *tajine*. Equally recognizable is the two-layered *keskas* or *couscoussière* (see Chapter 1), which steams the couscous with the sauce underneath.[17] Couscous is never served with bread, but is eaten with the hand or a tablespoon, usually on Fridays or Sundays.[18]

Some ingredients are never amiss in a Moroccan meal. For instance, my research participants agreed that the taste and smell of fresh parsley and coriander define savoury Moroccan dishes (cf. Hal 1996; Wolfert 1973). Not surprisingly, they are available at nearly every corner of the city. Most sweet or savoury-sweet main dishes such as *seffa* (sweet couscous with caramelized onions and raisins), *bastila* (chicken and almond pie) or lamb and prune *tajine* contain cinnamon. There are also clear rules about how to match ingredients. The most recurrent abhorrence

Figure 4.4. Earthenware *tajine*, which describes the cooking vessel and the dish, Marrakech, 2013. © Katharina Graf

during my fieldwork was related to chicken and sweet paprika, as described in the vignette (see also Mescoli 2016). All women taught me that chicken 'needed' turmeric and ginger and ideally *sa'fran al-horr* (real saffron) or colouring saffron; a yellow chicken is considered a crunchy chicken.[19] Thus, when Rachida stated that she put *all* spices, there was no doubt for her nor any other Moroccan cook about which spices she combined. By contrast, minced meat (*kefta*) 'needs' cumin and a lot of sweet paprika to enhance its taste and colour. Other red meats take either ginger and turmeric or cumin and paprika, depending on the process or the combination with other ingredients. For instance, when drying and preserving meat after 'Id al-kebir, turmeric was used to coat the raw meat owing to its antimicrobial effects.

Except for lentil or bean stews, which are considered poor people's food but were popular among all Marrakchis I interviewed, lunch dishes usually contain a small amount of meat. With a kilogram of beef costing about 80 dirham at the time, meat was expensive and often used only 'for the taste'. Most women informed me that red meat, especially the fattier mutton meat, was high in cholesterol and thus avoided preparing it in big quantities for everyday meals. Although Aylwin (1999) argues that vegetables are considered less important than cereals and meat, and this is certainly true when hosting visitors or celebrating the birth of a baby, in everyday cooking seasonal vegetables played a central role and were widely appreciated as nutritious and healthy food (see also Houbaida 2005).

There are also predictable successions of steps in Moroccan cooking, guided by a cook's multisensory taste knowledge (see Chapter 1). Most notably, meat is initially braised on high flame with oil and spices, then onions are added and the cook stirs occasionally (cf. Mescoli 2016). If it is a *tajine*, vegetables are evenly distributed on top of the meat and then covered by the lid. The flame is lowered. The cook ceases to stir at this point and most cooks preferred not to add any water or only enough not to burn the dish.[20] If it is couscous, water is added after the meat and onions are braised. When the water boils, vegetables are added in a standard succession depending on the time they need to boil to turn soft (see Interlude 2). While couscous grains are usually steamed three times, it depends on the taste of the cook at which stage salt is added or whether oil, butter or *smen* (clarified butter) are used (see Chapter 1).

Some gestures and techniques of the body are strikingly similar, especially the coordinated movement of the hands, wrists and fists in kneading and shaping bread (see Interlude 1). Just like walking or swimming (Bourdieu 1977, 1990; Mauss 1973), these everyday bodily movements bespeak the Moroccan cook's habitus and, in turn, shape the cook's body, as I argued in Chapter 3. All women I worked with also slapped the dough in a characteristic way to hear whether it has risen enough.[21] Couscous grains are massaged between the flat palms and mixed in circular furrowing movements in the *gsa'a* (a large plate for preparing and serving couscous) (see Figure 1.1).[22] Like bread dough, *msemen* (layered pancakes), a favoured afternoon snack, are kneaded and proved in the *qesriya*. They are portioned into small balls by squeezing a portion of dough with the palm and the last three fingers through a circle shaped by the index finger and thumb of the same hand. Then they are flattened with oil on the countertop with the palms and spread out fingers in rhythmic alternating movements until the dough forms a thin, translucent sheet. It is then folded from four sides into the centre and flattened again to form a square.

Every meal that is considered to be Moroccan is served and eaten from a shared plate placed at the centre of the table, though this does not necessarily imply that the whole family eats together as Newcomb (2017) suggests.[23] In fact, it is not unusual to eat separately. In urban Morocco in the past and in multigenerational households today, men and guests are often served first and at a different table from the women of the household.[24] Commensality – spiritually and morally speaking the ideal way to consume food – is generally subject to various religious discourses and rules, not all of which can be listed here. Most notably, every eater eats only from the corner in front of herself and uses the thumb, index and middle finger of her right hand to scoop food as the Prophet Mohamed supposedly did (Haleem 2010). In the case of *tajine* a small piece of bread is held against the index and middle finger, while the thumb pushes the soft food against the bread to scoop it. Couscous is similarly assembled with three fingers, but is then transferred in the upward-turned palm and tossed around until it forms a small ball that can be delivered into the mouth. The drinks served with lunch vary from family to family, but they usually exclude tea or coffee, which is served for breakfast or with snacks. Couscous is served with a bowl of *lben* (buttermilk) for each eater (see Figure 1.2).

Various *hadeeth* (reports describing words, actions or habits of the Prophet Mohamed) recommend that one begins to eat the vegetables closest to the edge of the plate and finishes by tearing off small pieces of the meat placed in the centre of the plate. It is considered rude to pick food not within one's own corner of the plate. When there a many eaters or guests, the lead cook will pick apart the meat and distribute it. The temperature and texture of the ingredients as well as the decoration of a plate thus also serve numerous practical functions and ensure everyone has access to all ingredients (see Figure 1.2). Finally, apart from very intimate family settings, a plate is never emptied, as this would indicate that the cook has not provided enough food and is a poor host. Moderation in eating, which is prescribed by the Qur'an (Haleem 2010: 31), is highly appreciated. Equally, salt or pepper are never offered. Indeed, asking for additional salt is considered an insult to the cook, resonating with Aicha's explanation that a Moroccan woman '*has to be* a good cook' (see Chapter 3).

Although these elements were taken for granted and rarely made explicit in the way Rachida did upon my probing, they proved remarkably similar from one family to the next, in Marrakech and beyond. The use of certain ingredients, their combinations, the shared gestures and processes and their predictable repetitions over time bespeak a shared Moroccan identity, quite like Sabry (2005) suggests in his piece about television and mental emigration that 'couscous is not merely a dish. It is also that against which the authenticity of a culture can be tested. The *couscoussière* is not a mere aluminium pot but is also responsible for reproducing the 'authentic' experience of what it means to be Moroccan, Arab, Amazigh, and Muslim' (ibid. 197, emphasis in original). This identity is reproduced every day in the making of a Moroccan meal.[25] The importance of these elements and processes for a typical lunch and for a shared Moroccan (culinary) identity more broadly becomes particularly obvious when contrasted with dinner preparations.

Dinner: Time for Convenience

It was past 11 pm on a hot night in June when Aicha began to make dinner. She searched the fridge for any remaining vegetables and found two red peppers, a tomato as well as fresh peas that she had peeled the day before. She found rice in one of the large drawers in the storage cupboard and placed all the ingredients on the small worktop next to her hob. She first rinsed and then swiftly cut the tomato in her hands over her pressure cooker and switched on the hob. She added vegetable oil, then sprinkled salt, black pepper, cumin and sweet paprika directly from each jar. She washed the red peppers and picked up the knife again. As the sauce started to sizzle, she stirred it with the knife and proceeded to cut the peppers in her hands over the pot. Finally, she added the peas, stirred everything once more, poured water and added two handfuls of rice. She tightened the lid and left the kitchen to continue with housework. It took her less than ten minutes to set up our dinner. One hour later, she served the pilaf rice on a large plate with forks for everyone. As we ate, she asked me why I had taken notes earlier, arguing: 'This is nothing. It doesn't even have meat!'

* * *

Whereas lunch is considered the main meal of the day and public institutions across Marrakech acknowledge this through lunch breaks lasting from two to three hours, dinner is no proper meal. The importance of lunch was perceptible in the streets of Marrakech: rush hour was not in the mornings and evenings, but around lunchtime. Ordinary dinner preparations are little structured and demonstrate by contrast what defines a good meal and *beldi* foodways generally. Whereas high expectations and standards existed for lunch – as a representative of Moroccan foodways – for dinner, a 'quick fix' was not only acceptable but mostly the norm. The women I worked with did not invest their bodies in making dinner, nor did their audience expect them to, unless for visits or special occasions. Dinner rarely figured as a topic of conversation among my research participants and was dismissed as nothing worth studying. Dinner does not serve a function in the daily structure of food preparation, except that of a negative against lunch (cf. Douglas 1972). Dinner is the time for convenience and as such helps us to understand the limited role that convenience foods and supermarkets play in the contemporary foodways of low-income households.

Aicha's reduced bodily and emotional engagement was noticeable in the absence of planning and in how she cursorily cut vegetables and combined spices. Sometimes, she was simultaneously on the phone chatting with friends, moved around the flat to tidy up or collected and folded the laundry. Her attention was not focused on preparing food; she was careless. Other times, she called Hassan on the phone to tell him to bring takeaway sandwiches after work while she fed yoghurts or leftovers from lunch to the girls. If she cooked, Aicha often prepared a pilaf as described, a tomato pasta or an omelette, all of which she called 'fast food'. She referred to these dishes by their international names: sandwich, spaghetti or omelette. Until the end of my stay, Aicha and everyone else I interviewed did not understand why I was interested in studying dinner preparations; perhaps this was also because I was presumed to know how to prepare 'European' dishes.[26] According to Aicha, food preparation that lasted less than one hour, did not contain meat, was eaten with a fork on separate plates and could be combined with cleaning the flat was not proper cooking. Taste did not matter in this context. The other women I worked with usually did not cook for dinner and ate only a yoghurt or leftover bread with butter. Wage-working women instead spent the evening preparing next day's lunch such as sorting, cleaning and cutting herbs and spices, fileting sardines or peeling peas.

For my research participants, convenience food denotes easily sourced or quickly prepared food, not processed or ready-to-eat foods from the supermarket. Moroccan supermarkets initially targeted high-income households and their emergence in the 1990s was linked to rapid urbanization (Codron et al. 2004). As a result, most supermarkets are located in high-income neighbourhoods and are designed to be reached by car rather than on foot or via public transport. Still, the reasons why low-income Marrakchis did not regularly shop in these supermarkets cannot be reduced to access and location or to price; indeed, many of my research participants knew from television or radio commercials that staple products such as vegetable oil or flour were cheaper in supermarkets than in most neighbourhood markets. Despite recent growth in supermarket retailing in urban Morocco, Codron et al. (2004) observe that consumers prefer product freshness and low prices, a domain where supermarkets cannot (yet) compete with traditional markets. Confirming my observations, the authors describe that consumers are used to choosing food and quantities individually, hence why packaging and related hygiene and safety claims have not been successful marketing strategies. Supermarkets generally fall short of meeting consumer expectations pertaining to taste, freshness, size and number of products (ibid.).

Amine and Lazzaoui (2010) add that although middle- and low-income consumers regularly frequent supermarkets and have a good idea of their products and prices, they only buy bulk products such as vegetable oil or flour. The authors note that 'practices related to traditional commerce ... are transposed to the modern retail format' (ibid. 572). Indeed, I often observed this transposition of shopping practices into supermarkets. These authors list mainly symbolic and social reasons for practices that involve breaking open flour bags, coming regularly to supermarkets without buying anything or speaking with staff about food. In my view, this transposition rather echoes Geertz's (1979) 'information game' and is due to shoppers trying – if not entirely succeeding – to invest their bodily knowledge in the identification of food products that they deem good for their family.[27] Overall, supermarkets do not (yet) speak to low-income Marrakchis' understanding of convenience, which relates to practices rather than to products and stands in contrast to everything that I described as *beldi* foodways above.

Street food, which has a long history in Marrakech due to its importance as a regional and (inter)national trade hub (Deverdun 1959; Raddadi 2012), speaks much more to low-income Marrakchis' understanding of convenience. Although it is not common for low-income Marrakchi wives and mothers to visit and sit in cafés or restaurants, it is acceptable to rely on street foods and processed snack foods for a second breakfast on the way to work, as a takeaway option for an afternoon snack with unannounced visitors at home or a quick family dinner, as long as the household finances allow for such a treat.[28] Many of the more popular snack foods such as *msemen* or *baghrir* are prepared on demand by female vendors. Indeed, as I confirmed during my research in Beni Mellal, buying the homemade or locally prepared food of other women – often neighbours or distant relatives – can partially stand in for preparing these oneself (cf. Staples 2020).

Relative to lunch, dinner is 'fast' food but not necessarily 'fast food'. The investment of time goes hand in hand with bodily effort and care, neither of which Aicha or any other of my research participants invested in their routine dinner preparations. Moroccan dishes require time and bodily effort, while 'European' dishes do not. Although not explicitly labelled as such by my research participants, this comparison bears a striking resemblance to the distinction between *beldi* and *rumi*. In other words, the investment of time and bodily effort is not only a marker of taste knowledge, as I demonstrated in Chapter 1, but is also a crucial determinant of *beldi* foodways. Convenience foods and dinner, even if made from scratch as described in the vignette, therefore cannot qualify as *beldi* foodways and show, by contrast, what makes food good and typically Moroccan.

Conclusion: Situating Moroccan Food and People

Beldi foodways make it possible to overcome both a simplistic view of diet and of the consumer – and a fatalistic view of the future – and remind us that cooking is always embedded in wider networks, discourses and practices. These begin with the careful and ethical provisioning and processing of food to ensure quality. Furthermore, this chapter has argued that, on the one hand, what is called *beldi* or *rumi* depends on the specific confluence of body, space and time, and is therefore necessarily context-specific and situated; good food cannot be defined abstractly. On the other hand, *beldi* also indicates shared values and shows that a distinct Moroccan way of cooking does exist, involving not only predictable ingredients, combinations, processes and gestures, but also the investment of time and bodily effort, as the contrast between lunch and dinner preparations highlighted. There is a shared expectation that lunch consists of a proper Moroccan meal, usually based on homemade bread and *tajine* and a couscous on Fridays. For dinner, 'fast' and 'convenient' foods are not only acceptable but also often the norm.

Through their emphasis on homemade and wholesome food and the *bled* as a more abstract category of tradition and belonging, low-income domestic cooks are also shaping values that are increasingly shared across class. Although *beldi* and *rumi* are relative categories that depend on the temporal and spatial situatedness of foods and bodies, this chapter has also demonstrated that there are Moroccan-wide categories that make it possible to distinguish between local and global, domestic and foreign, or simply good and bad food. My spotting of labelled '*beldi* bread' in supermarkets in 2017 is emblematic of the broader import of *beldi* foodways for Moroccan identity. In this case, *beldi* referred to wholemeal rather than white bread and thus referenced the smallest common denominator of what *beldi* bread can mean, despite being industrially produced and packaged. Although wholemeal is the only material characteristic it shares with homemade *beldi* bread, through it '*beldi* bread' materially and symbolically evokes the many other meanings of *beldi*, including Moroccan rather than imported ingredients, artisanal rather than industrial products and wholesome rather than 'empty' foods. The adoption of *beldi* bread in supermarkets hence denotes a form of validation of low-income *beldi* foodways and of a shared identification with homemade quality and more wholesome being in the face of change (Graf 2018). This appreciation coexists with seemingly opposed values held by the middle and upper classes, who simultaneously associate *rumi* with everything they desire: modernity and European or global culture (Cohen 2004; Newcomb 2017; Rachik 1997).

More generally, in their concern to control the foods they eat, low-income Moroccan cooks are not that different from other increasingly concerned shoppers and eaters around the world. *Beldi* and *rumi* are one of many practical indices devised to distinguish between what are considered good and bad food products.[29] They harbour many more values referring to qualitative or ethical dimensions in our global food system. Yet, because low-income Marrakchis self-certify the foods they consume through their knowledgeable practices of provisioning, processing, preparing and serving food, *beldi* and *rumi* will likely remain a vernacular index that cannot be abstracted and marketed in supermarkets or similarly disembodied markets. So far, *beldi* is not an established category in supermarkets precisely because it embodies so many ambivalent values. It is not surprising that Moroccan food marketing and retail have not significantly picked up on the pair of *beldi* and *rumi*, nor, for that matter, replaced the bazaar economy as the central institution of everyday food provisioning in urban Morocco.[30] In this respect, the Moroccan case also differs from other market contexts where the distinction between regional, flavourful or artisanal foods with imported, tasteless or industrial products is enmeshed in marketing strategies that are often related to elitist, nationalist or governmental concepts and technologies (e.g. Caldwell 2002; Guthman 2008; Jung 2014; Trubek 2008; Welz 2015).[31]

Notes

1. Historian of technology Ruth Schwartz Cowan (1983) shows that despite more than a century of material and social change in US American kitchens and homes, and the ensuing division of domestic and wage work that declared unpaid female domestic work as passive consumption rather than as production, domestic cooks still *produce* meals and, in doing so, reproduce family life. For a similar but more ethnographic argument, see Abbots (2013).

2. In their report on food security and nutrition in the world, the FAO et al. (2020) have recently acknowledged that a healthy diet, according to current nutrition research, is globally much more unaffordable than diets that only satisfy the minimum human need for energy and nutrients.
 3. A *suiqa* usually contains one or two fresh fruit and vegetable shops or mobile stalls and a butcher. A *suq* is often partially open-air and located at the juncture of several neighbourhoods. It contains several fruit and vegetables shops and stalls, butchers for white and red meat as well as one or two dry foods shops and a small kitchen appliance store.
 4. Historically speaking, because they buttressed urbanization and political legitimacy, meat, dairy and certain cereal products have been more closely controlled by state representatives than other food products (Essid 2000; Holden 2009).
 5. When a customer is presumed to be unfamiliar with the pricing of fresh fruit and vegetables, and the multiple factors determining it – for instance, a tourist or returning Moroccan migrants (Salih 2003) – some vendors ask higher prices. When this happened to me at the beginning of my fieldwork, Fatimzahra's and Hajja's reactions of surprise and indignation revealed their expectation of a 'fixed' price.
 6. Comparative ethnographic research on provisioning practices demonstrates the context specific circumstances in which food acquires quality, such as through careful practices of choosing, stacking or transporting foods (Barnes and Taher 2019; Garth 2020; Klein 2013).
 7. For comparative examples of food standards and processes of standardization, see Bergeaud-Blackler, Fischer and Lever (2016); Jung, Klein and Caldwell (2014); Kjaernes, Harvey and Warde (2007); and West (2008, 2013a).
 8. Speaking of peasant markets, Alexander (1992) argues that it is supermarkets that are determined by a lack of information and transparency, since prices are usually set by managers and not in response to demand, whereas sales staff are deskilled owing to the reduction of their role to simply giving change. For accounts of shopping in supermarkets in highly industrialized contexts, see Koch (2012); and Miller (1998).
 9. This observation resonates with Fikry's (2022: 85) argument, whereby animals reared as food on Egyptian rooftops enjoy 'a certain level of agency' since they can refuse to become edible.
 10. This ability to identify or know good foods could be labelled as 'consumer competence' (Jung 2014: 109) or a bodily way of 'self-certify[ing]' (West 2013b: 216) food products.
 11. No one else I interviewed gave such a succinct overview of these terms, largely because defining them requires abstracting oneself from their situated meaning.
 12. See, for instance, Bestor (2001) on *kokusan* and *kata* in Tokyo, and Caldwell (2002) on *nash* and *ne nash* in Moscow.
 13. The terms also vary across class. Middle-income families in Rabat use the term *beldi* to refer to 'traditional' Moroccan dishes such as *tajine* or couscous and *rumi* to refer to their own 'modern' practices of making pasta or soups (Montgomery 2016). For a similar distinction in relation to furniture, see Rachik (1997).
 14. In the rural setting described by Simenel (2010), where the perspective of homegrown and industrially produced foods is shared by most villagers, *beldi* and *rumi* are more clearly associated with good and bad quality respectively.
 15. Except Hajja, my research participants referred to chemical colouring saffron when they meant *sa'fran*; they did not normally use real saffron threads (see Chapter 3).

16. Although there are many regional and transnational differences in ingredients and style in everyday cooking, the basic elements I list in this section are remarkably similar across Morocco.
17. Beji-Becheur and Ozcaglar-Toulouse (2008) argue that the etymology of the name is based on the sound of the steam '*ksskss*'. The name of the dish and its method of preparation are thus metonymically linked.
18. Moroccan family meals are ordered according to their importance across the day, the week and the lunar year, whereby couscous is comparable to the English Sunday roast (Douglas 1972). Following Douglas's structuralist approach, bread could be considered the basis of a system of 'repeated analogies' (ibid. 68; cf. Sutton 2001: 103ff), where the part recalls the whole and gains meaning in this way. Lunch is the most important daily meal. It usually consists of a stew such as *tajine*, is always served with (ideally homemade) bread and climaxes every Friday lunch in couscous, which resembles bread in that it is also cereal-based and complements the stew on top. Couscous in turn marks nearly every Muslim holiday throughout the lunar annual calendar, with a special topping and often complemented by a *harira* soup thickened with flour (cf. Buitelaar 1993). In households marked by a working week from Monday to Friday couscous is often prepared on Sundays.
19. Fassi cuisine does not combine ginger with chicken (Wolfert 1973).
20. See Sarter (2006: 78) for a detailed description of the multiple roles of a Moroccan sauce (*doauz*).
21. Harris' (2015) detailed account of sound in breadmaking and other recipes suggests the role of sound is not limited to Moroccan food preparation.
22. In cookbooks (e.g. Hal 1996; Wolfert 1973) the *gsa'a* is associated with kneading dough. However, my Marrakchi research participants distinguished between the typical plate for kneading and shaping bread, the earthenware *qesriya*, and the typical plate for preparing and serving couscous, the wooden *gsa'a* (cf. Harrell 2004). Since bread dough has different properties from couscous and is much stickier and elastic when processed, it would be difficult to knead bread in a wooden *gsa'a*.
23. Implicit in Newcomb's (2017) account of the 'end of the Mediterranean diet' is an idealized Western understanding of the family meal, which is not typical across Morocco. Murcott (1983, 2019) has long been an advocate for deconstructing the idealized notion of the family meal.
24. During my research in the rural Drâa Valley I noticed that men holding professional jobs often ate their lunch much later than women (Graf 2010).
25. Though focused on middle-class Moroccans, Gaul's (2019) methodology of 'kitchen histories' similarly highlights the importance of everyday food preparation to the historical creation of a shared Moroccan identity and Moroccan nationhood.
26. My research participants considered me European rather than German and equated various foods typically associated with France, Germany or Italy simply with Europe as a whole.
27. Not all supermarkets are equal in this regard. For instance, Aswak Assalam (which is Moroccan-owned) is more visceral and more accessible within the socioeconomic geography of Marrakech than Acima (French). Marjane (Moroccan-French), even though claimed to be especially 'modern' (cf. Amine and Lazzaoui 2010), is also more attuned to customers' desire to engage bodily with food.
28. Speaking about Casablanca, Zirari (2020b) argues that it is increasingly normal to buy rather than prepare afternoon snacks for visitors among low-income women. However,

she does not describe how snacking relates to other mealtimes such as breakfast, lunch or dinner.
29. Widespread concepts are foods of halal, organic, artisanal or craft production, fair trade or regional foods (e.g. Bergeaud-Blackler, Fischer and Lever 2016; Jung, Klein and Caldwell 2014; Meneley 2014; West 2008).
30. The only food product labelled as *beldi* across most supermarkets were lemons. *Beldi* lemons (*citron beldi*) were small, round and darker than the uniform and bright yellow *rumi* equivalent that was simply called 'citron'. High-priced supermarket products like saffron, *amlou*, argan oil or honey, which would be indexed as *beldi* or *rumi* among my research participants, were labelled as 'organic', 'free from' or 'sugar free' and, judging by their price, were marketed to customers with high purchasing power.
31. Similar to Caldwell's (2002) arguments for Russian consumer preference for *nash* foods, Rachik (1997) also argues that the choice of *beldi* over *rumi* furniture is a response to a perceived encroaching occidentalization, especially among the urban Moroccan middle classes.

INTERLUDE 5

Tasting

It was a late January morning in Gueliz, the *ville nouvelle*, where I was living alone at the time. After living and working with others during the previous months, I was keen to try to make my own lunch the way I had observed and helped to make it so many times. Without a doubt, it had to be a *tajine*, a vegetable-heavy stew prepared for nearly all lunch meals and so beloved by my research participants. In the morning I had already bought vegetables, herbs, spices and a small piece of beef in the *suiqa* (diminutive of *suq*, market). I placed all the ingredients and tools on the worktop of my small kitchen. I was not exactly sure how to proceed, so I decided to clean and separate the bundle of parsley and coriander as I had done many times before. However, what I had not done myself was to prepare the meal itself. With a small knife, I chopped an onion on a cutting board, for I did not yet trust my ability to cut it in my hands. Along the way, I slowly remembered what I needed to do, how and when, and grew more confident. My hands knew, and so did my nose, my ears, my eyes and my tongue.

I placed the meat directly in the *tajine* pot (a thick earthenware plate with a lid), on a high fire on the hob, added some vegetable oil and started to add ground spices to it, sprinkling them from the paper bags I had bought them in. I was not sure which ones to use for this meat. Whenever I had asked, I was given the same reply: '*koulhou* [all]'. Surely, Hajja would not use ginger with this meat?! I decided to add a lot of cumin, because I like it, and a little bit of sweet paprika, salt and pepper. I added the onion pieces, stirred everything and turned to cleaning and cutting the vegetables. I started by scraping the skin off two carrots with the knife, halved them, took their core out and halved them again. I added the eight pieces straight to the *tajine* by stacking them over the meat, similar to how one would stack logs of wood on a fire. I lowered the fire and closed the lid. 'Carrots come first'; in my head I heard Fatimzahra's advice that each vegetable needs its time.

I continued by washing and cutting a turnip and a courgette, laying them aside in a bowl filled with water until it was their turn. After what seemed like an indefinite amount of time, I added the turnip, placing each quarter between every second carrot. Later, I added the courgette, placing each piece in the remaining gaps between the carrot and turnip pieces. I sprinkled a few parsley and coriander leaves on top, closed the lid once more and waited. When I perceived that distinct smell of stew, when it smelled 'ready', I lifted the lid. For a split second, I noticed how early it was compared to the lunches I ate with others. Had I done everything right?! Only when I placed the entire pot on the small table in front of me did I realize that I had no bread. Why not use a spoon for once, I told myself unsuspectingly, and began to eat. I lifted the first spoonful to my mouth and burned my lips. Had I dipped my fingers with bread into it, I would have known the dish was too hot. When I finally could eat, it tasted nothing like *tajine*! It also felt nothing like it, for I did not feel it between my fingers and I did not recognize its texture on my palate. As I kept eating, it did not behave like *tajine* either; the spoon cut into the soft vegetables too neatly. Finally, it did not last like *tajine*; with the spoon I ate much faster than usual. Without bread, a *tajine* like this was not truly a meal. The taste of nearly every dish and the time it takes to prepare and eat it are determined by bread.

CHAPTER 5

Cereal Citizens
'Bread Does Not Come from a Store'

In mid-November 2017 I travelled to Morocco for my research project on bread. I visited regional grain markets in the Haouz and the Tadla, the agricultural hinterlands of Marrakech and Beni Mellal respectively. As I enquired about grain prices, I was repeatedly told that prices were above average due to a lack of rain, which delays the sowing season and critically reduces the period of winter cereal growth, normally between October and May. The autumn had been exceptionally hot and dry, and farmers and brokers expected a bad agricultural season.

A couple of days later, in a small town west of Marrakech on 19 November 2017, fifteen women – mostly mothers – died in a stampede trying to obtain privately distributed food aid in the form of refined flour, cooking oil and sugar. Five more women were critically injured as they queued along with roughly a hundred others to receive these staple ingredients of the Moroccan diet. These women, too, had been acutely aware that it had not rained in most of Morocco for nearly six months. The anticipation of a year of drought, and of higher prices of grain and flour as a result, drove too many women to this free annual distribution, taking the organizers by surprise. The national media reacted to this tragic event by communicating the offer of help by King Mohamed VI for the families of the deceased by paying for the funerals.

* * *

Like many of their Arab neighbours, Moroccans expect their government to provide cheap bread, if nothing else (cf. Barnes 2022; Martinez 2022). Bread accompanies nearly every meal, from breakfast to dinner. It is the tool of choice to pick up food with one's hands from the shared platter. It is the basis of physical satiation and of hospitality. Across the Arab-speaking world, bread is furthermore sacred and considered the primary gift of God (*al-ni'ama*) representing all food. As such, it demands respect. Even when it turns into waste, Marrakchis do not throw it away, but redirect it towards feeding other creatures.[1] In the context of frequent droughts and widespread poverty, bread is also the staple that assures the country's food security. For centuries it has constituted the material and symbolic basis of the social contract between the *Makhzen* (literally, granary; tellingly it also denotes the Moroccan monarchy and its political allies) and its poor subjects: the guarantee of cheaply available flour and bread through a complex subsidy system ensures the monarchy's legitimacy among the low-income population. Though it might not seem to be a moment of political unrest at first glance, the unprecedented event of the stampede reveals the risks that food insecurity poses both to the lives of low-income women and to political stability in Morocco. Taking this event seriously and tracing Moroccan flatbread, and the ingredients and practices required to make it, allows me to link the reproduction of women's cooking knowledge to the political economy of food in globalized Morocco.

Flour, cooking oil and sugar constitute the basic triad of domestic food preparation. Without these, low-income Moroccans would not survive. Although the underlying cause of the stampede – poverty and everyday food insecurity – did not instigate a public debate, the deaths of these women caused a murmur of discontent among my research participants. In particular, wives and mothers who understood the risk of food insecurity from their own experience were keen to share their opinions on food security, economic development and political legitimacy in Morocco with me. The gist of their comments echoed political opinions I had already heard during my previous fieldwork: 'The King can get away with doing nothing about our poverty so long as there is cheap bread'. Indeed, the historian Holden argues that the Moroccan monarchy has been in power for four centuries *because*, in the context of frequent droughts, it redistributed scarce resources and guaranteed the supply of flour and meat in its urban markets: 'Popular responses to the threat of famine shaped Morocco's political system' (Holden 2009: 7). The stampede illustrates to what extent the social contract is still in place today, despite nearly four decades of market liberalization. More implicitly, the stampede also illustrates to what extent this social contract is based not simply on cheap flour and bread, but also on women's domestic food work. In this final chapter I draw on my research project on bread to present an urgently needed political economic perspective on domestic cooking.[2]

In making their own flour and bread – rather than buying it more cheaply from one of the ubiquitous corner shops or bakeries, as most of their Arab neighbours do (Barnes 2022; Martinez 2022) – low-income Marrakchis ensure that they have good food. In doing so, they not only gain a sense of control over their lives, they also become political subjects. Their efforts to prepare homemade bread echo Crawford's observation in rural Morocco that 'Bread – and by extension life – does not come from a store' (2008: 4) and contrast with Newcomb's

(2017) urban middle-class 'citizen-consumer' described in Chapter 4. To conceptualize Marrakchi women's practices in relation to the state, I propose the notion of 'cereal citizenship', which suggests that by focusing on low-income women, and their everyday work to make good flour and bread, we can better understand the enduring but paradox stability of the Moroccan government at a time of regional upheaval.

Crucially to the notion of cereal citizenship, not all bread is equally good. Even though bread of all kinds can be purchased cheaply across Marrakech, it is significant that many low-income urban Moroccans insist on making their own flour and bread.[3] Not only is homemade bread usually made fresh every day, its ingredients are also sourced and processed carefully. The typical homemade loaf consists of equal measures of *fors* (soft wheat) and *gemh* (durum wheat) flour.[4] The explanations for combining *fors* and *gemh* always followed the same logic. *Fors* flour was appreciated for its low price, ranging between 3 and 5 dirham per kilogram, and its softness in handling and eating. At the same time, it was decried for its lack of nutrients, texture and taste. Most of my research participants were also aware and criticized that the bulk of *fors* was imported from North America or Europe and thus the product of a long and industrialized supply chain that obscured its provenance.[5] *Fors* flour was considered the material and symbolic representation not only of industrialized and globalized food production but also of dependence on the government's subsidy system for keeping prices low. The government, in turn, is increasingly dependent on international trade agreements and volatile food prices due to global events such as the food price spikes in 2008 and 2011, the current war in Ukraine, a major supplier of wheat to North Africa, or the most recent global food price inflation.

Gemh flour was often described as hard to knead and to chew, but its positive qualities outweighed the negative ones. It was valued for its wholesome texture and was considered to aid digestion and overall wellbeing. Although available as refined flour (*fino*) in most corner shops at a price ranging between 5 and 8 dirham per kilogram (in 2023, its price could be up to 10 dirham per kilogram), everyone preferred to source it in grains (see Figure 5.1). This allowed urban Moroccans to 'know what's in there': the grains were visually inspected, touched, smelled and chewed before they were bought and then processed by hand to ensure good quality (see Chapter 4). Shoppers could tell whether the wheat had been irrigated and also differentiated between the flavour of grains from one region to another. In doing so, the broader knowledge of a region's ecology and the material and social infrastructure of domestic food production were actively cultivated and reproduced. Similar to other *beldi* (of/from the countryside) food products, *gemh* also linked its consumers to their hometown and their past, sometimes literally, sometimes only symbolically. Even when produced on relatively high-tech, irrigated farms, consumers praised its artisanal networks of distribution, which in Marrakech's grain or wholesale markets seldom involved

Figure 5.1. Inspecting grains at a weekly grain market, Beni Mellal, 2018.
© Katharina Graf

more than one or two brokers between farmer and consumer. Lastly, due to the bodily labour and effort invested, homemade *gemh* flour became imbued with *baraka* (God's blessing) and was thus also spiritually superior to industrially produced *fors* flour (see Chapter 1).

Strictly speaking, then, in combining these two different flours, even homemade bread came partially from the shop in Marrakech. This may be why my research participants did not refer to homemade bread as *beldi* (see Chapter 4). Indeed, it is the combination of cheap, industrial *fors* flour with handmade, highly valued *gemh* in homemade bread that symbolizes and materializes the ambiguities and faultlines of cereal citizenship. To trace these faultlines and contextualize domestic food preparation in the wider political economy of food security, this chapter follows the movement of bread from the field to the table. The first section sketches the historical and contemporary context of wheat production in Morocco to explore how domestic breadmaking is central to the monarchy's political legitimacy and to political stability until today. The second section then defines cereal citizenship through following wheat cereals as they are provisioned and processed. The third section describes baking and explores how bread loaves, on their paths across the city, symbolically and materially mark the rhythms of everyday urban life and through it maintain vital elements of the urban food infrastructure. The final section explores the physical interactions of flour and bread with/in the eating body and relates these to low-income Marrakchi perceptions of family health and wellbeing against the backdrop of persisting poverty and food insecurity.

On the whole, this chapter sums up the previous chapters and brings them into dialogue with global issues such as the global nutrition transition, food (in)security, environmental degradation and political (in)stability. Connecting the level of the body to the level of the state and the globe, it makes the case for understanding domestic cooking as a vital, yet largely hidden political-economic practice of low-income women.

Bread and Political Stability in the Past and Present

Where and how the two wheats for bread were produced and sourced is intricately connected to the history of Morocco's globalized food system. *Gemh* has been produced on Moroccan soil for at least two thousand years and has constituted a major crop since Roman times, gaining North Africa the mythical reputation as Rome's bread basket (Davis 2007). Today, *gemh* is still mainly produced on rainfed subsistence farms and without government support (see Figure 5.2). Although its yields have always fluctuated depending on annual rainfall and groundwater levels, evidence from the Souss shows that its cultivation has significantly decreased since the 2000s due to competition with export crops over increasingly scarce resources such as water and arable land (Sippel 2014: 121, 265). *Fors* was introduced during the early French Protectorate (1912–56), fuelled by the desire to resuscitate the mythic 'granary of Rome'. It requires continuous investment in irrigation and mechanization because it is poorly suited to the semi-arid climate and the constant threat of drought (Swearingen 1987). Although its production has been unprofitable from the start, the Protectorate administration followed an export-oriented agricultural policy, which in the context of the Great Depression and coupled with a series of droughts in the 1930s led to a domestic economic crisis. Historians like Swearingen (1987) suggest that the French colonists thereby undermined and destabilized their own rule in Morocco, which eventually ended in 1956 (see also Pascon 1986). The colonialists' focus on mechanized cash-crop production for export rather than production for growing domestic demand also became the foundation of misguided agricultural policies to come (Akesbi 2014).

Under King Hassan II (1961–99), investment in and development of the traditional rainfed farming sector stagnated further, while large-scale irrigated agriculture on the most fertile soils for the production of export crops expanded at the cost of irreversible resource degradation (Payne 1986; Sippel 2014; Swearingen 1987). Simultaneously, *fors* has become the most important import crop in the form of food aid in the 1970s first and since the structural agreement programmes of the 1980s as a regular and ever-expanding item of government spending. The 2008 launching of the Plan Maroc Vert (PMV) by Hassan II's son and successor, King Mohamed VI (1999 to present) did not change this dual approach to agriculture: the exportation of cash crops and the importation of *fors* on the one hand, and the neglect of *gemh* and food production for the domestic market on the other. Although it recognizes the importance of domestic food production – if not of ecologically and culturally more adapted *gemh* – the PMV aims to make Moroccan export agriculture the main source of the country's economic growth, quite like it did during the Protectorate (Akesbi 2014; Davis 2006).

In other words, *fors* was never a major export crop, nor did it ever sufficiently feed the domestic population. Yet, it became the basis of national food security. The wheat branch of the national subsidy system (*caisse de compensation*) almost exclusively targets *fors* and remains a central institution to uphold the social contract between the monarchy and the poor since it was set up in 1966.[6] Indeed, Holden (2009) demonstrates that the centralized regulation of wheat (and meat) in urban Morocco has been a major element of the Alaouite monarchy's enduring rule for more than four hundred years. These subsidies – together with sugar and liquified petroleum gas (LPG) the only three consumer goods to remain heavily regulated after three decades of economic liberalization (Verme, El-Massnaoui and Araar 2014) – will even have contributed to relative political stability during the Arab Spring revolutions that rocked the region between 2010 and 2012 (cf. Harrigan 2014). Although the Moroccan government gradually ended most other subsidies within its cheap food policy, following structural adjustment agreements with the International Monetary Fund (IMF) in 1982 and a general liberalization of its economy since, the memory of urban bread riots in the mid-1980s and the recurring threat of drought seem to forewarn the government to retain its *fors* subsidies, despite the increasing strain caused by them on the national budget.[7]

Indeed, in combination with urbanization and population growth, measures to ensure food security encouraged the growing importation of *fors*, which further undermine cereal production of more adapted wheat such as *gemh* for the domestic market (Davis 2006).[8] This trend continues since the 2004 Free Trade Agreement (FTA) between the Moroccan Government and the United States (ibid.) and the 2013 Deep and Comprehensive Free Trade Agreement (DCFTA) between the European Union and Morocco (cf. Boeckler and Berndt 2014). Not only is the government's political legitimacy still tied to the whims of the global food market, but by disincentivizing local food production, it also continues to stifle agricultural production for the domestic market (Sippel 2014). In the context of rising global food prices – especially following the multiple global food price crises since 2007–8 and in view of the war in Ukraine as well as increased food price volatility due to financial speculation and increasing environmental degradation – the Moroccan food system and political legitimacy are thus increasingly dependent on factors beyond the government's control.

What is missing from this depiction, and without which it is impossible to understand how Morocco sailed through the recent crises, is the role of those relying on bread every day. This chapter seeks to fill that gap. In her history of flour and meat production and distribution in modern Morocco, Holden (2009) establishes the historical connection between the urban poor and the Alaouite monarchy. In particular, in the nineteenth and twentieth centuries, the government focused on urban food supply to secure the loyalty of workers and the poor, the masses on whom its authority rests. She describes this form of loyalty as: 'Participatory paternalism whereby the state heeds the specific needs of its people and bases its policy on *their system of moral values as well as their practical knowledge about the local economy*' (ibid. 13, emphasis added). In the next section I will show that participatory paternalism still rules strong despite decades of economic liberalization. I will show in particular how without women's knowledge and work to make *gemh* flour and homemade bread, low-income families would not be able to eat what they consider good bread and how the absence of such bread could critically destabilize the Moroccan government. In providing cheap *fors* flour to stretch homemade *gemh* flour, the government, in turn, allows low-income Moroccans to materially and symbolically uphold these important practices.

Provisioning and Processing Wheat: Crafting Cereal Citizenship

One day in spring 2013, Rachida invited me to watch her clean the grains that her parents had brought with them from the Haouz the week before. She poured the brown-yellowish *gemh* grains into a large bucket placed under the running tab in her small shower cubicle and then briefly rubbed the grains between her flat hands to separate the chaff from the grains. With a sieve, she scooped off the chaff that was floating on the water. She repeated this process three times and then inspected a handful of grains between her fingers. She was satisfied and called Ibtissam to help her take the heavy, wet bag of grains to the roof terrace and spread them in the sun to dry. Although she could have bought *gemh* flour, Rachida specified: 'I like doing this. It's better to do all this at home to know what's in it.' She explained that *gemh* flour from the store was not good quality; it was ground too fine and did not come with the *nukhala* (bran flakes) of the milled grains that was necessary to shape the bread into the widely preferred large flat loaves. To illustrate, she placed a handful of store-bought *gemh* flour, so-called 'fino', in my hand and let my fingers feel the softness of it. 'It is too soft and does not go with the *fors*, which is also soft and makes the whole bread too soft. [For bread] I prefer the rough texture and the taste of *beldi* flour', she concluded.

Rachida dressed herself and we left the house to buy *fors* flour. As soon as we turned from the quiet and narrow *derb* (a small, often dead-end alley) into the busy *suiqa* (local market), Rachida tightened the grip on her handbag, cast down her gaze and sped up her pace. She motioned for me to follow her by pulling gently at my sleeve. Her stride was firm as we walked past the extending tarpaulin of vegetables and fruits on display along the street. She aimed for the dry goods shop at the other end of the *suiqa*, where they stocked Maimouna, her favourite brand of *fors* flour. Without bargaining, since the price of commercial flour was fixed, Rachida bought a 10 kg bag, which we carried between us in a large shopping bag that she had brought from home.

When I visited the next time, Rachida told me how she had processed the *gemh* further: she had covered the floor underneath the low table in the salon, then spread a portion of the rinsed and dried grains on the low table and began, portion after portion, to rub the remaining chaff off the grains by pressing and rubbing her flat palms together. After this, she explained, she had asked her husband Mohamed to bring the cleaned grains to the *tahuna* (local electric mill) just outside her *derb*. The only remaining task, Rachida cheerfully reported, was to sieve the freshly milled wholemeal flour to separate the *nukhala*, a precious byproduct that poorer households often received for free from their local *tahuna*. As she went to the task of doing so in her kitchen, she marvelled at the positive health effects of bran-coated bread.

*　*　*

This vignette highlights the bodily knowledge and work invested in homemaking good bread and flour and expresses the desire to remain in control of the family's food along the entire food chain. In doing so, recently urbanized Moroccans like Rachida re-create their taste for *beldi* flour in the city (see Chapter 4). Their elaborate practices of provisioning and processing *gemh* grains symbolically and materially connect their bodies both to rural Morocco and to their government. In doing so, they become important political actors, albeit from within the largely invisible space of the home. While Morocco appears to have liberalized in economic terms – if not democratizing (Maghraoui 2002) – turning the urban middle and upper classes into 'citizen consumers' (Newcomb 2017) or into an alienated 'global middle class' (Cohen 2004), the moral values and practical knowledge of low-income urban Moroccans like Rachida around bread continue to shape not only the Moroccan food system but also a political system that is still based on the old social contract of providing basic food security in return for political legitimacy. The mutual dependence that is implicit in participatory paternalism is captured in the notion of 'cereal citizenship'. 'Cereal' refers to the multiple entanglements that are re-created through repeatedly provisioning and processing grains into flour and making good bread. 'Citizen' refers to how in doing so, low-income Marrakchis, in particular domestic cooks, contribute to political stability through what food Holden calls 'participatory paternalism' (2009).[9] Thus, cereal citizens not only ensure their own bodies and their families are well, but also contribute to maintaining vital urban food infrastructures, the Moroccan food system and political stability at large.

To understand the workings of cereal citizenship, it is important to distinguish between *fors* and *gemh*. The widespread practice of mixing *fors* with *gemh* symbolizes and materializes the mutual but ambivalent shaping of everyday practices and political-economic forces in the Moroccan food system. Rachida explicated this most clearly: '*Beldi* [here: locally provisioned and homemade] flour gives the taste and texture, *fors* flour allows you to stretch and knead the bread.' Every domestic cook I worked with cared deeply about where their flour came from and associated the provenance of wheat with specific values and practices. Certain regions, such as Sidi Ismail in the Tadla plains or Rahhemna in the Haouz, were renowned for the high-quality, non-irrigated grains they produced – qualities my research participants were able to taste (see Figure 5.2). When urban cooks had the financial means, they provisioned *gemh* through their relatives in the countryside like Rachida or, if that failed due to a lack of occasion or contact, in the weekly grain or wholesale market (*al-jumela*) in the city (see Figure 5.1). Despite their limited financial and temporal resources, the households I interviewed during my research preferably sourced *gemh* in the form of grains and processed them at home as described above. They made these efforts even though every dry goods shop sells *fino*, the industrially processed flour of *gemh* that is cheaper than homemade *gemh* flour.[10] As the notion of *beldi* in the previous chapters suggested, *gemh* was associated with the rural lives many urban Moroccans have left behind when moving to the city in the 1980s and 1990s and thus also harboured important nonmaterial values. Homemade *gemh* symbolically re-created ties to

Figure 5.2. Small-scale *gemh* farming in the Haouz, near Marrakech, 2018. © Katharina Graf

rural foodways and constitutes a key element of recently urbanized Moroccans' identity (Graf 2018).

By contrast, *fors* is mostly produced on irrigated, large-scale farms in northwest Morocco and benefits from various governmental support schemes to reduce the need for imported wheat.[11] My research participants bought *fors* in the form of industrially refined soft flour. It was added in order to stretch the more expensive and precious *gemh*. In the words of one interviewee in Beni Mellal: 'If you don't mix it, you don't eat.' Due to governmental price fixing, *fors* flour was significantly more affordable than *gemh*. Even though many of the higher-quality brands are fortified with minerals and vitamins, and marketed as such, most urban consumers were suspicious of this commercial flour's whiteness. Similar to past and present consumers comparing homemade to industrial bread in North America (Bobrow-Strain 2012) or Europe (Aistara 2014), they suspected the use of bleach and other toxic chemicals. Indeed, in the absence of standardized food labelling, it was impossible for low-income Moroccans to identify the origins of this flour and of other *rumi* (here: imported) products (see Chapter 4). In the words of Fatima, whom I interviewed in 2018: 'Who knows where *fors* is from, Midelt [a commercial brand], Spain or America?! Nobody knows where it's from!' *Fors* thus constitutes at once an affordable means to stretch homemade flour and a suspicious, undesirable ingredient in the daily staple food.

In combining both in their homemade bread, domestic cooks become cereal citizens and thus central participants in Morocco's relative political stability. Indeed, I furthermore propose that because of its cereal citizens, Morocco has not suffered from the same levels of political instability as its Arab neighbours have in the last decade. Although both Jordan's and Egypt's governments have a similar history of guaranteeing access to cheap bread, their urban consumers in Amman and Cairo, as Martinez (2022) and Barnes (2022) describe respectively, have long given up making their own bread. Both authors show how central good *baladi* (here meaning subsidized) bread and those who ensure its quality are in legitimizing the respective governments. Yet, both countries have also suffered from political upheavals and undergone unprecedented policy reforms around their staple foods. Perhaps it is not too far-fetched to conclude that, in establishing subsidized, commercially produced bread as the national staple food, the Jordanian and Egyptian governments have decoupled political stability from the much less governable practices of domestic cooks. In both cases it is too early to say whether these reforms will improve the lives of their poor urban majorities, but it is evident from the respective ethnographic descriptions that poverty and uncertainty are unlikely to disappear anytime soon. In comparison to the highly regulated work that Jordanian bakers and Egyptian consumers of *baladi* bread do to make their staple food and thus their government palatable, low-income urban Moroccans emerge as important participants in their government's paternalist and authoritarian rule. As we follow bread further, from the agricultural countryside into the city, the ambiguity of their participation becomes yet more tangible.

Baking Bread: Maintaining the Urban Food Infrastructure

It was mid-morning at the end of June 2013. I made my way down the narrow staircase from our first-floor flat and stepped into the sunny *derb*, the aluminium tray tucked under my right arm, feeling the rough texture of the cloth that wrapped the unbaked bread loaves. The sun was so hot already that I immediately sought the shade along the walls. I was on my way to the *ferran* (public oven), for the first time bringing Aicha's two freshly kneaded bread loaves to bake there (see Figure 5.3). I felt the heat radiating from the thick adobe walls that line the narrow *derb* and smelled our neighbours' lunch preparations. I followed the quiet *derb* until it joined the busy *zenqa* and I dove into the dense concoction of smells, sounds and sights so particular to the larger streets of Marrakech's medina at this time; the penetrating gases and noises of speeding scooters first, closely followed by the hawking cries of street peddlers and, finally, the subtler perfumes of the visually appealing fruit and vegetable shops.

142 *Food and Families in the Making*

Figure 5.3. Baker wielding homemade bread loaves at a small *ferran* (public oven), Marrakech, 2013. © Katharina Graf

I had to slow down and adjust my walking pace to the dense flow of bodies, donkey carts, scooters and minitrucks that delivered fresh food products to the many market spaces within the medina walls; my heart beat accelerated momentarily. No more than ten steps and I separated from that flow again, lowered my head, entered an open door on my left and stepped four steps down into a dimly lit single room. The shadowy and still air that welcomed me stood in sharp contrast to the bright and busy street. The delicious smell of burning palm wood and baking bread filled my nostrils, my stomach reacted instantly with hungry growling. I had arrived at the *ferran*. I greeted the baker who stood in a hole that levelled him with the oven's open mouth, wielding a long wooden peel to manoeuvre bread in and out of the two metre-long oven. I informed him of the state of proofing of Aicha's loaves and, heeding his suggestion, placed the tray in the indicated spot in a queue of similar trays on the flour.[12] Within seconds, I was on my way home again. As I turned into our small *derb* and saw the tiny corner shop, I remembered to buy half a litre of fresh milk for the coffee that Aicha had begun to prepare when I had left. The smell of coffee guided my last steps back.

* * *

Bringing bread to the public oven is possibly the most public act of domestic food preparation in Marrakech. This movement symbolically and materially

Figure 5.4. Homemade bread ready to be picked up from the *ferran*, Marrakech, 2013. © Katharina Graf

marks the rhythms of everyday life and through it maintains vital elements of the urban food infrastructure. No matter where I was in the city, nearly every morning I saw women, men or children carrying freshly kneaded bread loaves wrapped in coloured cloth on wooden trays on their heads or tucked under their arms. Unless one followed the bearers of bread, it was often impossible to spot public ovens, as they were hidden behind and below indistinguishable doors along both quiet *druba* (plural of *derb*) and busy *zenqat* (plural of *zenqa*) in the medina. They are among the oldest buildings, often below street level. As the neighbouring houses were being built and rebuilt over the centuries, and their debris slowly raised the overall street level, public ovens have largely withstood material change (Wilbaux 2001). Their age is thus still perceptible today, because one invariably has to climb down a few steps from street level to enter. Even in the new, purpose-built quarters in Marrakech's growing grid-like peripheries, public ovens were still built and constituted thriving nodal points of the daily movement of food and people. Their operation was closely attuned to the daily domestic preparation of food. Many women began the day by kneading bread, letting it rise while they ate breakfast and bringing the leavened loaves to the *ferran* on their way to the market or to work. A couple of hours later, a family member picked up the freshly baked bread on the way home for lunch (see Figure 5.4). The rhythms around baking bread at the public oven gave the most tangible sense of continuity of urban food infrastructures and of everyday life in Marrakech, and defy accounts of their demise.

'Whereas going to the public oven used to be the only way to bake daily bread, private ovens are now common. Young women no longer want to deliver leavening bread in the morning and pick it up before lunch; they prefer to own a gas oven, for prestige and convenience' (Kapchan 1996: 14). For Kapchan, working in Beni Mellal, the demise of the public oven is closely connected to the growing preference for modern flats in purpose-built quarters. Greiman (2012: 61, 63) speaks of similar changes in the city of Fes, north of Marrakech: 'The public oven is quickly disappearing from Moroccan streets. The fate of the furan [*ferran*], as well as homemade bread, highlights the broader social change occurring across Morocco ... as Moroccan women have emerged into the workforce, either out of choice or out of necessity.' Indeed, the question over the use of the public oven – and the baking of homemade bread – reflects processes of material and social change in urban Morocco, albeit in different ways than these authors suggest. Public ovens – and the laborious preparation of homemade bread that warrants their existence – were far from 'disappearing' in Marrakech. Their continuous relevance in everyday domestic food preparation and their role in the urban food infrastructure further contextualize the complex entanglements between local and global processes, rural and urban places, and between low-income bodies and their government.

My fieldwork took me to three Marrakchi neighbourhoods. The first two were located in the medina, in Riad Zitoun in the south and in Bab Ailen in the east. The third was located in Socoma, in Marrakech's rapidly growing frontier in the far west. As the name suggests, Riad Zitoun (olive grove) is leafy and less dense than other medina quarters. Due to its location between the central marketing area around Jemaa el-fna in the north and the formerly Jewish Mellah and the royal residence in the south, it is a highly frequented and busy marketing area. Owing furthermore to its rich historic architecture, Riad Zitoun attracts foreign residents and tourists since the 1980s and has been one of the first medina neighbourhoods to benefit from paved streets and individual connections to running water and electricity (Ernst 2013).[13] At the same time, tourist boutiques and the opening of yet another tourist café drove out businesses aimed at its low-income residents. In the course of one year, I witnessed the transformation of a local *hanut* (small corner shop) frequented by Fatimzahra and of a vegetable shop frequented by Aicha into tiny tourist boutiques. My research participants judged this change according to their stakes in the tourist economy. While Hajja and Fatimzahra regretted to see their neighbourhood turned over to the tourist economy, and eventually sold their *riad* to a foreigner and moved to Socoma like many of their neighbours, Aicha and her husband benefited from increasing streams of tourists.

Bab Ailen is named after the gate (*bab*) that connects the medina with the adjacent rural hinterland of Marrakech, the Haouz, once reputedly the grain basket of the whole country (Pascon 1986). Now the Haouz supplies Marrakech's food markets with cereals, fruits and vegetables (Pennell 2000). Despite its reputation as a *cha'abi* (popular, traditional) neighbourhood that is home to poor migrant Imazighen from the Haouz, Bab Ailen is changing rapidly like the rest of the medina. In 2012 and 2013 I witnessed how nearly the entire quarter was equipped with new pipes and each *derb* paved with mortar and bricks. Almost every small house was being rebuilt in cement and the whole neighbourhood looked like a single construction site. In 2017 Rachida was finally able to secure a government grant to rebuild her small adobe house in cement just like her neighbours had done in 2013 (thus saving her house from damage during the earthquake in September 2023). Despite these material signs of change, the ongoing importance of and connections to the agricultural hinterland were still noticeable in Bab Ailen. For instance, on my way to Rachida's house in the early mornings, I often passed a small vehicle at the entrance to her *derb* delivering raw milk from the Haouz. The comparatively large gate and streets of Bab Ailen materially invited the many vehicles and people from outside the city and thus enabled exchange between urban and rural space (see Chapter 4).

After only a couple of years in existence in 2012, Socoma resembled other purpose-built quarters that mushroom all over Marrakech's periphery in their grid-like material layout and their multi-storey apartment blocks. For those who can afford to move, these neighbourhoods provide more space and privacy than the medina and other older neighbourhoods, while offering the comfort of air-conditioning and a parking lot for those wealthy enough to own a family car. At first glance, Socoma appears to mark a contrast to the medina and the daily life within it. Yet, at peak marketing times of the day, residents gathered in great numbers to cruise the *suiqa* just like in the medina, inspecting the fresh food delivered via mule-drawn carts or on trucks from the agricultural hinterlands; together they blocked local traffic during the late morning and early evening hours (see Figure 5.5). When following the ebb and flow of food as it moved through this neighbourhood, the multisensory experience of everyday life was surprisingly similar to the medina. In both new neighbourhoods such as Socoma and old ones in the medina, the combined movement of food and the everyday practices of people sourcing and processing food determine the urban space in ways that are not accounted for when planning the city.[14]

From Fatimzahra's perspective, it was not the existence of private ovens or modern apartments that prompted urban change, but the tourist economy and a lack of centralized urban planning that endangered the continuous movement of people and foods across the city. She did not bake her bread at the *ferran*, although she also preferred bread baked with palm wood. Fatimzahra blamed her

Figure 5.5. Socoma, one of many newly built neighbourhoods, Marrakech, 2012. © Katharina Graf

choice of baking at home on the disappearance of public ovens in her medina neighbourhood. The only *ferran* that remained in her *zenqa* was more than a ten-minute walk away, too far for her to walk every day. This prompted her to complain: 'In Riad Zitoun everything on the *zenqa* is now for tourists, and we have to walk further to bake our bread.' I asked her whether there was a public oven in Socoma. 'Of course there is! There has to be a *ferran* in every quarter!' According to her, public ovens did not disappear because Moroccan residents no longer needed them, but because economically more viable tourist businesses were allowed to replace everyday commerce in tourist hotspots of the medina such as her (former) neighbourhood Riad Zitoun.[15]

Still, in most residential neighbourhoods of Marrakech, the *ferran* remains a material marker of continuity in the context of change. The reasons for still using the public oven are more complex than those suggested by Kapchan (1996) or Greiman (2012) and link the urban food infrastructure to the wider food system. Although Aicha mentioned that she enjoyed going out at every occasion, this was not her main motivation to use the *ferran*. While most owned a private gas oven, all women I worked with over the years claimed that the main motivation for using the palm wood-fired public oven was that homemade bread baked in them tasted better. Whenever possible, they preferred to bake their bread there. This preference was part of a broader desire to control the foods they consume.

Eating Bread: Shaping the Moroccan Body

At the beginning of my fieldwork in October 2012, when I was still living and working with Hajja, Aicha invited me to her newly rented flat. She proudly showed me around the small apartment made from grey concrete, with windows that overlooked the *derb*, a rarity in the medina at the time, where the predominant old adobe houses opened towards an inner courtyard rather than towards the street. She finished the tour next to a brand-new sporting machine, which I had almost stumbled over when entering the flat – a sight even less common than the outward-facing windows. Aicha confessed, slightly angered by the machine as if its mere presence accused her: 'I am too fat, look at me! I need to do sports to lose weight after Rita's birth.' When I moved in with her and her family in late May 2013, the sporting machine still looked brand-new, but it had moved to a less assuming place in the flat. I enquired whether she had managed to lose weight. 'Aww, I don't have the time! I am too tired at the end of the day; working here, working there, the girls always by my side. Anyways, I eat too much bread. Moroccans eat too much bread!'

Upon a return visit in March 2017, as I prepared for my fieldwork around bread, Aicha similarly showed me around her newly rented flat. This one had a larger salon, 'to invite more people', and a bit more space for the fourth child she was expecting that month. It was fairly early in the day and despite her swollen body, she insisted on serving me her bread, which she knew well I had missed since my last visit. Holding her belly, she slowly bent over to pull out yesterday's bread from underneath the gas oven, where she kept it inside the *qesriya* (a large earthenware plate for kneading bread) in a plastic bag; at least until the fresh bread she had already kneaded would return with her husband from the public oven for lunch. She cut a quarter into half, grilled it briefly in a pan on the gas hob and served it with *beldi* olive oil and coffee. We sat down to chat. 'You know, I am thinking of making my own starter culture for bread, to make it even healthier. I was listening to a radio programme the other day, explaining how to make our bread more nutritious. My mother used to have one, you know, with the stone of a date in it and only wholemeal *gemh*. It was delicious. We didn't have industrial yeast in the village.' When it was time for her to go to work that morning – which she was intent on doing right until birth – Aicha concluded: 'Bread is so important; bread is our life.'

* * *

This vignette highlights the central but ambiguous place that bread holds in everyday life and the role that knowledge plays in handling it. Bread and other wheat products provide more than 50% of the average daily calorie intake per person, making Moroccans one of the most wheat-dependent nations in the world (Benjelloun 2002; Garcia-Closas, Berenguer and Gonzalez 2006). Yet, although the Moroccan food system provides its population with enough calories based on soft wheat, between 2017 and 2019, food insecurity affected on average a quarter of Moroccans (FAO et al. 2020: 165).[16] This high proportion is largely due to a recent redefinition of food insecurity as malnutrition not only in the form of hunger und undernourishment but also in the form of overweight and obesity.[17] This situation reflects the global trend of stagnating (high) levels of hunger *and* rising levels of overweight and obesity. Previously established correlations between low income and malnutrition no longer hold; noncommunicable diseases are on the rise across all income groups in Morocco.[18] Given its centrality in everyday diets, the daily bread and the breadmaking body take centre stage in perceptions and markers of poverty and health. Disentangling bread and the practices that produce it allows us to see the many substances and meanings of wellbeing beyond normative and one-dimensional understandings of health as nutrition.

There are three main types of bread low-income Marrakchis consume regularly. The most valued one is the large homemade flatbread (*khubz dyel dar*), usually containing yeast, water, salt, a mixture of *fors* and *gemh* flour, and a coating of *nukhala*. It is typically prepared daily in the morning, baked at the local *ferran* or in some cases at home and served with lunch, the most important meal of the day (see Figure 5.4). Many families also buy commercially baked baguette (*kumir*) from their local *hanut* or from a public oven that also makes and sells bread. Baguette is only sold and served for breakfast, often before the homemade bread is ready. It contains 100% *fors* and is preferred by children because of its sweetness and softness. It is decried for its lack of nutrients, fibre and taste by their mothers. Lastly, a variety of small round loaves are bought whenever homemade bread is insufficient or unavailable, for instance, when guests show up unexpectedly or as a convenient snack.[19] The standard and cheapest store-bought bread (*khubz 'adi*) consists of 100% *fors* and a coating of fine semolina. Through fieldwork until the time of revising this text in mid-2023, its price was fixed at 1.2 dirham. Often it contains sugar to aid leavening and was described as 'grey', 'bland' or 'empty' food by my research participants. It is particularly popular among (unemployed) young men. Furthermore, a commercial baker told me that most of this bread is actually delivered directly to restaurants. But store-bought bread can also contain *gemh* or barley flour. In some neighbourhoods in Marrakech – and in the case of Beni Mellal on many corners of the street – female peddlers sold small quantities of large homemade loaves for 4 dirham. This bread is considered almost as good as self-made bread; it is purchased by women whose long hours of wage work prevent them from baking during the working week, but who cannot afford a housemaid.

Due to the continued importance of bread in everyday cuisine and hospitality, the Moroccan diet has undergone a rather different nutrition transition compared to other countries (Batnitzky 2008; cf. Popkin 1998). In her nutritional study,

Benjelloun (2002) describes the main changes of the Moroccan diet: between 1990 and 1998, when wages grew relative to inflation, Moroccans consumed more animal products and oils. At the same time, the consumption of cereals and sugar remained steady due to 'dietary habits' such as dipping bread in sauce and drinking sweetened tea. In fact, Benjelloun (2002: 137) observed that with the economic betterment of a household and an increased intake of meat and vegetables, cereal consumption also increased, since bread is served with nearly every meal.[20] The result is an overall growing intake of calories, yet without necessarily improving diets from a nutritional perspective. Coupled with increased urbanization since the 1980s and a change towards a less physically active lifestyle, this contributed to overweight and obesity in children and adults, especially among urban women. Her research confirms not only that bread is the most affordable staple food for most low-income Moroccans but also that it remains culturally significant across class, despite material and social change. To recall the previous chapter, bread and wheat are the smallest common denominator of Moroccan cuisine. Homemade bread and other cereal-based dishes thus also carry immense symbolic weight.

In this chapter I emphasize the more material dimensions of bread, most notably how the type and quality of flour matter to perceived and actual health and wellbeing. MacPhee's (2004: 388) rural Moroccan interlocutors expressed my own research participants' suspicions when referring to industrially processed soft white bread, the only one that is controlled and subsidized by the Moroccan government, as 'plastic bread' devoid of nutrients, fibre, texture and taste: 'I eat a lot of this bread but I'm still hungry.' Most of our respective interviewees complained about constipation caused by 'white' flour and contrasted this with the health benefits of wholemeal *gemh* flour, mostly related to improved digestion and a longer-lasting feeling of physical satiation. Although some of the commercially available *fors* flours are fortified and certified according to the standards created by the International Organization for Standards (ISO), most of my research participants explained that they cannot afford these higher-grade branded products and have to resort to middle or lower-grade products, which adhere to less clear standards.[21] These perceptions were commonly expressed to justify why low-income cooks strove to make their own bread and added homemade *gemh* flour whenever they could afford to.[22] Interviews were often concluded by stating that homemade *gemh* flour has *baraka* (God's blessing) (see Chapters 1 and 4). Yet only together could *gemh* and *fors* ensure everyday wellbeing and food security.

In addition to their own bodily experience of good bread, through their lived experience in the city as well as via radio, television and, increasingly, social media, low-income Moroccans gradually incorporate new forms of knowledge about food standards, nutrition and the role of food for health. Nearly every family I worked with throughout my research in both rural and urban Morocco had at least one family member affected by diabetes, high cholesterol levels or high blood pressure and recounted how they had to adapt their everyday food preparation to counter the health risks. Foods such as wholemeal flour, fruits and fish – alongside physical activity – were identified as a main source of health and wellbeing.[23] Many of my research participants sought to prepare and consume a balanced diet that takes account of the role of fibre, minerals and vitamins for a healthy life. Yet, healthy foods, however they are defined, are still hard to come by, as the event on 19 November illustrates.[24] Indeed, the national subsidy system for wheat is almost exclusively based on *fors* and thus still adheres to a calorie-based understanding of diet and nutrition that disregards vernacular as well as scientific understandings of wellbeing and good health.[25] In this context, and as the notion of *beldi* foodways in Chapter 4 demonstrated, domestic cooks' bodily efforts to provision and prepare good food remain crucial instruments of family insurance against health risks, illness and death.

Conclusion: Life and Death

The stampede and the ethnographic examples given throughout this chapter illustrate to what extent low-income Moroccans reflect upon and actively engage in the Moroccan food system. The Marrakchi women I worked with closely followed domestic harvests and Morocco's trade relations, and their impact on domestic food prices, and thus their everyday survival. Countless conversations throughout years of fieldwork revealed that domestic cooks were keenly aware of the effects of the government's dual approach to agriculture, favouring export over domestic production, and how it affected their everyday diet. For instance, when she came back from a shopping trip in Socoma early in September 2012, Fatimzahra told me that flour and bread prices were expected to rise during the coming year because of a poor domestic cereal harvest in the preceding agricultural season. Instead of 50 dirham for a 10 kg bag of soft flour, vendors would soon have to ask 60 dirham, she reported.[26] I mentioned that I had read that even the North American cereal harvest was not as good as usual, to which she replied: 'That's even worse, because they help Morocco with cereals.'

At the same time, most Marrakchis viewed export negatively. For instance, according to Fatimzahra, in January 2013 the prices of tomatoes were much higher than they should be, '[e]ven though they are in season'. When I asked her to explain why, she pointed the finger at me accusingly and said: 'You Europeans get all our good tomatoes and we have to pay more but for bad tomatoes.'[27] From television and radio as well as conversations with shopkeepers and marketers, she knew, like many other Marrakchi women, of the pending trade negotiations between Morocco and the European Union, and presumed that this process was driven by demand and thus higher-income consumers like me. This sentiment was especially strong with respect to fresh foods such as fruits, vegetables and sardines – the main source of omega-3 that low-income Moroccans could afford, which they were well aware of – and directly reflects the described policies favouring large-scale (irrigated) production for export to the detriment of small-scale (rainfed) production for the domestic market. In this context, it is not surprising that low-income Moroccans continue to rely on cheap flour and remain ambivalent about bread. My research participants understood the changing Moroccan body as reflective of this broader political economy of food.

This chapter also showed how through cultivating and reproducing the moral values and the relevant bodily knowledge around the production, distribution and processing of two such distinct grains and flours into bread, low-income urban Moroccans generally, and women in particular, contribute to a fragile but effective form of everyday food security. The stampede in 2017 is an unprecedented example of this life-giving work and how it can end life at the same time. It symbolizes both the ongoing importance of staple foods for the life and death of Morocco's still too large low-income population and the knowledgeable work it takes to prepare it in culturally meaningful ways, ensuring poor families' wellbeing and health in the absence of affordable healthy foods.

This knowledgeable work around flour and homemade bread in Marrakech also distinguishes the Moroccan case from other regional food systems based on bread, most notably in urban Egypt and Jordan, where bread has long since come from the store (Barnes 2022; Martinez 2022). In their detailed ethnography of provisioning bread, Barnes and Taher (2019) argue that through caring for *baladi* bread in the process of conveying it from the shop to the home – through airing, stacking, packing, choosing or returning it – Cairene women, men and children care for their families. This 'casual care' (Barnes and Taher 2019: 437) helps to explain why low-income Egyptians' expectations towards their government for good bread are met. By inversion, in doing so, these ordinary people can also be considered to (unwittingly) care for their government; 'palatable' bread makes for a palatable government (cf. Caldwell 2014). If bread from the store can express the symbolic and material work of low-income urbanites towards economic and political stability, then surely the work of those who *make* their own flour and bread, as low-income Moroccans do, bespeaks a remarkable level of involvement in shaping their own bodies, their families, their city and their government.

Notes

1. For instance, when finding a piece of bread on the ground, most Moroccans would pick it up, kiss it and place it somewhere high, closer to God. Leftover bread is either soaked in water and fed to the birds on the rooftop or donated to a mobile peddler who collects old bread and sells it as animal feed.
2. Fieldwork for this project was carried out between December 2016 and November 2018 during three separate trips and with assistance from Monia Alazali from the University of Cadi Ayyad. She found and contacted fifteen low-income households in Marrakech and

Beni Mellal and joined me for all interviews with them. Field visits, participant observation and interviews with bakers, millers, traders and farmers were mostly carried out without her help. For more details, see: https://www.axa-research.org/en/project/katharina-graf (retrieved 18 September 2023).
3. They are not alone, as studies in Rabat (Dike 2021) and rural Morocco (Crawford 2008; MacPhee 2004) confirm.
4. *Fors* is the plural of *farisi*, meaning Persian (*bled al-fors* denotes Persia). In Marrakech *fors* denotes only the flour. In Beni Mellal *fors* is also used to describe the grain. I thus specify whether I mean the flour or grains of *fors*. *Gemh* is the generic Modern Standard Arabic term for wheat. In Morocco it refers to the grains and to homemade, wholemeal flour, hence why I specify which of the two I mean.
5. In Beni Mellal, a *fors* growing region since the French Protectorate, many interviewees preferred to source *fors* in the form of grains, called *farina* (referencing the French term *farine* for flour), and processed *farina* like *gemh* to circumvent the flour industry altogether.
6. Although dubbed subsidies, the regulation of wheat through the system of the *caisse de compensation* relies on a complex system of flexible import tariffs, agricultural extension, governmental administration of storage and milling as well as price controls of grains and *fors*-only bread. They also mark the attempt to keep jobs in the agricultural sector: although it produces only 14% of GDP, agriculture employs around 40% of the national labour force (Telleria Juarez and Dhehibi 2017). Keeping these jobs is crucial to slowing rural to urban migration and thus to countering rising rates of urban unemployment (cf. Crawford 2008; Sippel 2014). By contrast, the domestic *gemh* value-chain is not regulated by the government.
7. See also Harrigan and El-Said (2010) for a comparative approach to the impact of IMF and World Bank programmes in Middle East/North Africa (MENA) countries. The authors further describe the positive correlation between agricultural performance and economic growth in Morocco, which suggests the ongoing importance of agriculture to economic and political stability.
8. On average, 50% of the roughly 10 million metric tons of domestically consumed *fors* is imported annually, depending on rainfall and domestic production (Akesbi 2014; United States Department of Agriculture 2020).
9. Cereal citizenship echoes Martinez's (2022) experiential approach to the state as performed in and through mundane everyday practices, and thus differs from more mainstream political scientists' understanding of civil society as constituted through deliberate public protest (Hegasy 1997; Sater 2007).
10. During fieldwork *fino* cost 6–8 dirham per kilogram. After deducting weight loss in the form of chaff, small stones and sand, and including the cost of transport – often a reduced bus fare or petrol for a borrowed scooter – and milling, the price per kilogram of *gemh* flour processed by hand is nearly double that of commercial *fino*. This calculation does not consider the time and energy it takes or the cost of electricity and water to process grains (and neither does it include the price increases of *gemh* grains, along with food in general, since early 2023).
11. Despite this, the domestic production of *fors* cannot keep up with increased consumption due to population growth and urbanization (Arrisueno et al. 2016).
12. In small public ovens like this one, the baker manages both the queuing and the baking of several hundreds of loaves alone. He recognizes a household's bread by the colour of

the wrapping cloth and the size of the loaves. I only once witnessed a mismatched batch of baked bread. Regular customers pay a monthly fee, so no money is exchanged in daily transactions. Larger public ovens also make their own bread for sale, in which case an assistant manages the queues of private and commercial loaves.
13. Tourists and foreign residents have different effects on medina space. The movement of tourists is naturally restricted by the impenetrable maze of the many *druba* throughout the medina and centralized around Jemaa el-fna and adjacent *zenqat* (Schmidt 2005). In these areas tourist boutiques outnumber daily needs shops. Foreign residents, by contrast, live across the entire medina and their engagement has often contributed to the improvement of sanitation, road infrastructure and safety (cf. Ernst 2013).
14. This argument follows de Certeau's (1984) assertion that 'practised place' is made every day by those who move through it. For de Certeau, it is not the institutional and physical structure of space embodied in the infrastructure of signs, streets and traffic regulation, but the anti-discipline that constitutes it; the often hidden, habitual practices of ordinary people. This devious form of production is not manifest in products or material place, but in the ways of using them, echoing phenomenological theories of space (Casey 1997).
15. The newly built *ferran* in Socoma is less than a five-minute walk away from their new home. Yet, Fatimzahra continued baking her bread at home. The bodily pain she suffered due to her disability made her carefully weigh up every decision to leave the house.
16. On average, 4.3% of all Moroccans were affected by severe food insecurity in the form of undernourishment between 2017 and 2019. A total of 26.1% of all adults and 10.9% of all children under five were affected by overweight and obesity in 2016 and 2019 respectively (FAO et al. 2020: 165).
17. The way in which malnutrition is understood has changed over time. It used to be equated with hunger, i.e. a lack of calories or macronutrients. More recently, the FAO widened its definition to include overweight and obesity, i.e. a lack of micronutrients despite an abundance of calories (Carolan 2013; FAO et al. 2020). See Yates-Doerr (2015) for an anthropological critique of the implied ethnocentricity in understanding and discussing diet and health. Critical nutrition studies provide interdisciplinary critiques of normative definitions of healthy foods and diets (Guthman 2014).
18. In the 1990s overweight and diabetes were predominant among the middle- and upper-income groups, but today they increasingly affect all income groups (Benjelloun 2002; Global Nutrition Report 2020).
19. It is common to buy additional bread for guests, since considerate visitors do not announce their visit in order to avoid that their hosts feel obliged to prepare a lavish meal as Moroccan rules of hospitality prescribe.
20. Per capita consumption of wheat doubled from 138 kg/person/year in 1960 to 288 kg/person/year in 2019 (Telleria Juarez and Dhehibi 2017; United States Department of Agriculture 2019).
21. The lowest-grade flour available in Morocco is called *farine nationale*, flour of variable provenance that the government stores and regulates as a security against drought or other crises. It is sold at nearly a quarter below market value. Until recently, it made up about 10% of national cereal consumption, but its share has been reduced to 7% and is expected to decrease even further (cf. United States Department of Agriculture 2020). Where and when this flour is processed, stored and distributed is heavily regulated. According to interviews I carried out between 2017 and 2018, even millers who process *farine nationale*

stressed the significantly lower quality of this usually old flour and admitted to stretching it with the byproducts of their commercial flour.

22. Two out of the 15 low-income Marrakchi households I interviewed between 2017 and 2018 considered it a luxury to make their own bread. Their limited financial resources allowed them to buy flour and yeast and pay for the public oven only once a week. According to their calculations, homemade bread was almost double the cost of subsidized *fors* bread (cf. Graf 2018).

23. However, physical activity outside of the home was deemed inappropriate for married women in Marrakech, and certainly for those with a low income. This stands in contrast to the Fassi middle class described by Newcomb (2009), for whom it was fashionable to subscribe to a women-only gym.

24. According to the FAO et al. (2020), a key reason for global malnutrition lies in the significantly higher price of a healthy diet, which less than half of the global population can afford. In Morocco, 13.1% of the total population cannot afford a healthy diet, which would make up 67.4% of all domestic expenditure (ibid.: 165). Given the ubiquity of informal markets and informal provisioning practices, these numbers likely underestimate the real cost of food.

25. This technical understanding of food security is not limited to Morocco and emerged with the second global food regime in the 1970s (Friedmann 1993). See also Carolan (2013) for a critical engagement with simplistic definitions of food security.

26. Indeed, that year the United States Department of Agriculture (2012) reported a poor harvest in Morocco in 2011 and 2012, raising the quantity of cereal import and thus government spending.

27. As also shown by Sippel (2014: 102).

CONCLUSION

Moroccans in the Making

A couple of days before the end of Ramadan, towards the end of my fieldwork, the thermometer was hovering around 45°C. The hot, dry air carried only silence into the courtyard. My stomach was growling of hunger and my tongue was dry, while I prepared French *crêpes* to break the daily fast (*al-ftour*). This was the hardest moment of the fasting day: I smelled, saw, felt and heard delicious foods and drinks in the making, yet had to restrain myself for a couple more hours before tasting them. Standing next to me, Halima, Aicha's visiting sister-in-law, was cutting lettuce and tomatoes for a small salad. Aicha had turned her back to us; she was already busy with dinner preparations, to be served a couple of hours after *al-ftour*, around midnight. We worked in silence; in the course of that month, we had established a routine.

It was only after *al-ftour*, when everyone had drank water and *harira* soup, eaten a date and a few *shebbakiya* biscuits, that we all revived and began to converse. As we proceeded to eat my *crêpes* and Halima's salad, amid the joyous cries of Halima's and Aicha's children running around the courtyard, Aicha and I talked about the purpose of fasting. When I asked her why she fasts, she explained:

> We fast not for us but for God. We try to show him that we are *qashiyn* [tough] and *sebbar* [patient]; that we can endure. The first four to five days are always difficult but then you get used to it. In the beginning your body has to adapt but then you feel good. People who don't stop smoking or drinking alcohol are not really fasting; many men are weak. I even know of some who don't fast, Moroccans! That's horrifying! I don't want to talk to such a person!

Aicha shook herself as if the idea of knowing or talking to a Moroccan Muslim who does not fast was making her physically unwell. She continued:

> During Ramadan people are not supposed to fight or to argue over things. And men should not disturb us women and vice versa. We should pray and think about God. . . . Allah wants us to see and feel how poor people feel every

day – not just during Ramadan – who have only tea and a bit of bread. He wants us to remember what it means to have few things to eat. When you prepare food during Ramadan you should make enough and share it with the poor; that way you gain more *baraka* [God's blessing]. You should realize how precious food is and be grateful for what you have!

* * *

In this conversation Aicha conveyed a strong sense of common belonging, based on a very individual but also shared bodily experience of being Moroccan, connected in the fasting body. At the same time, Aicha stressed differences: between those who fast and those who do not, between low-income families like her own and those she considered to be really poor, between those who have enough to eat and those who do not. The motivation to fast is a very personal and bodily act, yet in eating together at the setting of the sun, everyone shares food and feasts together. The daylight hours are spent quietly at work in the home and in the workplace, while at night the city teems with promenading families, visiting friends and countless beggars. The spiritual held these contradictions together, the daily realization that food is the most precious gift that God gives (*al-ni'ama*), an acutely felt appreciation of food's importance in everyday life and for everyone. Ramadan is intrinsically contradictory and hence provides an ideal way to conclude this book.

During Ramadan, a cook's taste knowledge was called on to make ever more food. Although nominally it is all about fasting, this month centres around food: during the day, domestic cooks are busy provisioning, processing and preparing good food; during the night, families and friends gather to eat, drink and spend time together. Everything that defines domestic cooking knowledge in low-income urban Morocco comes together, from the taste of the cook to the persisting scarcity of good food in the country. In Chapter 1 I argued that although taste knowledge refers to a cook's multisensory engagement with food and the wider material and social environment, including temporality as a sixth sense, it is equally shared with others. Thus, especially in the context of rapid material and social change, taste knowledge also refers to the broader cultural values associated with domestic cooking. Even though most low-income women worked for a wage to make ends meet, they continued to invest considerable time into making homemade food, because only food that has been cooked 'As long as it takes' is deemed good food. Rather than being transmitted or passed on from one generation to the next, these values are regrown in younger generations of cook through what I called participant perception in Chapter 2. Indeed, my own participant perception, recounted in the five interludes, proved the basis on which I was able to understand how domestic cooks know how to and learn cooking.

Ramadan was an unexpected occasion for me to fully join daily food preparation. Throughout my previous eleven months of fieldwork, I had been considered a novice cook, too inexperienced to replace Fatimzahra, Rachida or Aicha, and even a liability to their reputation (Chapter 3). Yet, within the first few days of Ramadan, my presumed expertise in European food preparation was suddenly incorporated into the daily preparations for *al-ftour*. I proposed various dishes and, once approved, prepared countless 'German' apple pies, *flammkuchen* (Alsatian pizza-like thin dough topped with cream, onions and bacon, in this case substituted with minced meat), 'French' *crêpes* and 'Italian' pizzas. I temporarily became a partner in planning, shopping, processing, cooking, baking, serving, cleaning and disposing of food. Ramadan reversed previously established routines and created new experiences.

To share the limited space, tools and appliances, my doughs and batters had to be coordinated with Aicha's doughs and batters. We became increasingly aware of the temporalities of each other's food in the making. Previously, Aicha had always attended to my tasks, to what I did with food, how and when, as all expert cooks do when cooking with others. During Ramadan, I, too, began to attend to her processes, for instance by taking over a gesture such as turning a *msemen* in the pan when she was busy with another task. Through the shared use of kitchen space, tools and appliances and our simultaneous and reciprocal engagement with food's multiple transformations, Aicha and I created a shared taste environment and reached a phenomenological unity similar to that between Hajja and Fatimzahra described in Chapter 1: once I became aware of Aicha's perception, I began to switch my focus to the objects of her perception and vice versa. Although she retained her position of lead cook and her taste guided our joint preparations, my own taste knowledge impacted on hers. The last step in achieving a shared taste environment was reached when one day I required nutmeg for making *flammkuchen*, but ours had finished. I went to ask our neighbour Rqia. Suddenly Aicha came out, too, and saw me waiting at Rqia's door. She started laughing and, when she had caught her breath, told me that she also wanted to ask Rqia for a missing item: 'That's it, now you're just like us, going around asking neighbours for this and that!' In relying on her social network to provision a missing food item, I temporarily incorporated Aicha's 'culinary connections'.

My participant perception allowed me to grasp that domestic cooking is learnt in more diverse ways than just through observation and instruction, often despite a novice's intention to learn, and that mothers or mothers-in-law are not the only ones who teach it. Instead, learning to cook takes many different forms and it begins long before a novice seeks to learn by simply growing up in a certain material and social environment, by 'being there' and playfully absorbing a taste of food with all her senses. This is the case for both girls *and* boys. When a learner more actively seeks to attune to her food environment, she bodily knows something already. And she needs to, for when she begins to engage with food in her first attempts to prepare a dish, 'food teaches' her as it transforms. Mothers and experienced cooks teach mainly through setting up situations for learning through 'replacement' and convey a broader set of values as they do so. As exemplified by Aicha's words, womanhood is still associated with the hardworking and patient wife and mother who spends hours every day preparing good food for her family. Although quietly questioned, these values are not (yet) actively challenged by younger low-income women. However, with the availability of new technologies such as blenders or smartphones, senior cooks are increasingly just one of many sources of expert knowledge, including neighbours and friends, but also cookbooks or social media. The reproduction of taste knowledge in contemporary Marrakech thus also reveals a reversal of knowledge flows from younger generations of cooks to older ones.

Again, it is Ramadan that brings forth the subtle negotiations around what constitutes expertise, womanhood and the family meal, as the example of *amlou* preparations in Chapter 3 showed. The shared experience of Ramadan emphasizes the family and the importance of a cook's culinary connectivity; cooking, commensality and love become one and the same thing. More food is prepared for more family members, friends and guests. To do so, lead cooks still enforce a strict management regime in the kitchen and reinforce the division of labour according to hierarchies of taste knowledge. Aicha had to coordinate Halima and myself in the kitchen – occasionally aided by her mother and her brother – and plan meals while keeping in mind the different preferences of all family members and the changing number of eaters. A cook's taste knowledge and social status are on display every day. Yet, simultaneously, Ramadan makes it possible to negotiate existing hierarchies of taste knowledge and create new social configurations, as Aicha's *amlou* and my own becoming as expert of European foods show respectively.

Indeed, only during Ramadan did my research participants realize that I, too, knew how to cook and that over the course of my fieldwork I had learned something from them. As I – literally and metaphorically – cooked my way into their families during Ramadan, I became more of a person; more than that, I became a specific person, a woman with a history, a family and a material and social place somewhere. Until then, as becomes both a researcher and an apprentice, I had asked everyone about their experiences and their perspectives and perceptions. Once I began fasting, feasting and properly cooking alongside these women and men, people began asking how and what *I* knew. Although arguably my motivations to fast were different, the acutely shared bodily experience of fasting – of fatigue and frustration, of hunger and thirst – and of feasting – the joy of tasting the first bite and drinking the first sip, ending with eating too fast and too much – was a bodily and intersubjective manifestation of just how much cooking and eating means being.

As I argued in the Introduction and described throughout the interludes, my experience of learning to cook suggests to embrace the bodiliness of learning and becoming for analytical purposes, and also constitutes an attempt to overcome some of the limits of representations resulting from more visual and verbal forms of ethnographic learning and knowing. As I stood sweating in the hot and moist kitchen alongside Aicha and Halima, preparing food for several hours without a break in the afternoon heat of Ramadan 2013 – exhausted from a lack of sleep and frustrated with not being able to taste, hungry and thirsty – I understood through/with/in my body that cooking and being in Marrakech is both a challenge and a joy. Sharing these moments, which were rarely made explicit verbally – nor could they have been – enabled me to feel and thereby grasp some of the sensations and contradictions that determine cooking knowledge and being a low-income woman in a changing Marrakech. Disembodying and re-embodying these feelings enabled me not only to think analytically about cooking-being and learning-becoming, but also to realize how much it shaped me along the way.

Cooking and being a woman in Marrakech is marked by negotiations and shifting understandings of the family. While women's taste knowledge is crucial to making good food, it is only through the investment of their bodies and their time that a meal can be considered proper and thus fulfil its central function of creating and maintaining a family and, in doing so, make them in turn. In Chapter 3 I demonstrated that although low-income women's education and wage work increases their financial independence, the family home remains their primary site of identification. Yet, what constitutes the ideal family home changes with women's financial independence, shifting away from the multigenerational household dominated by senior women and towards the conjugal household wherein young wives and mothers can realize their ideal of womanhood by being the lead (and often only) cook. To hone and improve their growing cooking knowledge in this context, women not only mobilize new social relations and new material sources of knowledge, but also inadvertently alter gender relations. Although food preparation is still marked by the ideal of complementarity between husband and wife even in the conjugal household, with women's wage work, men's role as the main breadwinner is curtailed, whereas women's role as the family maker is increased. As a consequence, women often work even harder, and gender relations become imbalanced. Thus, it is not only during Ramadan that women demonstrate they are *qashiyn* and *sebbar*; every day, they re-enact these values when they lovingly knead their bread and literally and symbolically reproduce their families.

Beyond the family, Aicha's words also illustrate that Ramadan gives people a sense of national belonging: the shared experience of fasting and feasting makes them feel part of a shared Muslim *maghriby* (Moroccan) culture. Provisioning, preparing and eating recognizably Moroccan foods are crucial to creating this feeling of a shared Moroccan identity. It is when invoking the nation that the connection between the bodily sensations of low-income Moroccans and their government became palpable. This connection is established spiritually. While being privately connected to Allah during the five daily prayers the rest of the year, during Ramadan my research participants invoked God more actively in multiple conversations. He demands restraint in eating and continuous reflection about mundane but life-giving practices such as eating and drinking. In turn, he blesses those who share their bounties with others. Importantly, as Aicha's thoughts reveal, these are not considered individual acts, but social and cultural practices that unite all Moroccans. At this juncture, the Moroccan monarch becomes the binding link between low-income Moroccans and God, for he styles himself as 'commander of the faithful' and as representative of God on Earth (cf. Combs-Schilling 1989). Thus, while the practices around Ramadan are directed at Allah and gaining *baraka* for the afterlife, low-income Moroccans also invoked their obligations as Moroccan citizens. In fasting and sharing food with family and those in need (*zakat*; religiously prescribed alms), they do what it takes to be Moroccan. At the same time, they invoke their rights, exemplified in bread as the primary gift of God (*al-ni'ama*). As the representative of Allah, it is the monarch's duty to provide his citizens with sustenance.

This is where everyday cooking becomes more than a bodily and cultural practice of making food and the family, and in placing food practices in the broader context of poverty and food insecurity, this book is more than a phenomenology of practical knowledge in a locally circumscribed place. To understand why low-income Marrakchi women continue to cook despite material and social change, cooking also needs to be understood as a political economic practice through which low-income Moroccans can gain some control over their lives. The last two chapters described how in provisioning and making what they deem good food, Marrakchi cooks situate themselves within their city and their nation and enact their citizenship. Chapter 4 introduced the notion of *beldi* foodways to demonstrate that low-income Marrakchi cooks are concerned about the quality of the foods they eat, including where it comes from, how it has been processed and how it tastes. They continue to prefer homemade and locally produced foods despite the additional physical and financial resources this often entails compared to more convenient and cheaper foods. Chapter 4 introduced the whole range of networks, discourses and practices that mark typically Moroccan ways of preparing and eating food to argue for a more holistic and situated approach to food, taste and place based on the Moroccan notion of *beldi* (of/from the country). It showed that what and how people consider *good* food inevitably changes and varies not only from one body to another, but is also the result of each domestic cook's continuous and critical engagement with the entire food system. *Beldi* foodways therefore also point towards the broader social, ecological, economic and political factors of poverty and food (in)security and how these shape, and are shaped by, the everyday food work of low-income cooks.

This argument is brought to its logical conclusion in the final chapter on breadmaking by suggesting that the domestic (and thus largely hidden) work of low-income urban women is also a political economic practice. For centuries, bread has constituted the material and symbolic basis of the social contract between the *Makhzen* (granary; today this term denotes the monarchy and its political allies) and its poor subjects, whereby the guarantee of cheaply available flour and bread ensures the monarchy's legitimacy among the low-income urban population. In tracing bread, the staple of Moroccans across income and class, from the field to the table, I approached this social contract from the phenomenological perspective of the cook's body. I described the intimate, bodily connections that cooks establish with their government through cultivating their rural heritage, their city's food infrastructures and their families' health and wellbeing when they decide which wheat and flour to use in their homemade bread. Indeed, what grains and flours are used to make good bread, and how, is indicative of the mutual dependence between low-income urban Moroccans and their government. This relationship is captured in the notion of 'cereal citizenship': in preparing and eating homemade flour and bread, low-income domestic cooks shape their own bodies and urban life, and they shape their families and the Moroccan food system. In continuing to do so despite the availability of cheaper alternatives, they literally play a *vital* role in upholding the ruling Alaouite monarchy's long legacy of 'participatory paternalism' (Holden 2009). Through their knowledgeable work, domestic cooks are thus contributing to the maintenance of political stability in Morocco.

Overall, Ramadan ties together the different themes underlying this book but also challenges static or romantic representations. It brings to the fore women's multisensory knowledge and emphasizes its recognizable elements as well as the inherently situated and idiosyncratic nature of Moroccan cuisine (*al-makla al-maghribiya*). Ramadan in Morocco highlights the interconnectedness of knowing cooking and being, and acknowledges that neither is stable nor predictable, but rather infused with dissonance and uncertainty, including forces beyond the self. By preparing all food as best as they can – down to the simple but no less important daily bread – and by treating food with respect along the way (including a respectful treatment of food waste), Marrakchi cooks seek every day to do their part in ensuring a good life amid poverty and food insecurity. Ramadan reminds fasting and feasting low-income Moroccans that everyday life and change is both hard and beautiful.

More abstractly, in writing about and theorizing women's bodily knowledge, this book is also a more general call to value the vast amount of knowledge that is embodied in little gestures and everyday practices of every domestic cook and that persist not despite but *because of* material and social change. At the time of writing, not much seems to have changed since Giard has argued that even the French, who attribute such high value to cuisine, 'exclude it [cooking knowledge] from the field of knowledge' (1998: 156).[1] By writing and thinking about cooking knowledge and women's domestic work, this multisensory ethnography of *Food and Families in the Making* hopes to give dignity to and elevate domestic work and women's food knowledge into the field of knowledge, and to recognize low-income women as a major driving force of everyday life and thus of the future.

Note

1. The field of knowledge is itself hierarchical and gendered: science, considered a male domain, is often depicted as the purest, most powerful form of knowledge and the driving force of modernity (Bray 2007).

Glossary

Below is a glossary of foreign words that appear in the volume.

'Id al-kebir	'Great feast': commemorates Ibrahim's sacrifice of his son to God; Muslim families sacrifice a ram
abaya	A loose, usually black over-garment that covers the whole body
al-ftour	Meal breaking the fast during Ramadan; also refers to breakfast throughout the rest of the year
al-gheda	Lunch
al-ni'ama	Food as God's gift
al-shor	Last meal before fasting begins during Ramadan
Amazigh (pl. Imazighen)	'The free man'; refers to the indigenous peoples of Morocco and North Africa
baraka	God's blessing, though more abstractly refers to a supernatural power
bastila	Sweet and savoury pie with almonds and chicken
beldi	Literally from the country; describes people or objects from the village or countryside; with respect to food refers to homegrown, homemade or flavour-intensive food
berrad	Plump silver tea pot
cha'abi	Popular, traditional
couscous	Denotes both the small crushed grains or semolina that are steamed and the resulting dish, including the sauce or stew
darija	Moroccan Arabic dialect
derb	Small alley, usually dead-end
dirham (Dh)	Current Moroccan currency (0.07 GBP=1 Dh=20 Riyal=100 francs)
djaja	Hen, female animal
farush	Cockerel, male animal
ferran, pl. fraren	Public oven, either made of adobe or of cast iron

fors	Soft wheat
francs	Currency used during the French Protectorate, occasionally in use
fusha	Modern Standard Arabic
gemh	Durum wheat
gsa'a	Large wooden plate used for preparing and serving couscous
hadeeth	Reports describing words, actions or habits of the Prophet Mohamed
hanut	Shop; denotes small corner shops
harira	Soup, usually differentiated between white porridge-type soup with milk and red tomato-based soup with meat
hijab	Headscarf covering head and neck
jama'a daret	(Women's) saving group
jellaba	Outer garment with hood and long sleeves that covers the entire body
Jemaa el-fna	Central public square in Marrakech's medina
kaskrut	Afternoon snack, from the French *casse-croûte* for 'snack'
keskas (or couscoussière)	Two-part pot used for steaming couscous grains above the stew
lben	Buttermilk
Madaq or *legout* (French), iduq	Taste (noun), taste (verb)
Maghrib, maghriby/a	Morocco, Moroccan
Makhzen	Granary; today denotes the monarchy and its political allies
makla	Food or, depending on context, cuisine
medina	Old town, historic quarter
mehraz	Pestle and mortar
messous	Tasteless, usually refers to food that lacks salt
msemen	Layered pancake, without leavening
msiyr	Preserved lemons
muezzin	Person calling Muslims to prayer
nukhala	Wheat bran
qashiyn	Tough, hard, strong
qesriya	Large (usually earthenware) plate used for kneading dough, especially bread
raha taqlidiya	Traditional or hand-operated grinding stone
riad	House with an open courtyard
riyal	Currency used before the French Protectorate, still widely used today
rumi	Literally 'Roman'; describes foreign people or objects, with respect to food refers to industrially or mass-produced food

sebbar	Patient
sellou	Sweet snack, mostly prepared during Ramadan
sharif	Designates descendance from the Prophet Mohamed. Bestows a religiously endowed nobility passed on via the patrilineage
siyar	To spend money, here: chopmoney
smen	Clarified butter
suiqa	Small, local market, diminutive of suq
suq, pl. swaq	Market
tahuna	(Electric) mill
tajine	Earthenware thick plate with a conical or convex lid; also denotes the dish cooked within it
Tamazight	Generic term to describe various Amazigh language dialects
tanjiya	Earthenware urn used for slow-cooking meat in the ovens heating public baths; also denotes the dish, typically prepared only in Marrakech and by men
tayyib (t'ab, tyb, tyyeb)	Good, e.g. food (cooked/ripe food, pleasing, cooking)
tifinagh	Amazigh script
zenqa, pl. zenqat	High street

References

Abarca, Meredith E. 2006. *Voices in the Kitchen: Views of Food and the World from Working-Class Mexican and Mexican America Women*. College Station: Texas A&M University Press.
Abbots, Emma-Jayne. 2013. 'Investing in the Family's Future: Labour, Gender and Consumption in Highland Ecuador', *Families, Relationships and Societies* 2(3): 143–47.
———. 2017. *The Agency of Eating: Mediation, Food and the Body*. London: Bloomsbury.
Abu-Lughod, Lila. 2002. 'Do Muslim Women Really Need Saving? Anthropological Reflections on Cultural Relativism and Its Others', *American Anthropologist* 104(3): 783–90.
Adapon, Jay. 2008. *Culinary Art and Anthropology*. Oxford: Berg.
Aistara, Guntra. 2014. 'Authentic Anachronisms', *Gastronomica: The Journal of Critical Food Studies* 14(4): 7–16.
Akesbi, Najib. 2014. 'Which Agricultural Policy for Which Food Security in Morocco?', in Jörg Gertel and Sarah Ruth Sippel (eds), *Seasonal Workers in Mediterranean Agriculture: The Social Cost of Eating Fresh*. London: Routledge, pp. 167–74.
Alexander, Paul. 1992. 'What's in a Price? Trading Practices in Peasant (and Other) Markets', in Roy Dilley (ed.), *Contesting Markets: Anthropology of Ideology, Discourse and Practice*. Edinburgh: Edinburgh University Press, pp. 79–96.
Amine, Abdelmajid, and Najoua Lazzaoui. 2010. 'Shoppers' Reactions to Modern Food Retailing Systems in an Emerging Country', *International Journal of Retail & Distribution Management* 39(8): 562–81.
Arrisueno, Gabriel, et al. 2016. *Moroccan Food Security and the Wheat Value Chain*. Research briefs. Duke MINERVA.
Avakian, Arlene Voski, and Barbara Haber (eds). 2005. *From Betty Crocker to Feminist Food Studies: Critical Perspectives on Women and Food*. Amherst: University of Massachusetts Press.
Aylwin, Zohor S. 1999. 'The Cuisine of Morocco: Origins and Ritual Significance', Ph.D. dissertation. London: SOAS University of London.
Barnes, Jessica. 2022. *Staple Security: Bread and Wheat in Egypt*. Durham, NC: Duke University Press.
Barnes, Jessica, and Mariam Taher. 2019. 'Care and Conveyance: Buying Baladi Bread in Cairo', *Cultural Anthropology* 34(3): 417–43.
Batnitzky, Adina K. 2008. 'Obesity and Household Roles: Gender and Social Class in Morocco', *Sociology of Health and Illness* 30(3): 445–62.

Beji-Becheur, Amina, and Nil Özcaglar-Toulouse. 2008. 'Couscous Connexion: L'Histoire d'un Plat Migrant', *Journées Méditerranéennes*, Marseille, France, July 3–4. Marseille: Euromed.
Benjelloun, Sabah. 2002. 'Nutrition Transition in Morocco', *Public Health Nutrition* 5(1A): 135–40.
Benkheira, Mohammed Hocine. 2000. *Islam et Interdits Alimentaires: Juguler l'Animalité*. Paris: Presses Universitaires de France.
Bennett, Jane. 2010. *Vibrant Matter: A Political Ecology of Things*. Durham, NC: Duke University Press.
Bergeaud-Blackler, Florence, Johan Fischer and John Lever (eds). 2015. *Halal Matters: Islam, Politics and Markets in Global Perspective*. Abingdon: Routledge.
Bestor, Theodore C. 2001. 'Supply-Side Sushi: Commodity, Market and the Global City', *American Anthropologist* 103(1): 76–95.
Blend, Benay. 2001. 'I Am an Act of Kneading: Food and the Making of Chicana Identity', in Sherrie A. Inness (ed.), *Cooking Lessons: The Politics of Gender and Food*. New York: Rowman & Littlefield, pp. 41–61.
Bobrow-Strain, Aaron. 2012. *White Bread: A Social History of the Store-Bought Loaf*. Boston: Beacon Press.
Boeckler, Marc, and Christian Berndt. 2014. 'B/ordering the Mediterranean: Free Trade, Fresh Fruits and Fluid Fixity', in Jörg Gertel and Sarah Ruth Sippel (eds), *Seasonal Workers in Mediterranean Agriculture: The Social Cost of Eating Fresh*. London: Routledge, pp. 23–33.
Bogaert, Koenraad. 2018. *Globalized Authoritarianism: Megaprojects, Slums, and Class Relations in Urban Morocco*. Minneapolis: University of Minnesota Press.
Boni, Zofia. 2023. *Feeding Anxieties: The Politics of Children's Food in Warsaw*. Oxford: Berghahn Books.
Bordo, Susan. 1993. *Unbearable Weight: Feminism, Western Culture, and the Body*. Berkeley: University of California Press.
Borneman, John. 2007. *Syrian Episodes: Sons, Fathers, and an Anthropologist in Aleppo*. Princeton: Princeton University Press.
Bourdieu, Pierre. 1977. *Outline of a Theory of Practice*. Cambridge: Cambridge University Press.
———. 1990. *The Logic of Practice*. Cambridge: Polity Press.
———. 2010. *Distinction: A Social Critique of the Judgement of Taste*. London: Routledge.
Boutieri, Charis. 2016. *Learning in Morocco: Language Politics and the Abandoned Educational Dream*. Bloomington: Indiana University Press.
Bowen, Sarah, Joslyn Brenton, and Sinikka Elliott. 2019. *Pressure Cooker: Why Home Cooking Won't Solve Our Problems and What We Can Do about It*. New York: Oxford University Press.
Bray, Francesca. 2007. 'Gender and Technology', *Annual Review of Anthropology* 36: 37–53.
Buitelaar, Marjo. 1993. *Living Ramadan: Fasting and Feasting in Morocco*. Oxford: Berg.
Burgess, Jean, and Joshua Green. 2018. *YouTube: Online Video and Participatory Culture*. Cambridge: Polity Press.
Butler, Judith. 1993. *Bodies That Matter: On the Discursive Limits of Sex*. London: Routledge.
Cairns, Kate, and Josée Johnston. 2015. *Food and Femininity*. London: Bloomsbury.
Cairoli, Laetitia. 2011. *Girls of the Factory: A Year with the Garment Workers of Morocco*. Gainesville: University Press of Florida.

Caldwell, Melissa L. 2002. 'The Taste of Nationalism: Food Politics in Postsocialist Russia', *Ethnos: Journal of Anthropology* 67(3): 295–319.
———. 2014. 'Digestive Politics in Russia: Feeling the Sensorium Beyond the Palate', *Food & Foodways* 22(1–2): 112–35.
Caraher, Martin et al. 1999. 'The State of Cooking in England: The Relationship of Cooking Skills to Food Choice', *British Food Journal* 101(8): 590–609.
Carney, Megan A. 2015. *The Unending Hunger: Tracing Women and Food Insecurity across Borders*. Oakland: University of California Press.
Carolan, Michael. 2013. *Reclaiming Food Security*. New York: Routledge.
Carsten, Janet. 1995. 'The Substance of Kinship and the Heat of the Hearth: Feeding, Personhood, and Relatedness among Malays in Pulau Langkawi', *American Ethnologist* 22(2): 223–41.
Casey, Edward S. 1997. 'How to get from Space to Place in a Fairly Short Stretch of Time: Phenomenological Prolegomena', in Steven Feld and Keith Basso (eds), *Senses of Place*. Santa Fe: School of American Research Press, pp. 13–52.
Chafai, Habiba. 2021. 'Everyday Gendered Violence: Women's Experiences of and Discourses on Street Sexual Harassment in Morocco', *Journal of North African Studies* 26(5): 1013–32.
Chau, Adam Yuet. 2008. 'The Sensorial Production of the Social', *Ethnos* 73(4): 485–504.
Chekroun, Mohamed. 1993. *Famille, État et Transformations Socio-culturelles au Maroc*. Rabat: Editions Okad.
Citron, Lisa Nicole. 2004. 'Continuity and Change: Anthropological Perspectives on the Informal Economy of Marrakech'. Ph.D. dissertation. New York: Columbia University.
Clark, Gracia. 2014. 'From Fasting to Fast Food in Kumasi, Ghana', in Jakob A. Klein and Anne Murcott (eds), *Food Consumption in Global Perspective: Essays in the Anthropology of Food in Honour of Jack Goody*. London: Palgrave Macmillan, pp. 45–64.
Codron, Jean-Marie et al. 2004. 'Supermarkets in Low-Income Mediterranean Countries: Impact on Horticulture Systems', *Development Policy Review* 22(5): 587–602.
Cohen, Shana. 2004. *Searching for a Different Future: The Rise of a Global Middle Class in Morocco*. Durham, NC: Duke University Press.
Collier, Jane F. 1997. *From Duty to Desire: Remaking Families in a Spanish Village*. Princeton: Princeton University Press.
Combs-Schilling, M. Elaine. 1989. *Sacred Performances: Islam, Sexuality, and Sacrifice*. New York: Columbia University Press.
Connerton, Paul. 1989. *How Societies Remember*. Cambridge: Cambridge University Press.
Conway-Long, Don. 2006. 'Gender, Power and Social Change in Morocco', in Lahoucine Ouzgane (ed.), *Islamic Masculinities*. London: Zed Books, pp. 145–60.
Coslado, Elsa, Justin McGuinness and Catherine Miller (eds). 2013. 'Introduction', in Elsa Coslado, Justin McGuinness and Catherine Miller (eds), *Médinas Immuables? Gentrification et Changement dans les Villes Historiques Marocaines, 1996–2011*. Rabat: Centre Jacques Berque, pp. 27–41.
Counihan, Carole M. 2004. *Around the Tuscan Table: Food, Family and Gender in Twentieth Century Florence*. New York: Routledge.
———. 2009. *A Tortilla Is Like Life: Food and Culture in the San Luis Valley of Colorado*. Austin: Texas A&M University Press.

Coy, Michael W. 1989. 'Being What We Pretend to Be: The Usefulness of Apprenticeship as a Field Method', in Michael W. Coy (ed.), *Apprenticeship: From Theory to Method and Back Again*. New York: State University of New York Press, pp. 115–36.

Crawford, David. 2008. *Moroccan Households in the World Economy: Labor and Inequality in a Berber Village*. Baton Rouge: Louisiana State University Press.

———. 2009. 'How Life Is Hard: Visceral Notes on Meaning, Order, and Morocco', *Journal of North African Studies* 14(3–4): 523–41.

Csordas, Thomas J. 1993. 'Somatic Modes of Attention', *Cultural Anthropology* 8(2): 135–56.

———. 1994. 'Introduction: The Body as Representation and Being-in-the-World', in Thomas J. Csordas (ed.), *Embodiment and Experience*. Cambridge: Cambridge University Press, pp. 1–24.

Davis, Diana K. 2006. 'Neoliberalism, Environmentalism, and Agricultural Restructuring in Morocco', *Geographical Journal* 172(2): 88–105.

———. 2007. *Resurrecting the Granary of Rome: Environmental History and French Colonial Expansion in North Africa*. Athens, OH: Ohio University Press.

Davis, Susan S. 1983. *Patience and Power: Women's Lives in a Moroccan Village*. Rochester: Schenkman Books, Inc.

De Certeau, Michel. 1984. *The Practice of Everyday Life*. Berkeley: University of California Press.

Desmond, Matthew. 2006. 'Becoming a Firefighter', *Ethnography* 7(4): 387–421.

DeVault, Marjorie L. 1991. *Feeding the Family: The Social Organization of Caring as Gendered Work*. Chicago: University of Chicago Press.

Deverdun, Gaston. 1959. *Marrakech: Des Origines à 1912*. Rabat: Editions Techniques Nord-Africaines.

Dike, Ruth M. 2021. '"The Machine Does It!" Using Convenience Technologies to Analyze Care, Reproductive Labor, Gender, and Class in Urban Morocco', *Economic Anthropology* 8(2): 311–25).

Dodson, Leslie, Revi Sterling and John K. Bennett. 2013. 'Minding the Gaps: Cultural, Technical and Gender-Based Barriers to Mobile Use in Oral-Language Berber Communities in Morocco', *ICTD'13: Proceedings of the Sixth International Conference on Information and Communication Technology* 1: 79–88.

Douglas, Mary. 1972. 'Deciphering a Meal', *Daedalus* 101(1): 61–81.

Douglas, Mary, and Baron Isherwood. 1978. *The World of Goods: Towards an Anthropology of Consumption*. Harmondsworth: Penguin.

Early, Evelyn A. 1993. *Baladi Women of Cairo: Playing with an Egg and a Stone*. London: Lynne Rienner.

Edwards, Elizabeth, Chris Gosden and Ruth Phillips (eds). 2006. *Sensible Objects: Colonialism, Museums and Material Culture*. Oxford: Berg.

Eickelman, Dale F. 1985. *Knowledge and Power in Morocco*. Princeton: Princeton University Press.

El Hamel, Chouki. 2013. *Black Morocco: A History of Slavery, Race, and Islam*. Cambridge: Cambridge University Press.

Ernst, Ingrid. 2013. 'La Medina de Marrakech dans le Contexte de sa Gentrification: Un Jeu Virtuel et Paradoxal', in Elsa Coslado, Justin McGuinness and Catherine Miller (eds), *Médinas Immuables? Gentrification et Changement dans les Villes Historiques Marocaines, 1996–2011*. Rabat: Centre Jacques Berque, pp. 161–88.

Errazzouki, Samia. 2014. 'Working-Class Women Revolt: Gendered Political Economy in Morocco', *Journal of North African Studies* 19(2): 259–67.
Essid, Yassine. 2000. 'Les Métiers Alimentaires dans l'Économie Urbaine d'après les Ouvrages de Hisba', in Yassine Essid (ed.), *Alimentation et Pratiques de Table en Méditerranée*. Unknown place: Edition GERIM, pp. 255–67.
Fikry, Noha. 2022. 'Today's Children, Tomorrow's Meals: Rooftops as Spaces of Nurturance in Contemporary Egypt'. *Gastronomica* 22(2): 81–91.
Fischer, Johan. 2008. *Proper Islamic Consumption: Shopping among the Malays in Modern Malaysia*. Copenhagen: NIAS.
Food and Agriculture Organization et al. 2020. 'The State of Food Security and Nutrition in the World 2020: Transforming Food Systems for Affordable Healthy Diets'. Retrieved 20 September 2023 from https://www.fao.org/documents/card/en/c/ca9692en.
Friedmann, Harriet. 1993. 'The Political Economy of Food: A Global Crisis', *New Left Review* 197: 29–57.
Garcia-Closas, Reina, Antoni Berenguer and Carlos A. Gonzalez. 2006. 'Changes in Food Supply in Mediterranean Countries from 1961 to 2001', *Public Health Nutrition* 9(1): 53–60.
Garth, Hanna. 2020. *Food in Cuba: The Pursuit of a Decent Meal*. Stanford: Stanford University Press.
Gaul, Anny. 2018. 'Cooking "Civilized" Sauces in Egypt and Morocco', *Kitchening Modernity Blog*. Retrieved 20 September 2023 from https://kitcheningmodernity.wordpress.com/2018/01/23/cooking-civilized-sauces-in-egypt-morocco/#more-2421.
———. 2019. '"Kitchen Histories" and the Taste of Mobility in Morocco'. *Mashriq & Mahjar: Journal of Middle East and North African Migration Studies* 6(2): 36–55.
Geertz, Clifford. 1971. *Islam Observed: Religious Development in Morocco and Indonesia*. Chicago: University of Chicago Press.
———. 1979. 'Suq: Bazaar Economy', in Clifford Geertz, Hildred Geertz and Lawrence Rosen (eds), *Meaning and Order in Moroccan Society*. Cambridge: Cambridge University Press, pp. 124–236.
———. 1988. *Works and Lives: The Anthropologist as Author*. Cambridge: Polity Press.
Giard, Luce. 1998. 'The Nourishing Arts', in Michel de Certeau, Luce Giard and Pierre Mayol (eds), *The Practice of Everyday Life. Volume 2: Living and Cooking*. Minneapolis: University of Minnesota Press, pp. 151–70.
Gieser, Thomas. 2008. 'Embodiment, Emotion and Empathy: A Phenomenological Approach to Apprenticeship Learning', *Anthropological Theory* 8(3): 299–318.
Goodman, David, E. Melanie DuPuis and Michael K. Goodman. 2012. *Alternative Food Networks: Knowledge, Practice and Politics*. Abingdon: Routledge.
Global Nutrition Report. 2020. *Action on Equity to End Malnutrition*. Retrieved 20 September 2023 from https://globalnutritionreport.org/reports/2020-global-nutrition-report.
Graf, Katharina. 2010. 'Drinking Water Supply in the Middle Drâa Valley, South Morocco: Options for Action in the Context of Water Scarcity and Institutional Constraints', *Kölner ethnologische Beiträge* 34. MA dissertation, University of Cologne. Retrieved 20 October 2023 from https://kups.ub.uni-koeln.de/4171/.
———. 2015. 'Beldi Matters: Negotiating Proper Food in Urban Moroccan Food Consumption and Preparation', in Florence Bergeaud-Blackler, Johan Fischer and John Lever (eds), *Halal Matters: Islam, Politics and Markets in Global Perspective*. Abingdon: Routledge, pp. 72–90.

———. 2018. 'Cereal Citizens: Crafting Bread and Belonging in Urbanising Morocco', *Paideuma* 64: 244–77.

———. 2022a. 'Taste Knowledge: Couscous and the Cook's Six Senses'. *Journal of the Royal Anthropological Institute* 28(2): 577–94.

———. 2022b. 'Cooking with(out) Others? Changing Kitchen Technologies and Family Values in Marrakech', *Journal of North African Studies*, online early view.

Graf, Katharina, and Elsa Mescoli. 2020. 'Special Issue Introduction: From Nature to Culture?', *Food, Culture & Society* 23(4): 465–71.

Graouid, Said. 2004. 'Communication and the Social Production of Space: The Hammam, the Public Sphere and Moroccan Women', *Journal of North African Studies* 9(1): 104–30.

Grasseni, Cristina. 2008. 'Learning to See: World-Views, Skilled Visions, Skilled Practice', in Narmala Halstaed, Eric Hirsch and Judith Okely (eds), *Knowing How to Know: Fieldwork and the Ethnographic Present*. Oxford: Berghahn Books, pp. 151–72.

Grasseni, Cristina et al. 2014. 'Introducing a Special Issue on the Reinvention of Food', *Gastronomica* 14(4): 1–6.

Greiman, Lillie Ruth. 2012. 'Between *Harcha* and *Harira*: Moroccan Women's Relationships to Food and Kitchenspace', MA dissertation. Missoula: University of Montana.

Guthman, Julie 2008. 'Bringing Good Food to Others: Investigating the Subjects of Alternative Food Practice', *Cultural Geographies* 15(4): 431–47.

———. 2014. 'Introducing Critical Nutrition', *Gastronomica* 14(3): 1–4.

Gvion, Liora. 2012. *Beyond Hummus and Falafel: Social and Political Aspects of Palestinian Food in Israel*. Berkeley: University of California Press.

Hal, Fatima. 1996. *Les Saveurs et les Gestes: Cuisines et Traditions du Maroc*. Paris: Stock.

Haleem, Ayman M. 2010. *The Qur'an: A New Translation*. Oxford: Oxford University Press.

Haraway, Donna. 1988. 'Situated Knowledges: The Science Question in Feminism and the Privilege of Partial Perspective', *Feminist Studies* 14(3): 575–99.

Harrell, Richard S. (ed.). 2004. *A Dictionary of Moroccan Arabic*. Washington, DC: Georgetown University Press.

Harrigan, Jane R. 2014. *The Political Economy of Arab Food Sovereignty*. Basingstoke: Palgrave Macmillan.

Harrigan, Jane R., and Hamed El-Said. 2010. 'The Economic Impact of IMF and World Bank Programs in the Middle East and North Africa: A Case Study of Jordan, Egypt, Morocco and Tunisia, 1983–2004', *Review of Middle East Economics and Finance* 6(2): Article 1.

Harris, Anna. 2015. 'The Hollow Knock and Other Sounds in Recipes', *Gastronomica* 15(4): 14–17.

Hartblay, Cassandra. 2020. 'Disability Expertise: Claiming Disability Anthropology', *Current Anthropology* 61(S21): S26–S36.

Hegasy, Sonja. 1997. *Staat, Öffentlichkeit und Zivilgesellschaft in Marokko: Die Potenziale der sozio-kulturellen Opposition*. Hamburg: Deutsches Orient-Institut.

Hernandez, Michael, and David E. Sutton. 2003. 'Hands that Remember: An Ethnographic Approach to Everyday Cooking', *Expedition* 45(2): 30–37.

Hodges, Matt. 2008. 'Rethinking Time's Arrow: Bergson, Deleuze and the Anthropology of Time', *Anthropological Theory* 8(4): 399–429.

Holden, Stacey E. 2009. *The Politics of Food in Modern Morocco*. Gainesville: University Press of Florida.

Holtzman, Jon. 2009. *Uncertain Tastes: Memory, Ambivalence and the Politics of Eating in Samburu, Northern Kenya*. Berkeley: University of California Press.

Houbaida, Mohamed. 2005. 'Le Maroc Végétarien: Réflexions sur l'Histoire de l'Alimentation', in Said Ennahid et al. (eds), *Moroccan History: Defining New Fields and Approaches. Proceedings of the First Moroccan History Days, Ifrane 22–24 November 2004*. Rabat: Imprimerie el Maarif Al Jadida, pp. 98–108.

Howes, David. 1991. 'Introduction: To Summon all the Senses', in David Howes (ed.), *The Varieties of Sensory Experience*. Toronto: University of Toronto Press, pp. 3–21.

Ingold, Tim. 2001. 'From the Transmission of Representation to the Education of Attention', in Harvey Whitehouse (ed.), *The Debated Mind: Evolutionary Psychology Versus Ethnography*. Oxford: Berg, pp. 113–53.

———. 2011. *The Perception of the Environment: Essays on Livelihood, Dwelling and Skill*, 2nd edn. London: Routledge.

Jackson, Michael. 1996. 'Introduction: Phenomenology, Radical Empiricism, and Anthropological Critique', in Michael Jackson (ed.), *Things as They Are: New Directions in Phenomenological Anthropology*. Bloomington: Indiana University Press, pp. 1–50.

Janeja, Manpreet K. 2010. *Transactions in Taste: The Collaborative Lives of Everyday Bengali Food*. London: Routledge.

Jansen, Willy. 2001. 'French Bread and Algerian Wine: Conflicting Identities in French Algeria', in Peter Scholliers (ed.), *Food, Drink and Identity: Cooking, Eating and Drinking in Europe since the Middle Ages*. Oxford: Berg, pp. 195–218.

Joseph, Suad. 1999. 'Introduction: Theories and Dynamics of Gender, Self, and Identity in Arab Families', in Suad Joseph (ed.), *Intimate Selving in Arab Families: Gender, Self and Identity*. Syracuse: Syracuse University Press, pp. 1–17.

———. (ed.). 2018. *Arab Family Studies: Critical Reviews*. Syracuse: Syracuse University Press.

Jung, Yuson. 2014. 'Ambivalent Consumers and the Limits of Certification: Organic Foods in Postsocialist Bulgaria', in Yuson Jung, Jakob A. Klein and Melissa L. Caldwell (eds), *Ethical Eating in the Postsocialist and Socialist World*. Berkeley: University of California Press, pp. 93–115.

Jung, Yuson, Jakob A. Klein and Melissa L. Caldwell (eds). 2014. *Ethical Eating in the Postsocialist and Socialist World*. Berkeley: University of California Press.

Jung, Yuson, and Nicolas Sternsdorff Cisterna. 2014. 'Introduction to Crafting Senses: Circulating the Knowledge and Experience of Taste', *Food and Foodways* 22(1–2): 1–4.

Kantor, Hayden S. 2019. 'A Body set Between Hot and Cold: Everyday Sensory Labor and Attunement in an Indian Village', *Food, Culture & Society* 22(2): 237–52.

Kapchan, Deborah. 1996. *Gender on the Market: Moroccan Women and the Revoicing of Tradition*. Philadelphia: University of Pennsylvania Press.

Kaufmann, Jean-Claude. 2010. *The Meaning of Cooking*. Cambridge: Polity Press.

Khouri-Dagher, Nadia. 1996. 'The State, Urban Households, and Management of Daily Life: Food and Social Order in Cairo', in Diane Singerman and Homa Hoodfar (eds), *Development, Change, and Gender in Cairo: A View from the Household*. Bloomington: Indiana University Press, pp. 110–33.

Kirkwood, Katherine. 2018. 'Integrating Digital Media into Everyday Culinary Practices', *Communication Research and Practice* 4(4): 277–90.

Kjaernes, Unni, Mark Harvey and Alan Warde. 2007. *Trust in Food: A Comparative and Institutional Analysis*. Basingstoke: Palgrave Macmillan.

Klein, Jakob A. 2013. 'Everyday Approaches to Food Safety in Kunming', *China Quarterly* 214: 376–93.
Koch, Shelley L. 2012. *A Theory of Grocery Shopping: Food, Choice and Conflict*. Oxford: Berg.
Kondo, Dorinne. 1990. *Crafting Selves: Power, Gender, and Discourses of Identity in a Japanese Workplace*. Chicago: University of Chicago Press.
Korsmeyer, Carolyn, and David E. Sutton. 2011. 'The Sensory Experience of Food', *Food, Culture & Society* 14(4): 461–75.
Latour, Bruno. 2005. *Reassembling the Social: An Introduction to Actor-Network Theory*. Oxford: Oxford University Press.
Lave, Jean. 2011. *Apprenticeship in Critical Ethnographic Practice*. Chicago: University of Chicago Press.
Lave, Jean, and Etienne Wenger. 1991. *Situated Learning: Legitimate Peripheral Participation*. Cambridge: Cambridge University Press.
Lewis, Tania. 2018. 'Digital Food: From Paddock to Platform', *Communication Research and Practice* 4(3): 212–28.
Lewis, Tania, and Michelle Phillipov. 2018. 'Food/Media: Eating, Cooking, and Provisioning in a Digital World', *Communication Research and Practice* 4(3): 207–11.
Lupton, Deborah. 1996. *Food, the Body and the Self*. London: Sage.
MacDougall, Susan. 2021. 'Embodying Levantine Cuisine in East Amman, Jordan', in Anny Gaul, Graham Auman Pitts and Vicki Valosik (eds), *Making Levantine Cuisine: Modern Foodways of the Eastern Mediterranean*. Austin: University of Texas Press, pp. 151–69.
Maclagan, Ianthe. 1994. 'Food and Gender in a Yemeni Community', in Richard Tapper and Sami Zubaida (eds), *Culinary Cultures of the Middle East*. London: I.B. Tauris, pp. 159–72.
MacPhee, Marybeth J. 2004. 'The Weight of the Past in the Experience of Health: Time, Embodiment, and Cultural Change in Morocco', *Ethos* 32(3): 374–96.
Maghraoui, Abdeslam. 2002. 'Depoliticization in Morocco', *Journal of Democracy* 13(4): 24–32.
Maher, Vanessa. 1974. *Women and Property in Morocco: Their Changing Relation to the Process of Social Stratification in the Middle Atlas*. Cambridge: Cambridge University Press.
Mahmood, Saba. 2005. *Politics of Piety: The Islamic Revival and the Feminist Subject*. Princeton: Princeton University Press.
Mann, Anna, and Annemarie Mol. 2019. 'Talking Pleasures, Writing Dialects: Outlining Research on "Schmecka"', *Ethnos* 84(5): 772–88.
Mann, Anna et al. 2011. 'Mixing Methods, Tasting Fingers: Notes on an Ethnographic Experiment', *HAU: The Journal of Ethnographic Theory* 1(1): 221–43.
Marchand, Trevor H. 2009. *The Masons of Djenné*. Bloomington: Indiana University Press.
Martinez, José Ciro. 2022. *States of Subsistence: The Politics of Bread in Contemporary Jordan*. Stanford: Stanford University Press.
Mauss, Marcel. 1973. 'Techniques of the Body', *Economy and Society* 2: 70–88.
Meah, Angela, and Matt Watson. 2011. 'Saints and Slackers: Challenging Discourses about the Decline of Domestic Cooking', *Sociological Research Online* 16(2): 108–20.
Meneley, Anne. 1983. *Tournaments of Value: Sociability and Hierarchy in a Yemeni Town*. Toronto: University of Toronto Press.
———. 2014. 'Discourses of Distinction in Contemporary Palestinian Extra-Virgin Olive Oil Production', *Food and Foodways* 22(1–2): 48–64.
Merleau-Ponty, Maurice. 2001. *Phenomenology of Perception*. London: Routledge.

Mernissi, Fatima. 1987. *Beyond the Veil: Male-Female Dynamics in Modern Muslim Society*. Bloomington: Indiana University Press.

Mescoli, Elsa. 2016. 'Is There an Alphabet of Moroccan Cuisine? Notes on the Materiality of Cooking and Eating', *European Association of Social Anthropologists Conference*, Milan, 22 July.

———. 2020. 'Between Food Practices and Belongings: Intersectional Stories of Moroccan Women in Italy', in Raul Matta (ed.), *Food Identities at Home and on the Move: Explorations at the Intersection of Food, Belonging and Dwelling*. Abingdon: Routledge, pp. 49–61.

Miller, Daniel. 1995. 'Consumption and Commodities', *Annual Review of Anthropology* 24: 141–61.

———. 1998. *A Theory of Shopping*. Ithaca: Cornell University Press.

———. 2010. *Stuff*. Cambridge: Polity Press.

Mintz, Sidney. 1986. *Sweetness and Power: The Place of Sugar in Modern History*. London: Penguin.

———. 2006. 'Food at Moderate Speeds', in Richard Wilk (ed.), *Fast Food/Slow Food: The Cultural Economy of the Global Food System*. New York: Altamira Press, pp. 3–12.

Mintz, Sidney, and Christine M. du Bois. 2002. 'The Anthropology of Food and Eating', *Annual Review of Anthropology* 31: 99–119.

Mokhtar, Najat et al. 2001. 'Diet Culture and Obesity in Northern Africa', *Journal of Nutrition* 31: 887S–892S.

Monqid, Safaa. 2011. 'Violence against Women in Public Spaces: The Case of Morocco', *Égypte/Monde Arabe* Troisième Série(9): 105–17.

Montgomery, Mary. 2016. Personal communication, 6 June. LSE, London.

———. 2019. *Hired Daughters: Domestic Workers among Ordinary Moroccans*. Bloomington: Indiana University Press.

Munn, Nancy. 1992. 'The Cultural Anthropology of Time: A Critical Essay', *Annual Review of Anthropology* 21: 93–123.

Murcott, Anne. 1983. 'Women's Place: Cookbooks' Images of Technique and Technology in the British Kitchen', *Women's Studies International Forum* 6(2): 33–39.

———. 2019. *Introducing the Sociology of Food and Eating*. London: Bloomsbury.

Naguib, Nefissa. 2015. *Nurturing Masculinities: Men, Food, and Family in Contemporary Egypt*. Austin: University of Texas Press.

Newcomb, Rachel. 2009. *Women of Fes: Ambiguities of Urban Life in Morocco*. Philadelphia: University of Pennsylvania Press.

———. 2017. *Everyday Life in Global Morocco*. Bloomington: Indiana University Press.

O'Connell, Rebecca, and Julia Brannen. 2016. *Food, Families and Work*. London: Bloomsbury.

Ossman, Susan. 1994. *Picturing Casablanca: Portraits of Power in a Modern City*. Berkeley: University of California Press.

Papacharalampous, Nafsika. 2019. 'The Metamorphosis of Greek Cuisine: Sociability, Precarity and Foodways of Crisis in Middle-Class Athens'. Ph.D. dissertation. London: SOAS University of London.

Pascon, Paul. 1986. *Capitalism and Agriculture in the Haouz of Marrakesh*. London: KPI.

Paxson, Heather. 2013. *The Life of Cheese: Crafting Food and Value in America*. Berkeley: University of California Press.

Payne, Rhys. 1986. 'Food Deficits and Political Legitimacy: The Case of Morocco', in Stephen K. Commins, Michael F. Lofchie and Rhys Payne (eds), *Africa's Agrarian Crisis: The Roots of Famine*. Boulder: Lynne Rienner, pp. 153–73.

Pennell, C.R. 2000. *Morocco since 1830: A History*. London: Hurst and Company.

Pilcher, Jeffrey M. 2002. 'Industrial Tortillas and Folkloric Pepsi: The Nutritional Consequences of Hybrid Cuisines in Mexico', in Warren Belasco and Philip Scranton (eds), *Food Nations: Selling Taste in Consumer Societies*. New York: Routledge, pp. 222–39.

Pink, Sarah. 2009. *Doing Sensory Ethnography*. London: Sage.

Pink, Sarah, and David Howes. 2010. 'The Future of Sensory Anthropology/the Anthropology of the Senses: Debate Section', *Social Anthropology/Anthropologie Sociale* 18(3): 331–40.

Popkin, Barry M. 1998. 'The Nutrition Transition and Its Health Implications in Lower-Income Countries', *Public Health Nutrition* 1(1): 5–21.

Portisch, Anna. 2010. 'The Craft of Skilful Learning: Kazakh Women's Everyday Craft Practices in Western Mongolia', *Journal of the Royal Anthropological Institute* 16(May): S62–S79.

Prentice, Rebecca. 2008. 'Knowledge, Skill, and the Inculcation of the Anthropologist: Reflections on Learning to Sew in the Field', *Anthropology of Work Review* 29(3): 54–61.

Rachik, Hassan. 1997. 'Roumi et Beldi: Réflexions sur la Perception de l'Occidental à Travers une Dichotomie Locale', *Égypte/Monde Arabe* 30–31: 293–302.

Raddadi, Abdelkrim. 2012. *Maroc: L'Art Culinaire en Plain Air*. Rabat: Marsam.

Ray, Krishnendu. 2022. 'Hands on Food', Theorizing the Contemporary, *Fieldsights*, 1 December. Retrieved 20 September 2023 from https://culanth.org/fieldsights/hands-on-food.

Retsikas, Kostas. 2008. 'Knowledge from the Body: Fieldwork, Power, and the Acquisition of a New Self', in Narmala Halstaed, Eric Hirsch and Judith Okely (eds), *Knowing How to Know: Fieldwork and the Ethnographic Present*. Oxford: Berghahn Books, pp. 110–29.

Rosenberger, Bernard. 1999. 'Arab Cuisine and Its Contribution to European Culture', in Jean-Luis Flandrin and Massimo Montanari (eds), *Food: A Culinary History from Antiquity to the Present*. New York: Columbia University Press, pp. 207–23.

Royaume du Maroc. 2014. *Recensement Général de la Population et de l'Habitat 2014*. Rabat: Ministère de l'Aménagement du Territoire National, de l'Urbanisme, de l'Habitat et de la Politique de la Ville. Last retrieved 20 October 2023 from https://rgph2014.hcp.ma/.

Rumi, Jalal Al-Din. 1995. *The Essential Rumi*. New York: HarperCollins.

Sabry, Tarik. 2005. 'The Day Moroccans Gave up Couscous for Satellite: Global TV, Structures of Feeling and Mental Emigration', *Journal of Transnational Broadcasting Studies* 15(1): 197–221.

Sadiqi, Fatima. 2014. *The Shifting Status of Moroccan Languages in Morocco: Berber and Language Politics in the Moroccan Educational System*. Unknown publisher.

Sadiqi, Fatima, and Mohamed Ennaji. 2006. 'The Feminization of Public Space: Women's Activism, the Family Law, and Social Change in Morocco', *Journal of Middle East Women's Studies* 2(2): 86–114.

Salih, Ruba. 2003. *Gender in Transnationalism: Home, Longing and Belonging among Moroccan Migrant Women*. London: Routledge.

Salime, Zakia. 2018. 'Morocco', in Suad Joseph (ed.), *Arab Family Studies: Critical Reviews*. Syracuse: Syracuse University Press, pp. 75–95.

Sarter, Gilles. 2006. 'Manger et Élever des Moutons au Maroc: Sociologie des Préférences et des Pratiques de Consommation et de Production de Viande', Ph.D. dissertation. Paris: Université Panthéon-Sorbonne-Paris I.

Sater, James N. 2007. *Civil Society and Political Change in Morocco*. Abingdon: Routledge.
Sauvegrain, Sophie-Anne. 2009. 'Les Jeunes d'Alep Face à un Nouvel Horizon Alimentaire: Pratiques Sociales et Représentations Corporelles', Ph.D. dissertation. Marseille: Université de la Méditerranée Aix-Marseille II.
Schmidt, Thomas. 2005. 'Jemaa el Fna Square in Marrakech: Changes to a Social Space and to a UNESCO Masterpiece of Oral and Intangible Heritage of Humanity as a Result of Global Influences', *The Arab World Geographer/Le Géographe du Monde Arabe* 8(4): 173–95.
Schwartz Cowan, Ruth. 1983. *More Work for Mother: The Ironies of Household Technology from the Open Hearth to the Microwave*. New York: Basic Books.
Sebti, Mohamed et al. 2009. *Gens de Marrakech: Géo-Démographie de la Ville Rouge*. Paris: Ined.
Seremetakis, C. Nadia. 1994a. 'The Memory of the Senses, Part I: Marks of the Transitory', in C. Nadia Seremetakis (ed.), *The Senses Still: Perception and Memory as Material Culture in Modernity*. Chicago: University of Chicago Press, pp. 1–18.
———. 1994b. 'The Memory of the Senses, Part II: Still Acts', in C. Nadia Seremetakis (ed.), *The Senses Still: Perception and Memory as Material Culture in Modernity*. Chicago: University of Chicago Press, pp. 23–44.
Shapin, Stephen. 2012. 'The Sciences of Subjectivity', *Social Studies of Science* 42(2): 170–84.
Short, Frances. 2006. *Kitchen Secrets: The Meaning of Cooking in Everyday Life*. Oxford: Berg.
Silva, Elizabeth B. 2000. 'The Cook, the Cooker and the Gendering of the Kitchen', *Sociological Review* 48(4): 612–28.
Silverstein, Paul A., and David Crawford. 2004. 'Amazigh Activism and the Moroccan State', *Middle East Report* 233: 44–48.
Simenel, Romain. 2010. 'Beldi/Roumi: Une Conception Marocaine du Produit de Terroir, l'Exemple des Ait Ba'amram de la Région de Sidi Ifni', *Hespéris-Tamuda* LV 45: 167–76.
Sippel, Sarah Ruth. 2014. *Export(t)räume: Bruchzonen marokkanischer Landwirtschaft*. Bielefeld: transcript.
Smith, Pamela H. 2004. *The Body of the Artisan: Art and Experience in the Scientific Revolution*. Chicago: University of Chicago Press.
Sobal, José. 2005. 'Men, Meat and Marriage: Models of Masculinity', *Food & Foodways* 13: 135–58.
Spackman, Christy, and Jacob Lahne. 2019. 'Sensory Labor: Considering the Work of Taste in the Food System', *Food, Culture & Society* 22(2): 142–51.
Spiekermann, Uwe. 2018. *Künstliche Kost: Ernährung in Deutschland, 1840 bis heute*. Gottingen: Vandenhoeck & Ruprecht.
Spittler, Gerd. 2001. 'Teilnehmende Beobachtung als Dichte Teilnahme', *Zeitschrift für Ethnologie* 126(1): 1–25.
Staples, James. 2020. *Sacred Cows and Chicken Manchurian: The Everyday Politics of Eating Meat in India*. Seattle: University of Washington Press.
Stoller, Paul. 1989. *The Taste of Ethnographic Things: The Senses in Anthropology*. Philadelphia: University of Pennsylvania Press.
———. 1997. *Sensuous Scholarship*. Philadelphia: University of Pennsylvania Press.
Strathern, Marilyn. 2004. *Partial Connections: Updated Edition*. Oxford: Altamira Press.
Strava, Cristiana. 2021. *Precarious Modernities: Assembling State, Space and Society on the Urban Margins in Morocco*. London: Bloomsbury.

Sutton, David E. 2001. *Remembrance of Repasts: An Anthropology of Food and Memory.* Oxford: Berg.
———. 2006. 'Cooking Skill, the Senses and Memory: The Fate of Practical Knowledge', in Elizabeth Edwards, Chris Gosden and Ruth Phillips (eds), *Sensible Objects: Colonialism, Museums and Material Culture.* Oxford: Berg, pp. 87–118.
———. 2010. 'Food and the Senses', *Annual Review of Anthropology* 39: 209–23.
———. 2014. *Secrets from the Greek Kitchen: Cooking, Skill, and Everyday Life on an Aegean Island.* Oakland: University of California Press.
Swearingen, Will D. 1987. *Moroccan Mirages: Agrarian Dreams and Deceptions, 1912–1986.* Princeton: Princeton University Press.
Telleria Juarez, Roberto, and Boubaker Dhehibi. 2017. 'The Moroccan Wheat Sector: What if There Is No More Tariff Protection?', *Asian Journal of Agriculture and Rural Development* 7(4): 65–85.
Trubek, Amy. 2008. *The Taste of Place: A Cultural Journey into Terroir.* Berkeley: University of California Press.
———. 2017. *Making Modern Meals: How Americans Cook Today.* Berkeley: University of California Press.
Tsigkas, Alexios. 2019. 'Tasting Ceylon: Aesthetic Judgment Beyond "Good" Taste', *Food, Culture & Society* 22(2): 152–67.
Tsing, Anna L. 2015. *The Mushroom at the End of the World: On the Possibility of Life in Capitalist Ruins.* Princeton: Princeton University Press.
United States Department of Agriculture. 2012. 'Morocco: Grain and Feed Update'. *USDA Foreign Agricultural Service, Rabat.* Retrieved 20 October 2023 from https://voyager.fas.usda.gov/voyager/navigo/show?id=180ba2f4-e48b-5e0b-9ed6-147d79a4a7fb&disp=D176678659AD.
———. 2019. 'Morocco: Food and Agricultural Import Regulations and Standards Country Report'. *USDA Foreign Agricultural Service, Rabat.* Retrieved 20 October 2023 from https://agriexchange.apeda.gov.in/IR_Standards/Import_Regulation/Foodand%20AgriculturalImportRegulationsandStandardsCountryReportRabatMorocco662019.pdf.
———. 2020. 'Morocco: Food and Agricultural Import Regulations and Standards Export Certificate Report'. *USDA Foreign Agricultural Service, Rabat.* Retrieved 20 October 2023 from https://apps.fas.usda.gov/newgainapi/api/Report/DownloadReportByFileName?fileName=Food%20and%20Agricultural%20Import%20Regulations%20and%20Standards%20Export%20Certificate%20Report_Rabat_Morocco_12-31-2019.
Van Daele, Wim. 2013. '"Cooking" Life: An Anthropologist Blends in with Everyday Sustenance and Relationality in Sri Linka', *Food & Foodways* 21(1): 66–85.
Verme, Paolo, Karim El-Massnaoui, and Abdelkrim Araar. 2014. 'Reforming Subsidies in Morocco'. *Economic Premise* 134. Washington, DC: World Bank.
Vom Bruck, Gabriele. 1998. 'Kinship and the Embodiment of History', *History and Anthropology* 10(4): 263–98.
Wacquant, Loic J. 2004. *Body and Soul: Notebooks of an Apprentice Boxer.* Oxford: Oxford University Press.
Wagner, Daniel A. 1993. *Literacy, Culture and Development: Becoming Literate in Morocco.* Cambridge: Cambridge University Press.
Wajcman, Judy. 2015. *Pressed for Time: The Acceleration of Life in Digital Capitalism.* Chicago: University of Chicago Press.

Weiss, Brad. 1996. *The Making and Unmaking of the Haya Lived World: Consumption, Commoditization, and Everyday Practice*. Durham, NC: Duke University Press.

Welz, Gisela. 2015. *European Products: Making and Unmaking Heritage in Cyprus*. London: Berghahn Books.

West, Harry G. 2008. 'Food Fears and Raw-Milk Cheese', *Appetite* 51(1): 25–29.

———. 2013a. 'Appellations and Indications of Origin, Terroir, and the Social Construction and Contestation of Place-Named Foods', in Anne Murcott, Warren Belasco and Peter Jackson (eds), *The Handbook of Food Research*. London: Bloomsbury, pp. 209–28.

———. 2013b. 'Thinking like a Cheese: Towards an Ecological Understanding of the Reproduction of Knowledge in Contemporary Artisan Cheesemaking', in Roy Ellen, Stephen J. Lycett and Sarah E. Johns (eds), *Understanding Cultural Transmission in Anthropology: A Critical Synthesis*. Oxford: Berghahn Books, pp. 320–45.

Wilbaux, Quentin. 2001. *La Médina de Marrakech: Formation des Espaces Urbains d'une Ancienne Capitale du Maroc*. Paris: L'Harmattan.

Wills, Wendy et al. 2013. 'Domestic Kitchen Practices: Findings from the "Kitchen Life" Study'. Social Science Research Unit of the Food Standards Agency, Unit Report 24. Retrieved 20 October 2023 from https://www.food.gov.uk/sites/default/files/media/document/818-1-1496_KITCHEN_LIFE_FINAL_REPORT_10-07-13.pdf.

Wilk, Richard (ed.). 2006. *Fast Food/Slow Food: The Cultural Economy of the Global Food System*. New York: Altamira Press.

Wolfert, Paula. 1973. *Couscous and Other Good Foods from Morocco*. New York: Harper & Row.

Xu, Chenjia. 2019. 'Eating Things: Foodies, Bodies and Lives in Contemporary Urban Beijing', Ph.D. dissertation. London: SOAS University of London.

Yates-Doerr, Emily. 2015. *The Weight of Obesity: Hunger and Global Health in Postwar Guatemala*. Oakland: University of California Press.

Zirari, Hayat. 2020a. 'Entre Alimentation (Makla) et Nutrition (Taghdia): Arbitrages et Réinvention au Quotidien des Pratiques Alimentaires en Contexte Urbain', *Hespéris-Tamuda LV* 4: 385–407.

———. 2020b. '(S'en) Sortir de la Cuisine! Reconfigurations des Rapports de Genre et Pratiques Alimentaires à Casablanca', in Yount-André Soula et al. (eds), *Manger en Ville: Regards Socio-Anthropologiques d'Afrique, d'Amérique Latine et d'Asie*. Versailles: Quae, pp. 33–45.

Zvan Elliott, Katja. 2015. *Modernizing Patriarchy: The Politics of Women's Rights in Morocco*. Austin: University of Texas Press.

Index

✥ ✥ ✥

abaya (black overgarment), 116, 163
abstract time, bodily *versus*, 40, 50n15
Aicha (research participant), 9, 27–28, 30, 47, 77, 147
  family of, 6, 7, 29, 54, 56–57, 80, 89, 155
  financial management of, 84
  foodways of, 11
  kitchen of, 12
  taste knowledge of, 92
  womanhood for, 78
Allah (God), 34, 155, 159–160
alley, small (*derb*), 138, 145, 163
Amazigh (indigenous people), 4–5, 10–11, 24n6, 120, 163, 165
  language dialects (Tamazight) of, 7, 25n19, 165
amlou (almond-oil-honey spread), 11, 88–93, 127n30
apprenticeship, 15–16, 51, 54, 57, 59, 73n12
Arabization programmes, 13

baladi (subsidized), 112, 141, 151
baraka (blessing from God), 18, 31, 37–39, 41, 48, 111, 134, 149, 156, 160, 163
  temporality and, 37–39, 41
bastila (sweet and savoury pie), 10, 163
becoming, process of, 94
beldi (from the country, homemade), 23, 111–16, 125nn13–14, 127n30, 163
  foodways, 104–5, 107, 123–24

berrad (silver tea pot), 76, 163
bled (hometown or country), 108, 111, 113–15, 123
bodily movements, during cooking, 56, 62, 119
bodily senses, 26n26, 54, 59, 62, 72, 73n9
  food quality of, 110–13
  knowing from, 26n31, 55, 63, 77, 138
  taste and, 36, 48
  temporality of, 38, 40, 42, 46
boys, in food preparation, 55, 58–59, 71, 73n8, 157
bread, x–xi, 6, 11–12, 21, 27–29, 41, 50n12, 54–57, 63–67, 77–78, 96, 98n1, 99n21, 105, 111, 116–17, 119, 122–24, 126n18, 126n22, 130–31, 141, 147,151n1, 152n12, 153n19, 154n22, 161
  baking, 141–43
  bodily knowledge of making, 138
  homemade, 20–21, 23, 41, 64, 77–78, 126nn21–22, 133, 138
  importance of, 130–32, 148–49, 151
breakfast (*al-ftour*), 29, 155, 163
buttermilk (*lben*), 35, 120, 164

casse-croûte (afternoon snack), 11, 75, 86, 113, 164
cereal citizens, 23, 131, 133, 135, 141
cereal citizenship, 23, 133, 135, 137, 139, 152n9, 161
cereals, 10, 44, 118, 135, 145, 149–50

cha'abi (popular or traditional), 68, 145, 163
change, 12, 15, 72, 145
 in Moroccan bodies, 147, 151
 in Moroccan diet, 149
church (*église*), 5
citizen consumer, 107, 133, 139
clarified butter (*smen*), 80, 119, 165
cockerel (*farush*), 102–3, 163
collaborative performance, of food, 37
commensality, 111, 117, 119, 157
conjugal, 14, 78–79, 88, 98n11, 159
 households, multigenerational *versus*, 98n11
connectivity, culinary, 22, 77, 79, 94–97
consumer competence, 125n10
convenience, food and, 42, 45, 121–22
cookbook, as knowledge reproduction, 53, 57
cooking, 21–22, 46, 88, 156–58, 159, 160
 bodily movements during, 56, 62, 119
 domestic, 1–2, 10, 14, 20
 knowledge of, 30, 51, 161
 with research participants, 31–33, 36, 43, 102–3, 116–17
 temporality of, 30–31, 39–41, 48–49, 50n11
cooks, 4, 37, 38, 39, 49n3, 71
 bodily movements of, 119
 multisensory memory of, 115
cosmopolitan marketplace, Marrakech as, 8
country, homemade or from (*beldi*), 23, 111–16, 125nn13–14, 127n30, 163
couscous (grains or dish), 49n2, 49n5, 51, 102, 120, 163
 preparing, 31–35, 46–47, 52
covered market (*marché couvert*), 101–03
COVID-19, 9, 25n13, 84, 97
cuisine or food (*makla*), 90, 104, 114, 148–49, 161, 164
culinary connectivity, 22, 77, 79, 94–97
currency, Moroccan, 24n3, 101, 103n1, 163–64

darija (Moroccan Arabic dialect), 3–4, 6, 13, 17, 24n2, 76, 103n1, 163

DCFTA. *See* 2013 Deep and Comprehensive Free Trade Agreement
death and life, due to food systems, 150–51
2013 Deep and Comprehensive Free Trade Agreement (DCFTA), 137
dependence, mutual, of Moroccans and government, 161
derb (small alley), 138, 145, 163
descendant, from Prophet Mohamed (*sharif*), 5, 24n8, 114, 165
Dh. *See* dirham (currency)
dinner, 11, 75, 82, 120–23
digital,
 literacy, 11, 72, 92
 media, 22, 66, 68–70, 72, 73n14, 92, 96, 158
 technology, 22, 68, 70, 72, 74n19
dirham (currency) (Dh), 24n3, 24n9, 101, 103n1, 108, 118, 133, 148, 150, 163
djaja (hen), 103, 163
domestic cooking, 1, 2, 10, 14, 20
domestic hierarchy, 19, 56, 69–70, 72, 86, 93
domestic space, 50n16, 98n4
domestic space, as female, 82, 85
durum wheat (*gemh*), 64, 133–35, 139–40, 164

economy, 1, 2, 8–9, 19, 110, 132, 144–46
education, 5–6, 9, 13, 25n18, 48, 59, 62, 69–71, 73n8, 79, 86, 92, 98nn10–11, 159
église (church), 5
environment, of food, 18, 36, 41, 50n12, 157
ethics and spirituality, of provisioning food, 111
European food, fast food as, 74n20, 87, 121, 123
expectations, of men *versus* women, 83
experience, of food, multisensory, 17, 26n24, 38

faith and religion, in Morocco, 26n32
family. *See specific topics*
family law (*mudawana*), 14

farush (cockerel), 102–3, 163
fast food, European food as, 74n20, 87, 121, 123
fasting, 155–56, 159
Fatimzahra (research participant), 6, 10, 24n4, 43, 75–76, 102–3
  family of, 3, 9, 86, 108
feel (*kathess*), 28
female space, domestic as, 82, 85
feminized food preparation, masculinized *versus*, 82
ferran (public oven), 116, 141–46, 148, 152–53n12, 153n15, 163
food. *See specific topics*
food insecurity, 37, 132, 135, 148, 153nn16–17, 154n24
  poverty and, 1, 23, 132, 135, 160–61
food labelling, standardized, 110–11, 140
food preparation, rhythms of, x–xii, 58, 62
food quality, bodily senses and, 110–13
food security, 111, 125n2, 132, 135–36, 149, 151, 154n25
food system, Moroccan, 2, 19, 23, 37, 41, 105, 110, 135, 137, 139, 146, 148, 150, 160
foodways, 2, 10–11, 23, 45, 47, 72, 104, 115, 118, 121–24, 140, 160
  beldi, 104–5, 107, 123–24
foreign or mass-produced food (*rumi*), 23, 102, 107, 111–16, 123–24, 125nn13–14, 127n31, 140, 164
fors (soft wheat), 64, 133–36, 140, 152n8, 152n11, 152nn4–5, 164
francs (currency), 24n3, 103n1, 164
2004 Free Trade Agreement (FTA), 137
al-ftour (breakfast), 29, 155, 163
fusha (Modern Standard Arabic), 13, 92, 164

gemh (durum wheat), 64, 133–35, 139–40, 164
gender relations, 74n19, 78–80, 85
al-gheda (lunch), 116–18, 120–21, 123, 163
girls, boys *versus*, in food preparation, 55, 58–59, 71–72, 73n8, 157

good food (*tayyib*), xii, 1–3, 21–23, 30, 36, 44–45, 56, 65–66, 71, 79–80, 83, 88, 93, 96, 105–07, 110–111, 115–16, 122, 123, 125n10, 132, 137, 150, 156, 158–61, 165
  good cook or mother, 30, 39, 45, 47–48, 56, 66, 78, 120
grain prices, 131
grains, inspecting, 134
grains or semolina dish (couscous), 49n2, 49n5, 51, 102, 120, 163
  preparing, 31–35, 46–47, 52
granary (*Makhzen*), 132, 164
great feast ('Id al-kebir), 12, 118, 163
grinding stone (*raha taqlidiya*), 88–91, 164
gsa'a (large serving plate), 32–33, 39, 119, 126n22, 164
guide, as food, 56, 62, 63
gustemology, 30–31, 40

habitus, 15, 36, 119
hadeeth (reports on Prophet Mohamed), 120, 164
Hajja (research participant), 4–5, 12, 24n5, 39, 75–76, 101
  cooking of, 31–33, 36, 43, 103
haj (Mecca pilgrimage), 4, 75–76
hanut (shop), 11, 105–06, 144, 148, 164
harira (soup), x, 126n18, 155, 164
headscarf (*hijab*), 64, 87, 116, 164
hen (*djaja*), 103, 163
hierarchies, social, 19, 56, 69–70, 72, 85, 86, 93
high street (*zenqa*), 78, 105, 141, 143, 146, 165
hijab (headscarf), 64, 87, 116, 164
homemade, 67–68, 87, 116, 123–24, 126n18, 140, 156, 160, 164
  bread as, 20–21, 23, 41, 64, 77–78, 126nn21–22, 132–33, 135, 138, 143–44, 146, 148–49, 161
  from the country or (*beldi*), 23, 111–16, 125nn13–14, 127n30, 163
house, with courtyard (*riad*), 4–7, 56, 75, 144, 164

households, multigenerational, 78, 87, 99n17

identity, 9, 13–14, 24n6, 88, 93, 159
 baraka and, 38–39
 Moroccan, 124, 126n25, 159
 of women, 46, 104
'Id al-kebir (great feast), 12, 118, 163
IMF. *See* International Monetary Fund (IMF)
imitation, 16
indigenous people (Amazigh), 4, 24n6, 120, 163
individualism and relationality, 94, 99n19
infrastructure, of urban food, 141, 143–44, 146
intergenerational learning, technology and media in, 66, 68–70, 72
intergenerational reproduction, 91
International Monetary Fund (IMF), 9, 136, 152n7
International Organization for Standards (ISO), 149

jama'a daret (saving group for women), 6, 84, 164
jellaba (outer garment), 87, 164
Jemaa el-fna (Marrakech central public square), x, 103, 144, 153n13, 164

kaskrut (afternoon snack), 164
kathess (feel), 28–29
keskas (two-part pot for making couscous), 32–33, 51, 117, 164
kitchen, 12, 42–45
 space of, 41, 55, 82
knowing, from bodily senses, 26n31, 55, 63, 77, 138
knowing, learning before, 56, 58, 62
knowledge, 1, 26n31, 55, 63, 77, 162n1
 cooking, 30, 51, 161
 taste, 21–22, 31, 36–37, 39, 42, 44, 46, 48, 58, 70–72, 74n19, 90–91, 92, 119, 158
knowledge reproduction. *See specific topics*

labour
 division of, 22, 56, 66, 70, 72, 93, 158
 domestic, 19, 56, 70, 78, 93
 market, 13, 152n6
 of food, 46–47, 75, 134
last meal, before Ramadan (*al-shor*), 88–89, 163
lben (buttermilk), 35, 120, 164
lead cook, 4, 71
learning, through food, 56, 58–59, 61, 62, 65
legout (taste), 29, 34, 113, 164
lemons, preserved (*msiyr*), 80, 164
life and death, due to food systems, 150–51
liquid petroleum gas (LPG), 12, 136
literacy
 digital, 11, 72, 92
 and education, in Morocco, 13, 25n18
local or small market (*suiqa*), 64, 75, 105, 116, 125n3, 129, 138, 145, 165
low-income
 families, 8, 12, 19–21, 68, 71, 104–5, 122, 124
 women, 1, 3, 13–14, 22, 24n10, 24n12, 47–48, 73n7, 79, 83, 162
low-literate women, 5, 13, 25n18, 70, 74n17
LPG. *See* liquid petroleum gas (LPG)
lunch (*al-gheda*), 116–18, 120–21, 123, 163

madaq (taste), 30, 34, 164
Makhzen (Moroccan monarchy or granary), 132, 164
makla (food or cuisine), 104, 164
marché couvert (covered market), 102–3
market (*suq*), 31, 101, 105, 107, 109–10, 125n3, 129, 165
Marrakech, x, 3–9, 12, 42, 68, 82, 104, 109, 111–14, 121–22, 133, 141–48
masculinized food preparation, feminized *versus*, 82
mass-produced or foreign food (*rumi*), 23, 111–16, 124, 125nn13–14, 127n31, 164
material environment, 18, 36, 41
materiality of food, 18, 38, 40, 63

Mecca pilgrimage (*haj*), 4, 75–76
media
　gap, 68, 74n17
　digital, 22, 66, 68–70, 72, 73n14, 92, 96, 158
　new, 54, 56, 66, 72, 74n17, 79, 92, 96, 149, 158
　social, 68–70, 72, 73n14, 92, 96–97, 109, 149, 158
mehraz (pestle and mortar), 32, 89, 164
men, 24n12, 59, 83
　in domestic spaces, 50n16, 98n4
　food and, 74n19, 79–85, 98n7
messous (tasteless food), 29, 34, 80, 164
middle class, global, 14, 124, 139
mill, electric (*tahuna*), 138, 165
minimum wage, monthly national, 5
Modern Standard Arabic (*fusha*), 13, 92, 164
monarchy, Moroccan (*Makhzen*), 132, 164
money, to spend (*siyar*), 82–85, 165
monthly national minimum wage, 5
Morocco (Maghrib), 124, 126n25, 147, 151, 159, 164
　Arabic dialect (*darija*) in, 3, 6, 13, 17, 24n2, 163
　currency of, 24n3, 101, 103n1, 163–64
　food of, 104–5, 123, 126n18, 148, 149, 150
　mother, role of, 30, 45–47, 56, 58, 64–66, 71, 74n19, 87
Moulinex electric blender, 32, 43–44, 88, 91
msemen (layered pancake), 11, 75–76, 119, 123, 157, 164
msiyr (preserved lemons), 80, 164
mudawana (family law), 14
muezzin (person calling Muslims to prayer), xi, 164
multigenerational households, 78, 87, 98n11, 99n17
multisensory experience, of food, 17, 26nn24–26, 110, 111, 115, 119

national subsidy system, 103n2, 132–33, 136, 150, 152n6

new media, 54, 56, 66, 68, 72, 74n17, 79, 92, 96, 149, 158
al-ni'ama (food, as gift from God), 66, 131, 156, 160, 163
nonverbal practice, 1, 14–15, 18
nukhala (wheat bran), 63, 138, 148, 164

observation, learning as, 16–17, 51, 53, 55, 59, 61, 71–72
older cooks, younger versus, 14, 22, 44–47, 49n3, 56, 66, 68–69, 72, 78, 93, 97, 156, 158, 49n3

pancake, layered (*msemen*), 11, 75–76, 119, 123, 157, 164
participant
　observation, 15–16, 18, 26n28, 51, 53, 55, 61, 71, 152n2, 157
　perception, 16–22, 53–56, 58, 65–66, 69, 71–72, 156–7
participatory paternalism, 2, 137, 139
patient (*sebbar*), 66, 99n18, 155, 158, 165
patriarchal connectivity, 95
perception, sensory, x, 30, 37, 56, 63
pestle and mortar (*mehraz*), 32, 43, 46, 89, 164
phenomenology, 15, 19, 23, 26n26, 31, 40, 59, 153n14, 157, 160–61
pizza dyel dar (homemade pizza), 11, 29–30, 41, 67–68
Plan Maroc Vert (PMV), 136
plate, 11, 117–19, 129–30, 165
　for kneading dough (*qesriya*), 27, 29, 55–56, 119, 126n22, 147, 164
　for making and serving couscous (*gsa'a*), 32–33, 39, 119, 126n22, 164
PMV. *See* Plan Maroc Vert
political economic practice, cooking as, 1–2, 23, 79, 97, 105, 132, 135, 160
politics, 1–2, 19, 132, 135
popular or traditional (*cha'abi*), 68, 145, 163
power dynamics, in family, 19, 43–44, 73n13, 79–80, 85–6, 92–93, 96–97, 98n10
power relationships, 18, 43, 79–80, 83, 85, 92, 96–97

practice theory, 15, 62
practice, nonverbal, 1, 14–15, 18
pressure cooker, xii, 11, 32, 45, 117, 120
prices, of grain, 131, 137, 150
process, of becoming, 56, 71, 78, 79, 94–95, 158–59
processing wheat, provisioning and, 12, 23, 63, 115, 135, 137, 139, 152n4
provisioning food, 4, 10, 12, 16, 17, 19, 23, 78, 86, 96, 99n12, 99n21, 101, 107, 109–11, 125n6
public oven (*ferran*), 116, 141–46, 148, 152n12, 153n15, 163

qashiyn (tough), 155, 159, 164
qesriya (large plate for kneading dough), 27, 29, 55–56, 119, 126n22, 147, 164
quality, of food, 23, 36–37, 83, 104–5, 110–15, 123–24, 125n6, 125n14, 133, 138–41, 149, 154n21, 160

Rachida (research participant), 9, 12
  family of, 5–7, 54, 60–61, 64, 67, 84, 99nn15–16
  foodways of, 10–11, 116–17, 138
raha taqlidiya (grinding stone), 88–91, 164
Ramadan, 156–58, 159, 160–61
réapprentissage (re-learning), 90
reciprocity of taste, 43–44, 65
relational connectivity, 95
relationality and individualism, 94, 99n19
relationships
  gender, 79–80, 85
  sociomaterial, 88, 90–93, 95–97
re-learning (*réapprentissage*), 90
religion and faith, in Morocco, 26n32
replacement, as learning, 63–5, 158
reports, on Prophet Mohamed (*hadeeth*), 120, 164
riad (house with courtyard), 4–7, 56, 75, 144, 164
riyal (currency), 24n3, 101, 103n1, 108, 164
rumi (foreign or mass-produced food), 23, 111–16, 124, 125nn13–14, 127n31, 164

rural, urban space *versus*, 23, 105, 112–15, 144–45

sa'fran al-horr (real or pure saffron), 114, 118
saving group, for women (*jama'a daret*), 6, 84, 164
sebbar (patient), 66, 99n18, 155, 159, 165
self and family, in cooking, 93–96
sellou (sweet snack), 92, 112, 165
seniority, 71, 78, 85, 93, 95
sensory anthropology, 16, 34
shared food, 11, 17, 86, 87, 157
sharif (descendant of Prophet Mohamed), 5, 24n8, 114, 165
shop (*hanut*), 11, 105–6, 144–48, 164
al-shor (last meal before Ramadan), 89, 163
siyar (to spend money), 82–85, 165
smen (clarified butter), 80, 119, 165
social media, 68–70, 72, 73n14, 92, 96–97, 109, 149, 158
sociomaterial relations, 88, 90–93, 95–97
soft wheat (*fors*), 64, 133–36, 140, 152n8, 152n11, 152nn4–5, 164
soup (*harira*), x, 126n18, 155, 164
Soussi cuisine, 25n16
space, 15, 18
  kitchen, 41, 55
  male, 24n12
spirituality and ethics, of provisioning food, 111
standardized food labelling, 110–11, 140
stew, prepared in earthenware plate (*tajine*), xii, 11, 117–19, 125n13, 126n18, 129–30, 165
street food, 11–12, 78, 105, 122, 141, 148
subsidized (*baladi*), 112, 141, 151
suiqa (local market), 64, 75, 105, 116, 125n3, 129, 138, 145, 165
supermarket, 12, 14, 19, 47, 93, 106, 110–11, 121–24, 125n8, 126n27, 127n30
suq (market), 31, 101, 105, 107, 109–10, 125n3, 129, 165
sweet and savoury pie (*bastila*), 10–11, 117, 163
sweet snack (*sellou*), 92, 112, 165

synesthetic experience, 30, 38, 42, 52
synesthetic perception, 16, 36
system, national subsidy, 103n2, 132–33, 136, 150, 152n6

tahuna (electric mill), 138, 165
tajine (stew on earthenware plate), xii, 11, 117–19, 125n13, 126n18, 129–30, 165
Tamazight (Amazigh language dialects), 7, 13, 24n6, 25n19, 165
tanjiya (earthenware urn), 79–82, 165
taste, 11, 20–21, 26n25, 34, 36, 42, 43–44, 65, 112–13
  acquired, 36
  bodily senses and, 36, 48
  legout, 34, 164
  madaq, 30, 34, 164
taste knowledge, 29–31, 36, 42, 44, 48, 90–92, 158
  and *baraka*, 18, 21, 31, 37
  cooking knowledge as, 21–22, 30, 51, 156
  development of, 58, 71
  of men, 74n19
  temporality within, 21, 30–31, 38–39, 42, 46, 48, 50n11, 57, 156
tasteless food (*messous*), 29, 34, 80, 164
taste of place, 112–13
tea, brewing, 75–76
tea pot, silver (*berrad*), 76, 163
technology,
  digital, 22, 68, 70, 72, 74n19
  kitchen, 14, 30, 42–45, 79, 90, 93, 97
technology and media, in intergenerational learning, 66, 68–70, 72
temporality, 42, 52, 57
  baraka and, 37–39, 41
  of cooking, 30–31, 39–41, 48–49, 50n11
  sense of, 38–39, 40, 42, 46, 50n11, 52, 57, 59

tifinagh (Amazigh script), 25n19, 165
time, 40, 42–45, 50n15, 120–21
  cooking, 11, 29, 33, 39–41, 46–48, 66, 123
  investment of, 129, 156, 159
  phenomenology of, 40
tough (*qashiyn*), 155, 159, 164
tourist (informal) economy, 8–9, 144–46, 153n13
traditional or popular (*cha'abi*), 68, 145, 163
two-part pot for making couscous (*keskas*), 32–33, 51, 117, 164

United Nations Educational Scientific and Cultural Organization (UNESCO), 8, 23
urban, food infrastructure, 37, 141, 143–44, 145, 146
urn, earthenware (*tanjiya*), 79–85, 165

wage work, of women, 45–47, 50n15, 83–88, 93, 96–97, 99n17, 124n1, 159
wheat, 12, 23, 63, 103n2, 115, 133, 135, 137, 138, 152n6, 153n20, 164
womanhood, 2, 8, 21–22, 47, 58, 66, 71–72, 73n11, 77–9, 87–88, 93, 97, 98n5, 158–59
women, 45–46, 74n17, 83, 85, 99n14, 104
  food knowledge of, 2, 53, 162
  low-income, 1, 3, 13–14, 22, 24n10, 24n12, 47–48, 73n7, 79, 83, 162
  wage work of, 47, 50n15, 83–88, 93, 96–97, 99n17, 124n1, 159

younger cooks, older *versus*, 14, 22, 44–47, 49n3, 56, 66, 68–69, 72, 78, 93, 97, 156, 158
YouTube, 60, 67, 69–70

zenqa (high street), 78, 105, 141, 143, 146, 165

Printed in the USA
CPSIA information can be obtained
at www.ICGtesting.com
JSHW051957140324
59245JS00003B/8